AMERICA'S
FORGOTTEN CASTE

America's Forgotten Caste

Free Blacks in Antebellum Virginia and North Carolina

Rodney Barfield

Library of Congress Control Number:		2013906131
ISBN:	Hardcover	978-1-4836-1965-1
	Softcover	978-1-4836-1964-4
	Ebook	978-1-4836-1966-8

This book was printed in the United States of America.

Rev. date: 05/10/2013

To order additional copies of this book, contact:
Xlibris Corporation
1-888-795-4274
www.Xlibris.com
Orders@Xlibris.com
130809

CONTENTS

To The Memory Of

Jennings L. & Pauline Barfield

INTRODUCTION

Thomas Day was twenty-nine years old in 1830 when he finally married Aquilla Wilson. Day lived in Milton, North Carolina, a small village in Caswell County on the banks of the Dan River near Danville. He had moved there seven or eight years earlier from Southside Virginia to start a business with his brother, John. His betrothed lived across the state border in nearby Halifax County, Virginia.

Day was a master cabinetmaker who was on his way to "doing well in the eyes of the world," in the words of his brother. Cabinetmaking was a respected vocation in antebellum America that required skills beyond that of most village artisans. Day had done well with his furniture in Milton in a few short years. He eventually owned valuable property on the main street of town, a respectable house, a shop for his furniture making, and a farm outside town. The artisan formed strong business and political ties in both states with plantation owners and businessmen of means and his furniture was in great demand.

Aquilla Wilson, however, could not immigrate to North Carolina to live with her chosen. She was, in the parlance of the day, a free person of color, as was Thomas Day. They were part of an American caste system that placed severe restrictions on the liberties and mobility of blacks and nonwhites who were not slaves, though to call these people "free" was a misnomer of serious proportions.

Specifically, both states had enacted laws to deny the entry of free blacks and the colored into their borders. Virginia's law had been on the books since 1795; North Carolina did not enact a similar law until 1826. All slave states enacted similar laws in the 18th and 19th centuries and codified them into their legal systems. The purpose of the laws was to rid states in the South of their recently freed slaves whom they considered a threat to the "peculiar institution."

The theory behind the laws was that by denying freed blacks a home, they would leave the South. Ordered to leave their native states yet denied the right to cross borders in the South, freed blacks would have no choice but to migrate to free northern states and to western territories, areas that did not allow slavery, or maybe they would choose to go to Africa or to Haiti. The laws were conceived for the benefit, comfort and protection of the white majority, and they were reworked, reworded, enhanced, and extended for fifty years to no good effect. To the constant chagrin of the white power elite, the free-black class was the fastest-growing segment of the population, and free blacks showed little inclination to leave their home states.

Thomas Day, like many of his caste contemporaries, was neither free nor black, though the courts considered him a "free Negro." He was not free because of the restrictive state laws against his caste that legally prevented him and his family from voting, from participating in politics, and from moving freely from state to state, and even county to county, among other legal deterrents. He was not black by virtue of his Caucasian-tainted ancestry.

Even so, as an accomplished artisan and businessman, Day had the confidence of his community and of its business and political leaders. When the Caswell County community realized the potential economic loss of Day's defection to Virginia to be with his wife, the leading citizens of the county rose to his defense. In the manner of the day and in a democratic process in which Day could not participate, the good citizens of Caswell County solicited the aid of their affluent and connected citizens to petition the state's legislature for an exemption for Aquilla Wilson from the state's immigration law of 1826 in order to accommodate the master cabinetmaker. The petition to the General Assembly read

> that Thomas Day, a free man of color, an inhabitant of this town, a cabinet maker by trade, a first rate workman, a remarkably sober, steady and industrious man, a high minded, good and valuable citizen possessing a valuable property in this town, did, on the 6th day of January last, intermarry with Aquilla Wilson, a free woman of color of good family and character, a resident of Halifax in the State of Virginia, who is prevented from migrating to this State and living with her husband because of said act [act of 1826 outlawing the immigration of blacks into the state]. Therefore your memorialists humbly petition your honorable body to pass an act, giving said Aquilla the privilege of migrating to this State free from the fines and penalties of said act.[1]

Without detracting from the importance of the Milton petition in Day's behalf, it should be noted that free blacks throughout the South sent hundreds of petitions such as this one to their legislatures in attempts to circumvent the harsh restrictions against them. Most of the petitions came from freed slaves who were vital to the economic well-being of towns and communities and had the support of influential whites in their efforts. In fact, white businessmen initiated many, perhaps most, of such petitions to the state's legislatures. So many petitions for free blacks, as well as for industrious slaves, were filed with the courts and with legislatures that the language in such appeals became boilerplate, generic prose designed to flatter legislators and to praise the object of their attentions (the free-black artisan or businessperson) while preserving some semblance, or at least an appearance, of objectivity.

Equally important as the petition itself were the names and reputations of the "memorialists" who presented it. In Day's case, he had in his corner the state's attorney general, Romulus Saunders, a native of Caswell County who had an interest in helping out his home county. Saunders was prominent in the state and well-known in the legislature, where he once served, and his name on the petition would have caught the attention of the right people. But the future minister to Spain went a step further and penned a note to the petition giving his personal recommendation to the bill in Day's behalf, describing him as a "free man of color of very fair character, an excellent mechanic [artisan], industrious, honest and sober in his habits."[2]

The bill to permit Aquilla Wilson to immigrate to North Carolina was read and passed in both houses of the General Assembly, and the young "free" black lady was allowed to enter the state as the wife of Mr. Day. Thomas Day, a free man of color and member of the most reviled caste in America, exhibited courage and confidence when in 1830, despite immigration laws against his class in both Virginia and North Carolina, he crossed the state line and married a woman of color who resided in Halifax County, Virginia. Marriage records of the state show that Thomas Day and Aquilla Wilson were married January 7, 1830 by Rev. David Street.[3] The couple would bear three children, and Aquilla would be a helpmate to Thomas Day for three decades, contributing to the family's economic well-being with a farm of her own.

Thomas Day was a man of means in the village of Milton, one of the prominent people of wealth and influence. He traveled out of state despite the state's restrictive laws, he was a member of the white Presbyterian church in Milton, he owned shares in the state bank, and he conducted business with governors and legislators and wealthy planters. But he could not marry the woman of his choice nor live where he chose without the blessings of the white community—without, literally, an act of the state's legislature.

11

Thomas Day's integration into the dominant antebellum culture of North Carolina and Virginia, while living in a nebulous world outside of accepted social customs, appears to be an anomaly in the context of America's slave society. At least part of the riddle of a quasi-legal free person of color receiving the attention and favor of a community's best citizens and the approval of the state's legislature lies in the subtle and complex social and legal scaffolding supporting the institution of slavery and the unexpected emergence of free blacks from its leaky barriers.

From a legislative act of 1681 in Virginia until the Civil War, the definition and meaning of *free blacks* and their role in American society would hover menacingly over America's political stability. The judicial act in 1681 and most of the restrictive laws that followed were designed to restrain blacks, free and slave, in their daily choices and to deny them civil rights and protection of the laws. These laws were drafted by a dominant white culture that feared the political and social ramifications of non-slave blacks and colored on the institution of slavery. The laws were designed to strengthen the institution of slavery and to remove manumitted slaves, or free blacks, from the boundaries of America.

At the start of the American Revolution, free blacks counted but a few thousand among the millions of whites and black slaves; eighty-five years later, at the outbreak of the American Civil War, the group numbered almost half a million. Of those, most lived in the states of the Upper South: fifty-eight thousand lived in Virginia, and some thirty thousand lived in North Carolina. There were only forty thousand or so in the seven Deep South states, where a strong plantation economy held sway. Virginia and North Carolina offer two examples of the complexity of the free-black community and of the relationships between whites and blacks, masters and slaves, and free blacks and slaves.[4]

By 1800 the revolutionary sentiments and ringing political slogans of freedom of the late eighteenth century and the liberal passions that sustained calls for manumission of slaves belonged to a former generation. The rebels and radicals of the eighteenth century who forged a sweeping new political system in colonial America had emerged as the establishment in politics and religion in twenty short years and were no longer interested in making changes in the social or political fabric of the nation. Few people in America cared about the civic rights of free blacks.

By 1820 free Negroes were restricted by 150 years of legislation and legal statutes that proscribed their movements, their ability to assemble, their social gatherings, their right to vote, their ownership of businesses, their education, where they could live, who they could marry, and whether they could arm themselves.

Free people of color were free mainly in the sense that they were not slaves, but even that status teetered on a very thin ledge. With a slip of the tongue, a careless look at a white woman, or a black business enterprise that threatened the profit of a white man, the "free" black could be jailed, fined, whipped, and sold off into slavery. Free blacks were free only if they displayed the proper deference to whites, as long as the economy was good, and as long as slaves were not making things difficult in the neighborhood. Otherwise, free blacks were the perfect scapegoat for the thinnest complaints by white Southern society. Free blacks existed for the convenience of and by the benevolence of the white ruling community.[5]

By the 1850s, the free Negro caste was the most despised and reviled element of the America population—albeit the fastest-growing section. Racism had so imbued itself in the American character that free blacks were completely outside the social contract, with a few exceptions of protected individuals. Their status and station in life were completely under the authority of a white ruling class that feared and resented their potential for equal civil rights and social privileges. They were, according to a British visitor of the era, "masterless slaves."[6]

The presence of free blacks was especially galling to the ruling class because they presumed in certain areas where whites determined they had no rights: education, religion, mobility, and politics. These were areas carefully controlled by elite landowners through money, influence, and very restrictive laws and local ordinances. Slave owners and political leaders understood that general enlightenment in any of those areas imbued blacks with self-esteem and a desire to become more equal with whites. Equality was a subversive sentiment that threatened the institution of slavery. Therefore, white political leaders restricted mobility, voting, teaching and eventually even preaching.

The ruling elite also resented and feared the caste for its alleged magnetic pull on the slaves. Most whites assumed that slaves wanted to achieve the status of "free" and that they looked to the free-black community as a model. And whites believed that slaves would revolt to achieve their freedom, just as the colonials did against the king of England, and that the free-black caste would be the catalyst. The free black was ultimately an anomaly in a society designed for just two races: black slaves and free whites.

Hence, the free black caste would usually carry the brunt of neighborhood revenge and reprisals occasioned by crime, rumors of revolt among the slaves, or even a general downturn in the economy. The caste was a convenient substitute for any anxiety in the body politic, and ruling whites seldom failed to exploit its pitiable situation. The historian David Dodge pointed out in the 1880s that the free black caste had a much greater notoriety than either its actions or its numbers would warrant, not unlike the position of Jews in Europe throughout history. "There is hardly another instance in the range of history in which a class as comparatively insignificant in numbers and as timid and unaggressive in spirit has been the occasion of so much alarm and disquietude."[7]

Layered under all the political and social issue concerning free blacks was the ultimate matter of color. Free Negroes in 18th and 19th century America ranged in color from coal black to white, including gradations that ran the gamut from mulatto to quadroon to octoroon, depending on ancestry and how intimate parents and grandparents were with either white slaveholders (not necessarily by choice) or with white indentured female servants. The black communities in America, slave and free, included an inordinate number of mulattoes, a stark reminder to all that racism and bigotry did not preclude sexual intimacy.

Thomas Day's family, initially residents of Southside Virginia, was one such "free" family. The Days traced their freedom back several generations in Virginia. As free people of color, they lived in and had business and family connections in the three abutting Southside counties of Dinwiddie, Greensville, and Sussex. Thomas's father spent time in Petersburg, perhaps as an apprentice cabinetmaker or a journeyman. They were very light in color, educated, and skilled, and they had numerous white associations and relationships.

But instead of passing their lives in the silenced anonymity of their caste, the Days lived in their communities as people of means and prominence, people who were as near politically free as it was possible for free people of color in nineteenth-century America. For at least three generations, the men in the family engaged in the trade of cabinetmaking that ultimately led to a major and superior company in North Carolina. The women owned farms and raised stock, tobacco, and produce. They intermarried with other prominent free-black families of Virginia and North Carolina. Sons and daughters of the third generation attended schools in the North. One of the brothers became an ordained minister and missionary, a teacher, and a court justice in Liberia.[8]

The Days were not the only free-black, high-level achievers in Virginia. Free blacks—and slaves for that matter—across the South and in the North acquired wealth and notoriety in their communities. Two of the Day brothers achieved an unusual and unlikely degree of prominence and distinction in North Carolina and Liberia, and many of their caste throughout the country did likewise, but their achievements were recognized only insofar as they reflected well on their white communities. The Day brothers' stories can be told today because their associations with prominent people, organizations and businesses created paper documents that were archived. Few black inventors or writers or gifted artisans or artists who lived in antebellum America received public recognition that would assure them a place in the chronicles of America.

Americans remain strangers to the nation's slave history, which includes the history of free blacks. This work is a small recounting of a few successful free blacks in Virginia and North Carolina, whose purpose is to introduce college-level students and the general reader to the complexities of free-black life in the slave era. As pioneer historian John Hope Franklin wrote many years ago, the story of the people and the historical era of slavery "cannot be completely told until there is available an adequate account of these quarter of a million people [free blacks] who often influenced the attitude and policies of the communities in which they lived to a degree all out of proportion to their numbers."[9]

This history is about some of those unusual people who, despite their low social standing as a caste, made major contributions to their communities. It raises questions rather than provides answers. How did a minority of free blacks in the first half of the nineteenth century rise above the restrictions on their caste and achieve positions of social and economic standing typically reserved for whites? How did they function in a white society determined to limit their rights and privileges, even to the extent of exiling them from the country? What motivated the likes of Thomas and John Day to rise above caste, and how did they perceive their place in the American South?

Chapter One

Slavery in the Making

The first Africans to make land in England's American outpost sailed into Jamestown, Virginia, on a Dutch man-of-war in 1619. The Dutch ship had seized the Africans, some one hundred of them, from a Spanish frigate it had raided in search of gold. Spanish ships bringing gold from Central and South America back to Europe were favorite targets of pirates and privateers from other nations at war with Spain, including the Dutch.

The Dutch raiders found no gold on the Spanish ship and so took the Africans and some ebony as plunder. The privateer then encountered heavy weather in the Atlantic, beat about the coast for some weeks, and finally put into the puny English settlement of Jamestown with only twenty of the Africans still alive, all of whom were sold to the English colonists.[1]

America's first slaveholders handled their charges with some uncertainty. The legal and social status of Virginia's first Africans would require a couple of generations to harden into law and custom. The colonists treaded carefully with their first bondsmen and women, writing much of the script as they went. True, they had the tradition of indentured servitude in England and in the colonies and the experience of slave societies in the Caribbean to look to for guidance, but their hands-on experience came by trial and error.

The "Muster Rolls of Settlements in Virginia" in 1624-1625 lists twenty-three African "servants" in the colony, being the same twenty delivered by the Dutch privateer, plus three, who were addressed by the same title as white indentured servants and who were treated as such in that their terms of service were limited.

The few colonists who bought and worked Africans initially mimicked the conventions of indenture in practice and in nomenclature. White servants, largely from Ireland, filled the role for menial labor in the earliest years of the Virginia colony. Agents recruited groups of immigrants, from Ireland and other European countries, with the promise of a trip to Virginia in return for a limited term of service to a master, usually from five to seven years, but the terms might vary.

A generation after the Dutch delivered the first twenty Africans to Jamestown, there were some five hundred Africans in the colony, a growth that resulted from the odd slave ship coming ashore but mostly from natural increase. Even by 1670, just shy of two generations after the first landing, there were a mere two thousand Africans in Virginia, roughly the same number of Indians who occupied the same area.[2]

The slow increase in the African population the first half of the seventeenth century was due in part to the dominance of the slave trade by the Dutch, who preferred to trade in the West Indies, where the markets were well established and more profitable. The Dutch trade was slow to develop in the American colonies also because English companies supplying white indentured servants from the British Isles opposed the African trade as competition and worked against it.

There were far more white indentured servants than Africans working the land of seventeenth-century Virginia, and most planters preferred that arrangement to slavery, at least in the beginning. It would be many years before the English and the colonists worked out their differences over the indenture trade and accepted the profitability and efficacy of bringing black labor to America from Africa and the Caribbean.

Distinctions were not always clear between slave and indentured servant in the American colonies of the early seventeenth century. Servants were bought, sold, traded, rented out, and even bequeathed as property, as were slaves. They held few rights and those but what their masters afforded them. They shared their work with slaves, drank with them, and yielded to the same hardships and abuse from masters. Yet their claim to a status of "free men and women" was that their servitude was contractual and limited; at some point they would be the social equal of other free working whites.

As the number of white planters in Virginia increased and the number of plantations grew and the comfort level of the colonists with slavery grew, black indenture was increasingly tested and abused. Black-servant status in the American colonies took on the characteristics of slavery, gradually extending black servitude to a state of permanency. By 1700 there was no question as to the meaning of *slavery* in America. The differences between an indentured servant and a slave had been long settled: the former was white and the service was temporary; the latter was black and the service was for life.[3]

Regardless of the abuse they suffered while indentured, servants could absolutely count on a day of freedom in the future, whether at the end of the standard five—to seven-year indenture or on some other agreed term. Servants also had the use of the courts, and their marriages were recognized by the church. At the end of their term, the master was obligated to provide a new set of clothes and a bonus to help the released worker begin life as a free man or woman.

The servant carried papers as proof of his or her freedom lest they be placed again in servitude. Indeed, it was fairly assumed that all indentured workers would eventually fulfill the obligations of their indenture and then live in the colonies as free people. The indenture system created the major labor supply for the American colonies during the first half of the seventeenth century in a land in dire need of labor.[4]

The economics of indenture took a turn in the second half of the 17th century. Indentured servants from Europe were harder to get and were more expensive. Once large-scale farmers and planters calculated the economics of the issue, indentured servants fell out of favor, and African labor became more acceptable. Black slaves were often cheaper than white servants from England, and owners managed to extend the terms of service of blacks without having the courts interfere.[5]

The colonists learned quickly that Africans worked harder than the English or the Indian and that they brought many skills from their native land. The women cooked and wove and tended gardens much as they did in their homelands; the men farmed, handled cattle and horses, and fished and hunted without much training. Their familiarity with crops prepared them to cultivate tobacco and rice, the major colonial cash crops. They were trained by owners and overseers for the more skilled plantation jobs. Africans were quick learners and ultimately assumed almost complete operation of large colonial farms.[6]

The African also resisted English diseases, to which the Indian had scant immunity. They brought their own medicinal remedies with them and shared them with their owners. English colonials came to appreciate the assets of their new labor source and to realize the advantages of an endless supply of fresh labor that did not speak the language and would not understand how to approach a court or magistrate to complain about brutish treatment.

White slave owners learned early to disparage slaves and their work ethic, much as they did European servants, for their own selfish purposes. This frequent criticism of black slaves became the default position of slave owners in whose interest it was to belittle everything African so as to accelerate and to justify the process of enslavement. There are anecdotes about the first Africans

19

to America using the wrong end of a hoe and their fear of farm animals. Africans were farmers in their own lands; they were also potters and musicians and artists and builders. [7]

A few of the more ambitious Africans mastered the labor of colonial plantations and eventually even joined in its exploitation of land and labor. Early in the formation of slavery in America, perhaps with the original twenty, Africans received a plot of land on which they produced crops for themselves. They could sell the crop to the owner or to their neighbors or keep it for their own use. They kept cows, hogs, and chickens and maybe hoed an acre or two of tobacco that was for their personal use or for sale. Eventually, they were allowed to accumulate capital, to buy and sell goods, and to trade at market.[8]

The "slave's acre" quickly became a fixed custom fiercely defended by slaves and acknowledged by most slave owners. The early acceptance of the arrangement suggests that the custom came to America from Barbados and the other Caribbean islands intact as a tenet of the institution of slavery. Owners resisted the slave plot on occasion and even denied the slave his plot on occasion, but it remained a common right that was allowed by most owners down to the Civil War.[9]

Slave owners hardly supported the slave acre out of altruism. Those who did allow the custom did so for self-serving reasons, calculating that the practice encouraged their slaves to remain on the plantation and to spend their time productively. The practice became routine by the eighteenth century, a well-accepted custom in most of the colonies, so common that many slaves assumed it to be their common right.[10]

A visitor to southeast North Carolina in the 1770s described the slave routine on a large coastal plantation. Work for the master began at sunrise with an assignment of the day's tasks. The slaves worked the master's field until one or two o'clock and then spent the remainder of the day working their own plots of two to four acres, hoeing corn, tobacco, beans, and potatoes. Some raised cattle, hogs, poultry, and horses, from which they enriched their own diets and made a small profit by selling to their masters or to their neighbors.[11]

The visitor to North Carolina painted a rosier picture of plantation life than most observers recorded. That would have been a very lenient plantation and planter who worked his slaves a mere ten hours daily. Smaller plantations, the ordinary run-of-the-mill operations, worked slaves from sunup to sundown or from "day clean to first dark." When crops were ripe for harvesting, they might work well into the night. Private plots, when they were available, were worked on Saturday afternoons or Sundays. Planters did not like to see their slaves idle, which they considered an aid to mischief. Some owners insisted that slaves repair their cabins and other plantations buildings on Sunday and perform other "light" duties outside the field.[12]

As slaves and servants absorbed the methods of colonial farmers and the basics of farm capitalism, some of their garden plots became so efficient and prosperous that whites complained and petitioned the courts to stop the practice. White farmers found that slave and servant produce sold cheaper than their own and undercut their profits. Subsequently, North Carolina passed a law in 1741 against slave bartering and selling in the marketplace. Slaves in that colony could not "buy, sell, trade, barter, or borrow 'any Commodities whatsoever' or to raise horses, cattle, or hogs 'on any Pretense whatsoever.'"[13] Laws against slave and free-black competition were enacted wherever blacks succeeded to the point of annoying whites. Whites railed against black competition and filed petitions against it with the courts up to the eve of the Civil War, an indication that the complaints and petitions were ineffective.

Market Day. Free blacks and slaves took advantage of town markets to sell their private produce and other staples. The "slave's acre" was a plot of land allotted by owners for their servants' personal use. Many slaves saved enough money from these "private enterprise" endeavors to purchase their freedom and that of their families. *(Courtesy of the Library of Congress, Prints & Photographs Division, Washington, D.C. No Use Restrictions)*

When the early-seventeenth-century black servant worked off a typical term, he or she cleared the contract debt. Freed African servants at that time, in the youthful years of the system, then had the rights of any freeholder: they acquired land, built houses, planted tobacco, and even purchased slaves. They asserted their rights as landowners and a few as slaveholders, sued in the courts for their property, married within the community, and were accepted by some whites as legal residents.[14]

These early African property owners in Virginia and elsewhere in the South gained confidence and status by acquiring property. Some of them managed to acquire land and other property even during their years as slaves from profits made by planting their own small vegetable patches and small plots of tobacco or by hiring out their spare time to other planters and merchants. They acquired personal property and saved money, not unlike the small slave holders who may have owned them.

Anthony Johnson, one of the original twenty Africans to land at Jamestown, apparently adapted quickly to Virginia's plantation economy. He obtained his freedom within a few years, quicker than the usual indentured servant, married an African woman, and acquired his own property. Johnson followed the routine of white planters in the colony, clearing land and planting tobacco. He was very successful at it.

Taking advantage of the English headright system of land distribution, the former slave in 1651 imported his own servants, four white and one black, and received 250 acres in Northampton County on the Pungoteague River. The resourceful freedman eventually put together a plantation with a dozen other Africans, who had also earned their freedom, in what was probably the first African American community in America. It would not be the last. By choice and by white-inspired segregation, all-black villages appeared as the numbers of free blacks increased.[15]

Johnson and other Africans with English names had been baptized into the English religion, accepted American marriage rites and the capitalist system of property ownership. Ship captains sometimes baptized captured Africans aboard ship, and they arrived in Virginia with names like Angelo and John Pedro. By 1664 there were probably forty-plus African American freeholders in Northampton County out of the 144 documented blacks living there. These freedmen had worked their indentures and were released by their masters to find their own livelihood. Sebastian Cane, Philip Mongum, Manuel Rodriggus, and other black freeholders found their destinies as tobacco farmers.[16]

Anthony Johnson became successful as a planter by imitating the capitalistic system of the slave society that was evolving in the Southern colonies. He enlarged his estate and passed his ambition and legacy as a landowner and slave owner to his son and grandson, though by then the family had moved to Maryland to escape Virginia's harsh slave codes. Both of his progeny were free-black planters and property owners. The grandson named his plantation Angola.[17]

A sizeable number of seventeenth-century servants worked off their obligations and bequeathed freedom, property, and sometimes slaves to their heirs. Sebastian Cane, Francis Paine, and Anthony Longo gained their freedom from slavery. Longo is in the court records for defying a subpoena to appear in court. He cursed and berated the server of the document and gave the man "some blows." Longo and his fellow black freedmen demonstrated their equality with their white neighbors in their physical resistance to white authority.[18]

Other Johnson freedmen, either former slaves or servants of Anthony or of his master, joined the Pungoteague River community. Richard Johnson, a free-black carpenter, brought two white servants to Virginia in 1654 to qualify for 100 acres on the river. John Johnson, another former slave, brought in eleven servants, which qualified him for 550 acres adjoining Richard Johnson's farm. Other blacks, upon obtaining their freedom, acquired property under the headright system by importing their own servants in Surry, New Kent, and York Counties. Benjamin Doyle in Surrey County received 300 acres for importing servants in 1656. Emanuel Cambrew of James City County received 50 acres in 1667. These were former servants who paid their indenture, understood and accepted the capitalistic nature of colonialism, and saw "liquid capital not only as a means to attach their paternity—and hence, their identity as persons—to something even their masters would have to respect."[19]

For those enterprising servants who had free time to do with as they chose, and if their owner agreed, there was money to be made. Some chose and were allowed by their owners to hire out their labor to other slave owners who might need their particular talents and skills. Hired labor was at a premium in seventeenth-century Virginia, and a servant or even a slave could make good money, even after paying his owner a percentage, by hiring out at harvest time or hiring out a particular skill, such as carpentry, cooperage, or blacksmithing.

The labor practice expanded rapidly in the eighteenth and nineteenth centuries until most of Southern society employed slave labor. Hired-out slaves were used in mining, fishing, urban industry, mining, road building, and agriculture. Leased slaves were especially valuable to those who owned no slaves, filling a labor need without the expense and upkeep of ownership. The "hired out" leases were initially filled by males, but eventually, females and children joined the lease system.[20]

Hiring Out

The slave economy did not work on the capitalistic principle of the marketplace in regulating labor. Planters determined the labor market and bought slaves accordingly. It was an inefficient way to operate a labor system. Some harvests were lush, others were poor, but the labor pool remained constant. Rivers were unpredictable, either rising too high or falling too low to move freight barges, thus idling fishermen, freight movers, and boat pilots. At these slack economic times, slaves remained inactive or labored at makeshift work. Or, according to planters, at making mischief.

There were many aspects to farm life, oftentimes skilled work, for which slaves had to be trained or for which white craftsmen were hired. The requirements of a large farm or plantation often required work beyond the skill of farm hands, skills such as construction of barns and outbuildings, metal and leather work. Some of the tasks called for temporary workers. For example, once a barn was built, the planter might have no call for carpenters for months or years. In the early years of the slave economy, planters loaned slaves to neighbors to help them through a harvest or to get a well dug or a barn built. What began as a helping hand developed into a lease business that assisted a neighbor and found work for idle slaves, an advantage to the slave owner and to the farmer who needed a temporary worker. The practice spread due to its very success and found success in logging, road building, fisheries, manufacturing, and many other nonagricultural pursuits. By the 1780s, as high as 90 percent of whites in certain Virginia counties hired slaves, a system that became "an integral part of the institution of slavery" in the county.[21]

Ironically, hiring out eventually worked to the slaves' advantage as well. As the system matured, some planters allowed their slaves increasing responsibility over their work. When the slave proved reliable, a planter might allow him to find his own work away from the farm and even negotiate his own wages, provided he pay the owner a set sum for the time he was away. The practice of hiring out would evolve into a major part of the slave economy after the revolution, with planters and businessmen buying slaves for the primary purpose of lending them out. The practice prepared many slaves for economic independence, a large asset when post-revolutionary laws once again allowed private manumissions.

The extreme form of hiring out developed over time into quasi autonomy for some slaves, a situation of "self-hire." Slave leases at times extended into years, years that the owner seldom saw his bondsman. Such a lease might call for the slave or for his borrower to clothe and feed the laborer. In such a case, the owner might see his slave once a year, or if he dealt directly with the hiring person to renew the lease, he might not see his slave at all. Some owners finally left it to the slave to make his own contracts and provide his own clothes and food in return for an annual or monthly payment.

Self-hire required a very motivated, experienced, and often literate slave who could assume responsibility for himself, abstain from alcohol and other urban temptations, and operate a business or a trade that would pay not only the owner's fee but earn a living wage for the slave. A man might cut wood for sale, clean stables for a farmer, run errands for a businessman, clean boots for the public—all done after his regular workweek for some planter or merchant. Lunsford Lane in North Carolina sold firewood, was a messenger for the governor's office, and operated a small tobacco kiosk from which he sold custom-made smoking pipes along with a special tobacco he laced with molasses to sweeten it. He eventually made enough money to buy himself and his family.[22]

George Moses Horton of Northampton County and later Chatham County in North Carolina managed to eke out a miserly existence for himself and satisfy his owner's demands for a fee by, of all things, selling poems to students at the University of North Carolina. Horton made his initial association with university students circa 1820, selling his owner's produce at Chapel Hill. When students learned that the literate young slave was something of an orator, they collected around him to hear his florid speeches.

Poetry was Horton's true talent and his moneymaker. His acrostics, which he formed from the letters of the names of student sweethearts, sold each for a quarter, and Horton sold enough to eventually buy his time away from the farm to ply his trade in the university town. He achieved some notoriety in the region for his orations and his poems and found himself the feature of an article in the *Raleigh Register* in 1828. White sponsors published two books of his poetry before the Civil War, the first in 1829, both printed in hopes of raising funds to manumit the slave.[23]

Hired-out slaves were yet another complaint for white folks who wanted bondsmen and women kept in a distinct form of servitude easily recognized and unrelated to white mobility and work. Ironically, many of those same whites chose to rent slave labor rather than to become slaveholders.

Creating a Caste

> *Every day, my blood has frequently almost run cold within me to consider how many of your slaves had neither convenient food to eat, nor proper raiment to put on. Notwithstanding most of the comfort you enjoy is solely owing to their indefatigable labors.*
>
> —George Whitefield

Permanent servitude was never announced or proclaimed; it developed by custom and incident, and its progression is to be found in court records and documents that rule in the favor of planters almost without exception. Statutory recognition came later and merely codified a well-established institution. During this maturation period, in the first half of the seventeenth century, indentured blacks are always referred to as servants or Negroes in court records. The word *slave* did not appear until about 1661. And black servants continued to hold legal and property rights during that period of time. "The truth is that no attempt was ever made to supply legal grounds for holding negroes in a status of slavery. Custom supplied all the authority that appeared to be necessary, and legislation at first merely performed the part of resolving some uncertainties concerning a well-established institution."[24]

James Curtis Ballagh, a pioneer historian of slavery in Virginia, gave a similar description of the beginnings of slavery as "some essential or actual inequality between individuals or sets of individuals in their broad social relations. Such an inequality continued and intensified, gradually and almost imperceptibly creates a status marked by distinct incidents, which in time assumes the form of a definite social institution, recognized first in custom, then in law."[25]

Ballagh contends that servitude of Africans preceded their "subjection" but that it was the "historic base upon which slavery, by the extension and addition of incidents, was constructed."[26] Even so, the first generation of Africans in Virginia were treated more like indentured servants than they ever would be thereafter. Their time of servitude was limited, at the end of which they were released from bondage. They had certain legal rights and privileges equal to white servants that were gradually taken from them as white landowners discovered that they could subject Africans to lifelong labor without benefit of a contract.

There were other issues that disturbed slave owners. White planters and wealthy merchants in seventeenth-century Virginia tried to anticipate future conditions for their earnings. Even in the first decades of slavery, they were uneasy with the potential of an explosive population of slaves and of losing control of their labor. Even in mid-century, with only two thousand blacks working their plantations, owners were overly sensitive to threats of rebellion and regularly pushed for legislation to control the mobility and rights of bondsmen. They also sensed a future threat to white dominance in the nature of a potential prosperous free-black population, which was so small in the seventeenth century as to barely register in colonial statistics.[27]

Governor Sir William Berkeley responded to an inquiry by the English Lords Commissioners of Foreign Plantations in 1671 about the size and numbers of people, farms, rivers, forts, and other demographic issues in the

Virginia colony. He reported that the colony held about forty thousand people, six thousand "Christian servants," and two thousand "black slaves." He also enumerated the number of forts that were dilapidated, rivers that were clogged with debris, Indians that threatened the colony, and other hazards and threats. Nowhere was there mention of free blacks, not as an aside, certainly nothing about their numbers representing a threat to the colony.[28]

White slave owners mulled the future as former servants such as Anthony Johnson and his progeny gained their liberty, joined the property and slave-owning class, and passed their legacies to their children. The white slave owners' solution to this perceived threat of social leveling was to press for even more laws to circumscribe the liberties not only of their bondsmen and women but of free blacks as well.

A codification of slave laws coincided with a rise in slave numbers in America in the 1660s and with a hardening of white attitudes toward blacks. The majority of blacks by the 1660s were "homegrown," a second generation of Africans who knew little of Africa and who grew up more "American" than African. The colony entertained relatively few slave ships from either Africa or the Caribbean. Nonetheless, the number of black slaves and even free blacks continued to grow by natural increase in the colonies. From the 1660s white planters would constantly push for stricter laws to control black mobility and choice and to limit the increase in the free-black population.[29]

The tandem growth of slave numbers and the addition of slave codes took an upward spiral over the next century, marked by the racial issues and attitudes that would plague the nation down to 1861. As the number of black slaves grew at the end of the eighteenth century and the number of white indentured servants diminished, white planters and merchants insisted on more restrictive and rigid laws to circumscribe the mobility and behavior of slaves. By 1705 numerous laws and statutes of the previous quarter century were codified into Virginia's slave codes.

There were early signs that English racial attitudes toward Africans in America leaned toward racial bigotry. These feelings were reflected in the treatment of slaves by owners who determined laws and customs in their communities. Planters were not particularly aware that they were setting precedents for a new society; they were farmers looking for the best advantage to make money. But colonial courts followed the opinions of planters as they established custom and habit in the American colonies, unhampered by obstacles except their conscience and English common law.[30]

By the second generation of slavery in America, attitudes were already hardening toward blacks, and the courts were making legal distinctions between black and white indentured servants. A 1649 decision by the courts provided a clue to the future of the American slave system and the status of blacks in general. The jurists considered a case of three runaway servants, a Dutchman named Victor, a Scotsman named James Gregory, and a black named John Punch.

The two white runaways captured with the black were given an extra four years of service and thirty lashes for their escape from indenture. The court sentenced the black runaway servant to thirty lashes and a *life* of servitude. White planters already were in practice and in fact establishing slavery by binding blacks to increasingly lengthy indentures, making contracts for life terms, and deeding their servants to their "heyers and assigns forever."[31]

White attitudes toward blacks became more racial in the late seventeenth century with planter attitudes reflected in the increasingly rigid laws aimed at black servants and slaves. An act of the Virginia General Assembly in 1661 declared that "negroes are incapable of making satisfaction [for the time lost in running away] by addition of time," though addition of time was the customary punishment for runaway servants.

Under the new law, adding to "time served" as punishment for a slave had no meaning if a slave's term was already for life, and the General Assembly essentially recognized the meaning and settled the issue to the satisfaction of slave owners. This act has been termed the "first general sanction of slavery in Virginia," when a servant was sentenced to a life of servitude as punishment.[32] Ballagh calls the law the "point of institutional divergence, where slavery began a course of development more or less independent of the system of servitude from which it descended."[33]

If the 1661 law can be described as the first general sanction of slavery in America, an assembly act the following year may have laid the legal foundation for slavery. The law of 1662 determined that the legal status of a black child would be decided by the status of its mother. This law made a clear distinction between slavery and indentured servitude. Servitude remained a voluntary contract, regardless of how much it was abused. Its services were never meant to extend for the life of the servant. "The first essential element in the change of status [from servant to slave] consisted merely in . . . the extension of the terms of service from a period of years to that of natural life."[34]

Historians generally accept the decade between 1660s and 1670s as the "time of transition from slavery sanctioned by customary law to slavery defined by statute law." Most historians recognize that the first legislative act legalizing slavery in the American colonies was the Act XII of 1662 in the General Assembly that recognized children either free or slave according to the status of their mothers.

WHEREAS some doubts have arisen whether children got by an Englishman upon a negro woman should be slave or free, Be it therefore

*enacted and declared by this present grand assembly, that all children borne
in this country shal be held bond or free only according to the condition
of the mother, And that if any Christian shall commit fornication with a
negro man or woman, hee or shee soe offending shall pay double the fines
imposed by the former act.*[35]

The Act of 1662 made slavery hereditary in Virginia, a law duplicated by
Maryland (1662), Massachusetts (1698), Connecticut and New Jersey (1704),
Pennsylvania and New York (1712), Rhode Island (1728), and North Carolina
(1741). Southern states were not the first, however, to institute slavery. In
Rhode Island the practice of buying "slaves forever" was common by 1652.
The earliest sanction of slavery by *local law* occurred in Massachusetts in 1639.
It was in the South, however, that slavery first became vital to a one-crop
economy.[36]

Racial attitudes toward blacks developed alongside the growth of slavery
as an economic and social system. Ironically, white attitudes in some instances
followed those of indentured servants who began to leave the South as the
slave population grew and to differentiate themselves as "Christian servants,"
as opposed to "heathen Africans." Some white servants refused to work
alongside slaves.[37] At least one historian claims that racial contempt for
African Americans was muted as long as whites and blacks worked together as
servants. Racism developed in proportion to the loss of white servants and the
increase of black slaves.[38]

The year after designating children free or slave according to the status
of the mother, the Virginia Assembly passed a law forbidding "servants to go
abroad without a lycence," meaning that bondsmen and women must have a
paper or some other item to demonstrate their owners' permission to be away
from their farms.

Act XVIII—1663
*For better suppressing the unlawful meetings of servants . . . that all
masters of Families be enjoyned and take special care that their servants
doe not depart from their houses on Sundayes or any other dayes without
particular lycence from them.*[39]

On sight, free blacks were indistinguishable from slaves. Increased mobility
of slaves, especially those "hiring out," added to the unease of owners. Slave
owners opposed the practice of freeing blacks from slavery in the first instance
as a dangerous example to slaves. The increase in the number of free blacks
in the late seventeenth century began to raise multiple questions regarding
their relationship vis-à-vis slaves and whites servants. Would free blacks be a

catalyst to revolt by the slave communities in which they recently lived? And would free blacks feel emboldened to cohabit with white servants?

Slaveholders faced less tangible issues than slave rebellion and miscegenation. As Christians, Virginia planters often tried to justify their slave trade and the ownership of humans as a humane act that brought infidels and heathens out of their barbarous homeland into the "blessed light of Christianity." It was a dubious argument that could be self-serving and no doubt was for many planters. For the devout planter, however, the moral dilemma was a serious one for which he wanted religious validation and secular acceptance.[40]

The construct was both religious and cultural for slave holders and supporters of slavery in America: that being a slave in enlightened and Christian Virginia or North Carolina was preferable to being a prince in darkest heathen Africa. The arguments amounted to cultural hubris and religious arrogance that assumed European, especially English, superiority to other religions and cultures. Whether all slave owners subscribed to the twin pillars of colonial rationalization for slavery, few argued against them. And if religious and cultural excuses did not assuage the conscience, then surely the flow of history must carry some weight: "The barbarian, the heathen, and the heretic have been through all ages subjects of dominion." The adage was reassuring to slaveholders with a conscience and to politicians who wanted to justify a slave economy.[41]

George Whitefield, the Anglican priest who articulated the early tenets of Methodism, perhaps stated the seventeenth-century Christian slaveholder's theology best. Though he lamented the poverty of slaves, he agreed that it was "laudable to bring the negro under Christianizing influences, even if the only road lay through slavery; to save the heathen African souls at the expense of heathen African bodies."[42]

Other planters denigrated the notion of Christian slaves by claiming that a slave could not comprehend religion and that baptism would merely elevate his status and give him notions of equality that would lead to subversive emotions. These owners, often the elite of the planter class, wanted nothing to do with the Scriptures that read "all men are equal in the sight of the Lord." They frowned on slaves, servants, the poor, and middling whites equally.

By 1667 the planters had dealt with the religious issue to their satisfaction by getting a ruling in the legislature that a slave's religion had no bearing on his legal status. The 1667 act brushed the religious argument aside in stark language:

> An act declaring ye Baptism of Slaves doth not exempt ye from
> Bondage. Declared ye Baptism doth not alter ye condition of a slave.[43]

Virginia planters held sway in the General Assembly in the seventeenth century, so their wants concerning slaves and free blacks easily translated into legislation. Ever on the alert for situations that might favor free blacks, the assembly in 1668 opted to remind them that they were not equal to whites and to saddle them with a punitive tax in the bargain. By an act of the legislature in that year, the planters made free-black women "tithables" (taxable) to remind them that, "though permitted to enjoy their freedome yet ought not in all respects to be admitted to a full fruition of the exemptions and immunities of the English."[44]

The courts and the justice system in general steadily denied slaves redress of grievances. Slave owners could now punish their slaves or even kill them with slight chance of legal repercussions. In 1669 the House passed an act that declared "if any slave resist his Master or other by his master's order correcting him, and by extremity of the correction should chance to die . . . his death shall not be accompted a felony."[45]

The reality of colonial laws against slaves and free blacks may escape the sensibilities of our own century, especially when read in the euphemistic language of seventeenth-century English courts. The use of the phrase "by extremity of the correction" to refer to killing slaves intends to hide as much as it reveals. For an Englishman to kill a fellow human without fear of serious consequences speaks to the contempt the English held for Africans and African Americans under their care.

In a simple and stark example of planter justice, Robert Carter, member of Virginia's first families and one of its largest slave owners, petitioned the court to allow him to maim two of his slaves. Bambarra Harry and Dinah were the designated victims, presumably for their habit of leaving the plantation without permission. The court found for Carter and ruled "[i]t is therefore ordered That for the better reclaiming the said negroes and deterring others from ill practices That the said Robert Carter Esq. have full power according to Law to dismember the said negroes or Either of them by cutting of[f] their toes."[46]

The 1660s was the decisive decade that Virginia planters forced their views of blacks, free and slave, through the General Assembly, into the law books and into the social fabric of the colony. The laws dealing with blacks became more punitive than before and also more racial in nature. The 1660s set precedents for the restrictive and racially charged laws that followed over the next three decades.

In 1670 a law was enacted that forbade free blacks from owning white servants. To this point, free blacks had the rights of other freemen to buy slaves and to contract with servants for an indenture, black and white. First-generation black servants such as Anthony Johnson imported slave and white servants to fulfill the requirements of the headright system to acquire free land.

The 1670 act was the most blatantly race-based law to discriminate against free people of color. The statute barred blacks from purchasing any "Christian" (i.e., white person) as a slave or servant, as whites were permitted to do, but they could continue to buy people of color as servants and slaves. Or as the statute read, "any of their owne nation" and "of their own complexion." The law applied to blacks and Indians equally.

> *ACT V 1670 Noe Negroes nor Indians to buy Christian servants.*
> *WHEREAS it hath been questioned whither Indians or negroes manumitted, or otherwise free, could be capable of purchasing Christian [white] servants, It is enacted that noe Negroe or Indian though baptized and enjoyned their owne ffreedom shall be capable of any such purchase of Christians, but yet not debarred from buying any of their owne nation.*[47]

Twelve years later, Act I in 1682 of the Virginia General Assembly in James City repealed the Act of 1670, defining who would be slaves, to replace it with a more specific and demeaning law narrowing the definition of *slave*. The new act designated as slaves "all servants not being christian, being imported into this country by shipping shall be slaves, but what shall come by land shall serve if boyes and girls until thirty yeares of age [as servants], if men and women, twelve yeares and noe longer." That is, imported Africans, those imported "by shipping," were by definition slaves. The legislators assumed that those arriving by land were already on the continent and hence Christian and white.[48]

The act strengthened the previous law that declared converting to Christianity did not free a slave from his/her servitude, and it reversed an earlier law that protected Indians from slavery. The new law declared "all servants except Turkes and Moores . . . brought or imported into the country, either by land or sea, whether Negroes, Moors, Molattoes or Indians, who and whose parentage and native country are not Christian at the time of their first purchase of such servant by some Christian . . . are hereby adjudged, deemed and taken to be slaves to all intents and purposes."[49]

The act worked against slave owners who had baptized their bondsmen prior to the law. And it failed to give any consideration to Christianized blacks imported from the Caribbean and those reshipped from England and the English colonies. The inherent contradictions in slave laws, in their attempts to justify slavery by Christian doctrine, and the inconveniences such laws inevitably placed on certain sections of slave-owning planters led to constant tampering and tweaking of the laws.

The act of 1682 first blunted the religious doctrine of freedom inherent in Christianity and replaced it with a "more profitable social principle of fundamental racial difference"—the black as an inferior human. "The nominal test for slavery became original heathenism and present servitude resting upon the *prima facie* evidence of importation."[50] This neglect of the slave's moral soul would remain the general attitude of the colonial planter until the religious Great Awakening when a swell of evangelism would soften the slaveholder's harshness toward his slaves' religious needs for a brief time. It also allowed Indians, who had escaped slavery in the previous act of 1670, to engage in slavery and in the slave trade.

Every session of the Virginia Assembly in the remaining two decades of the century layered more laws against free blacks and further restricted their few remaining legal rights. The assembly in 1681 debated the issue of free blacks and their potential for harm amongst the slaves. White planters assumed that free blacks were sympathetic to slaves and would therefore assist them in any rising against servitude or perhaps take the lead in such subversive activities.

The response of the assembly was to ban all future personal manumissions and to order that all newly freed blacks remove themselves the colony within six months of their emancipation—at the expense of the owner. The legislators reasoned that creating an expense for owners would impede their propensity to free their slaves, not that the law or the apprehension of planters was justified by the miniscule numbers of free blacks. The act also prohibited, again, interracial marriage of whites to any "Negro, mulatto or Indian." The colony's legislative acts dealing with free blacks in the final decades of the seventeenth century were openly and unapologetically racial in nature.

Though the migration law was never effectively enforced—and in fact was generally ignored by magistrates, slave owners, and freedmen—planters never tired of debating the issue, and the Virginia Assembly continued to enact versions of the law throughout the eighteenth and nineteenth centuries. In 1691 the General Assembly enacted a more extreme version of the law that called for the end of private manumissions forever and for any cause.

> *And forasmuch as great inconveniences may happen to this country by setting of negroes and mulattoes free, by their either entertaining negro slaves from their masters service, or receiving stolen goods, or being grown old bringing a charge upon the country . . . Be it enacted . . . That no negro or mulatto to be after the end of this present session of the assembly set free by any person or persons.*[51]

An act of 1705 required hard evidence on the importation of Africans or any colored persons to show proof of "personal Christianity" in his/her native country "before capture" in order to escape the slave traders' clutches. The law all but eliminated the few blacks and mulattoes who might have been born of Christian parents in a Christian land, and those were extremely few. Most slaves came from African and Muslim or pagan countries. Thus, all potential avenues of freedom for blacks, whether coming into America from Asia, Africa, or "Christian lands," were shut down. Ballagh wrote that "It was easier for a camel to pass through the eye of a needle than for a negro or mulatto servant threreafter imported into Virginia to escape being made a slave if the law was enforced to its full extent.[52]

The 1705 law assigned penalties against any "Negro, mulatto, or Indian," slave or free, who raised a hand against any "Christian" (white person). It further enhanced white dominance of nonwhites and allowed whites to correct and even punish *any* nonwhite, whether they owned or had contracted such a person. The act and subsequent colonial laws that allowed the general white public to order about and punish nonwhites was a great assist to bind lower-class, non-slaveholding whites to slave owners and to the institution of bondage.

The law forbade Negroes, mulattoes, and Indians to own "any Christian servant" but allowed ownership of their "owne complexion," another repeat edict that separated, fundamentally, whites from nonwhites, giving whites by statute a higher social position in society. Consequently, African Americans and Native Americans owned slaves of their own and the others' race.

The law also reaffirmed bans on travel and weapons for blacks and forbade Indians and colored people from holding office and bearing witness in court. Equally significant in its march to statutory racism, the assembly in 1705 determined that slaves would no longer be held as chattel, personal property, but as real property that could be passed to heirs in the same manner as furniture, land and livestock.

The assembly further defined the parameters for recognizing the transition from black or colored to white, decreeing that the taint of "impure" blood could be reduced by four generations. The legislators enacted and declared "[t]hat the child of an Indian and the child, grand child, or great grand child, of a negro shall be deemed, accounted, held and taken to be a mulatto." Of course, the formula required the presence of a white parent in each generation, which in itself ran contrary to the law since interracial marriage was illegal. The act considered the Indian and the black on the same legal level but held that the stigma against the Indian lasted for two generations and against the black for four generations. Most colonial laws used four generations as a standard to determine when a mulatto lost his/her African blood.[53]

A section of the same act moved nonwhites further from judicial protections. "*Provided always* . . . That popish recusants convict, negroes, mulattoes and

Indian servants, and others, not being Christians, shall be deemed and taken to be persons incapable in law, to be witnesses in any cases whatsoever."[54]

Other laws of 1705 provided for punishment of female servants—white, black, and mulatto—who had bastards by their masters or other men. The punishment is most often directed at the female, calling for an extension of her servitude or enslavement and usually a fine. The children of such unions were most often bound out to the age of thirty, sometimes to the local church, often to the father who sired them.

> *If a woman servant is got by child by her master, the woman must fulfill her indenture, afterwhich she is sold for one year or pay 1,000 lbs. tobacco to the church. If the woman servant (white) has a bastard by a negro or mulatto, she pays 15 pounds "current money of Virginia" or be sold for five years and the same penalty for a "free Christian white woman."*[55]

White servants were no longer to be whipped naked as punishment; that indignity was now bestowed only on "brutish blacks," male and female. And while white servants were allowed to keep what livestock they had inherited, had bought, or were given while serving out a contract, by this act of the legislature slaves were now punishable by the seizure of their property by the church warden, which was transferred to poor whites for their upkeep.

An act of 1723 further restricted manumission of slaves to an act of "meritorious service." Such service often meant leniency to a slave who informed on purported slave insurrections. The law set the bar for freeing a slave so high that only a select few, to be determined by the governor and the council, would be freed. Since the landed gentry served on the council, the question of manumissions was effectively placed in their hands. The same act reinforced the disenfranchisement of free blacks and Indians.

The 1723 act put a larger burden on slave women by adding punishment and fines should they produce a bastard child, something that happened more frequently as slave owners gained absolute control of their charges. Ballagh points out that the law "unwittingly set a premium upon immorality" by extending the service of the offending woman to the owner, who might well be her seducer, and by placing the child under the guardianship of the owner, who might also be the father, for thirty-one years. Thus, the mulatto child was scarcely better off than a slave and in many instances eventually became a full-fledged slave. Hence, the act encouraged immorality by creating an economic advantage to the slave owner to impregnate his slaves.[56]

In case anyone should mistake the message of the Virginia Assembly to legislate against the interests of blacks, the governor of the colony spelled it out in the King's English in 1723, that blacks were destined to forever be separate and distinct from white. There must be "a perpetual Brand upon Free-negroes & mulattos by excluding them from the great Priviledge [*sic*] of a Freeman [to] make the free-negros sensible that a distinction ought to be made between their offspring and the Descendants of an Englishman, with whom they never were to be Accounted Equal."[57]

The General Assembly kept at its work to minimize the number of free blacks in the colony not only for the present but for the future. The assembly passed another revised law in 1748 to update the language of the act of 1682 that had included "all persons imported" to be slaves to read that "all persons who have been or shall be imported." The extremism of the law was so odious that even a prominent slave owner such as Thomas Jefferson took issue with it. The law would, according to Jefferson, make slaves "of the Jews who shall come from these countries [non-Christian] . . . Nay, it extends not only to such as those persons as should come here after the act, but also to those who came before and might then be living here in a state of freedom."[58]

By the mid-1700s, planters had rendered practically all black servants into slaves with little room for changing their status and had put severe restrictions on free blacks. Slave codes were in place in law and practice; custom supported those laws. Planters ruled the colonies both in economy and in legal administration. Professor Kulikoff has reduced the rule of slaves by mid-eighteenth-century to a primer of race relations:

> *First, they* [slaves] *had to accept the absolute power of their masters over their persons: they could be sold or transferred at any time, thereby suffering separation from kindred and friends. Not only did they have to refrain from assaulting or stealing from whites, they also owed every white complete deference. Slaves had to obey only their masters and work diligently for them and take in return only those goods their masters gave them. Finally, slaves had to avoid social contact with whites, and sexual relations with white women were forbidden.*[59]

Meanwhile, North Carolina and other slave colonies generally followed Virginia's lead in legislating slave codes, though North Carolina was often years behind and its laws were less harsh. For example, North Carolina's own "meritorious service" law was not enacted until 1741, likely in anticipation of Quaker initiatives in freeing slaves. Nonetheless, Quakers in Perquimans and Pasquotank Counties in North Carolina generally ignored the act and followed their conscience in the ambiguous business of slave manumissions.

The Revolutionary Upheaval

The second half of the eighteenth century wrought epochal change in the American colonies. The Great Awakening of Protestant revivalism swept through the colonies with a spirit of uplift and democracy. The movement lowered barriers between ministers and their congregations and gave the masses a sense of equality with their betters. It inspired a desire in the lower classes for literacy to put them in reach of the Bible. It brought a sense of fairness and right and wrong to the yeoman and the merchant. It, in short, inspired Americans to question authority and to reconsider their relations with Britain.[60]

Protestant revivalism was a primer for political democracy. As Protestants revolted against the established church, so did American colonials revolt against the British Crown. The ideas and principles of the Enlightenment propelled both movements, even if representatives of the new religion and the new politics selected those ideas that most served their causes.

By 1770 the frail antislavery sentiment in America was fortified by anti-British feelings wafting across the colonies. Virginia led the South in resistance to British rule. Caught up in the heady froth of revolutionary zeal, many planters in the South, especially in the border colonies, rashly embraced and espoused the radical ideas of John Locke's natural rights of man and the French political ideals of republicanism and liberalism. Liberty and equality were appealing ideas within the context of a break with Britain.

However, the inherent contradiction of American slaveholders urging war against British tyranny exposed itself, undermining the almost absolute influence of slave owners over the issue of slavery. Legislative bills found their way into the assembly proclaiming freedom as the "birth-right of all mankind" and that keeping Africans in bondage was a violation of that "unalienable right." 61

With America's success in the war, the new assembly of Virginia found a more forgiving attitude toward blacks. A sizeable number of whites, even slave owners, reconsidered their political and moral stance on the issue of slavery, and many agitated for an end to the practice. The state's legislature passed an act in 1782 that allowed for the personal manumission of slaves, a radical retreat from the slave codes that harked back to the early seventeenth century, specifically the act of 1691 that had banned private manumission. The bill would have enormous influence on the rapid growth of the free black caste.[62]

The act to end personal manumissions that had been law since 1723 was seconded by none other than Thomas Jefferson. Even Patrick Henry, prominent planter and revolutionary vanguard and slave owner, labeled the institution "repugnant to humanity . . . inconsistent with the Bible, and destructive to Liberty." The bill became law in Virginia in 1782, and by 1790 slave owners across the South, except in North Carolina, had regained the right to personally manumit their slaves.[63]

Virginia ended its slave trade in 1778 in a political gesture to the world that represented a new society, one whose support and legitimacy came from the people. While Virginians continued to hold slaves and domestic trading in slaves continued, slaves could no longer be imported directly from Africa or the Caribbean. In the heat of war and political revolution, republican ideals earned the colonies support of their own middling population and of international powers, such as France. But its themes of liberty and freedom excluded a half-million black people in bondage, half of those in the Virginia colony.

Henceforth, the freeing of slaves, though the process had to pass through the courts, became a much simpler action driven by owner release and slave self-purchase. Slaves no longer were held to meritorious service for their freedom. At this date, there were a mere 2,800 free blacks in the state. The new law created a burgeoning population of free blacks and, within a decade, a white backlash to the exploding caste.[64]

In the years after the 1782 manumission act, the white majority directed its fear and rancor not at slaves but at free African Americans. Revolutionary ideals concerning slavery eroded rather quickly in the South, and the draconian legislation used so heavily against slaves was now turned against free blacks. In 1793 the Virginia legislature, partly in reaction to the Toussant L'Ouverture rebellion in Saint Domingue, acted to "restrain the practice of Negroes going at large" by requiring urban free blacks to register with the clerk of court every year and rural blacks to register every three years. The law fixed a penalty for any free black to be about without a certificate as proof of his/her status.[65]

The registration of free blacks, while a racial indignity and curtailment of the civil rights of ostensibly free people, has provided historians, antiquarians, and genealogists with a treasure of information about American society in the antebellum South. The historical records reveal many surprises. For example, most of the free blacks who registered in 1793 had never been slaves. The majority of blacks who registered to comply with the law claimed freedom by birth, primarily from black fathers and white mothers. Eighty percent of people designated as "all other free persons" in the North Carolina censuses from 1790 to 1810 indicate that they were descendants of African Americans who were free in Virginia during the colonial period.[66]

Descendants of families which had been free during the colonial period continued to comprise a major part of the free African American population due to natural increase . . . . [In 1810] the Chavis family, free since the seventeenth century, headed forty-one households containing forty-six persons in Virginia, 159 in North Carolina, and twelve in South Carolina.[67]

Ironically, as American blacks, slave and free, became more acculturated and accepting of European/American values, as they became more estranged from newly arrived Africans, whites became more separated from blacks and more demanding of legal statutes to enforce their perspective. The aim of the early-nineteenth-century slave owner was to prevent the expansion of the free-black caste by preventing the manumission of slaves and the importation of free blacks. Their perspective was often shared by non-slave-owning whites, especially when laws forbade free-black competition with whites in particular areas of labor.

Southern lawmakers and planters colluded to keep blacks in America in ignorance and without skills by enacting restrictive laws against them, preventing them from acquiring education and basic civil rights. They then justified the institution of slavery and legal control of the free-black caste by pointing to their lack of education and skills. Planters appealed to lower-class whites by offering them reduced taxes and flattered them by implying that yeomanry and planters had a common enemy and a social inferior. They also instilled fear in lower-class whites by painting a scenario of hordes of unfettered blacks flooding towns and countryside, wreaking untold havoc and threatening rape and mayhem. It was a formula that served the ruling elite for generations.

Southern planters preached to a converted audience when they railed against the threats to slavery, having convinced the non-slaveholding populace of the virtues of bondage long ago. Though the slave system harmed white workers and small farmers in every way, they were frightened by the slave owners' dark prophecies of hordes of freed blacks running wild across the South, of the images of black satyrs molesting their wives and children, of black labor taking the jobs of white mechanics and farm workers. The subliminal notion that lay warmly cosseted in the white Southern psyche was spoken openly and succinctly by the *Columbus Times* (Georgia) as quoted by the Memphis *Tri-Weekly Appeal* in 1850:

> *It is African slavery that makes every white man in some sense a lord—it draws a broad line of distinction between the two races, and color gives caste .... Here the division is between white free men and black slaves, and every white is, and feels that he is a MAN.*[68]

As long as lower-class whites, farm workers, mechanics and laborers could demand of blacks their "certificate" and arrest them as runaways, punish them for infractions of the "Negro laws" and for their small indignities to whites and generally make their lives miserable at will, then non-slave-owning whites identified with slaveholders and were a mainstay of slavery. For however mean and low the white, he was not at the bottom of the social ladder; there was always a lower class that he could lord over. As John Quincy Adams framed it, "In the abstract [Southerners] say that slavery is an evil. But when probed to the quick on it they show at the bottom of their souls pride and vainglory in their condition of masterdom."[69]

There were many colonial political leaders who were slave owners but, caught up in the fervor of righteous indignation at the British and in the new ideologies of personal liberty and freedom, espoused the emancipation of slaves. Thomas Jefferson and James Madison, both owners of many slaves, nonetheless made impassioned speeches and wrote convincingly about emancipation. Though Jefferson did not free his slaves, nor did most slave owners, he understood and described for his peers the corrosive effects of slavery on Southern society.

> *The whole commerce between master and slave is a perpetual exercise of the most boisterous passions, the most unremitting despotism on the one part, and degrading submissions on the other. Our children see this, and learn to imitate it . . . . The parent storms, the child looks on, catches the lineaments of wrath, puts on the same airs in the circle of smaller slaves, gives loose to his worst passions, and thus nursed, educated and daily exercised in tyranny, cannot but be stamped by it with odious peculiarities.*[70]

CHAPTER TWO

The Free-Black Caste

We reside among you and yet are strangers; natives, and yet are not citizens; surrounded by the freest people and most republican institutions in the world, and yet enjoying none of the imunities [sic] of freedom . . . Though we are not slaves, we are not free.

Virginia had a free-black population of about 3,000 when the legislature passed the 1782 law allowing personal manumission, an increase in population that required about 150 years to achieve. By 1790, in a mere eight years, the number of free-black Virginians had soared to 12,766—more than twice the number of free blacks in the entire South before the Revolutionary War. The number of free blacks in the South that year was 32,357.

In the 1800 census the free-black Virginia population had increased to 20,124 while that of the entire South had mounted to 61,241. By 1810 the number of free blacks in Virginia had reached 30,570 and by 1830 was approaching 50,000. By 1810 the free-black numbers in the South amounted to 108,000 and was the fastest growing element of the Southern population.[1]

On the eve of the Revolution, there were still very few free blacks in relation to the black population as a whole in the Southern states. Restrictions on manumission of slaves had held the free-black caste to exceptional cases wherein owners would expend the energy and effort to slog through the process. Natural increase account for most of the remainder, minus those runaways who lost themselves in city ghettoes or in the swamps of the coastal plains. Maybe 1.5 % or 6,000 blacks, out of a population of 411,000, could qualify as "free" in Virginia by 1770.[2]

The explosion of the free-black population, ignited by the flames of the American Revolution and fanned by the emotionalism of evangelical religion, could not have occurred without the active involvement of the planter class. The spirit of the revolutionary era touched many slave owners and touched them deeply. Even slaveholders who held many bondsmen, the social and political elite, denounced the inherent evils of the system. The revolutionary slogans of liberty and freedom struck deep in the colonial psyche among all classes of people, planters and yeomen alike.

Numerous slave owners in the Upper South wished to escape the oppressive weight of slavery. Whether by political persuasion, religious conviction, financial considerations, or intrinsic moral choice—perhaps by a combination of all of these—thousands of slaveholders took advantage of more lenient manumission laws enacted in the wake of the Revolution to free or otherwise rid themselves of their charges. Across the South, the number of free blacks made a fivefold increase in twenty years.[3]

National political leaders such as Patrick Henry and Thomas Jefferson joined the chorus of voices denouncing human bondage, even as they held fast to their hundreds of slaves. Jefferson, the author of "all men are created equal," called slavery an "execrable commerce" and a "war against human nature." He joined forces with George Wythe, a signer of the Declaration of Independence and first law professor in the new country, to propose a plan to the Constitutional Convention for the gradual emancipation of slaves in Virginia, an idea that had been debated in Virginia for almost a century. The General Assembly rejected the proposal."[4]

Jefferson prophetically wrote after the failure of the plan that "It was found that the public mind would not bear the proposition, nor will it bear it even at this day. Yet the day is not distant when it must bear and adopt it, or worse will follow. Nothing is more certainly written in the book of fate than that these people are to be free."[5]

The contradictions of verbally supporting slavery while holding slaves may be explained in part by the very size and nature of the problem. Many planters discussed the failings of slavery and the need to rid the country of its influence, but their economy was so bound up in the holding of slaves that a ready remedy did not present itself. Immediate manumission presented a dread too stark to contemplate, of millions of illiterate, unskilled African Americans terrorizing the countryside. Also, whether immediate or gradual, emancipation threatened the greatest source of wealth for all slaveholders.

Still, private manumissions continued unabated for decades following the 1780s. The freedom bird had left the coop, never to return to the pre-1780s days of "meritorious service" standards. Not to say that service to the white community did not continue to win approval for black freedom. The tobacco manufacturer James Dunlop in 1822 freed his slave John Brander, a Petersburg boatman, for "uncommonly devoted attention to, and care of his late master during a most dangerous illness." Brander tended his owner after he fell seriously ill on a trip to Lynchburg, and the slave was credited with saving his owner's life. Dunlop gave a very personal and heartfelt plea for the emancipation of his slave, one which spoke of a personal relationship between slave and master.[6]

Scores of slaves were freed for their service in the Revolutionary War. The *Register of Free Negroes of Petersburg* lists several black veterans of the war in language similar to the following: "Jesse Scott a light Mulatto man about five feet eight inches high who served as a Soldier & a free man during the American Revolution about thirty four years old."[7] John Chavis, a noted Presbyterian minister and missionary from Virginia, boasted of his service in the American army to a North Carolina congressman.

Slave petitions for manumission for service in the Revolutionary War continued for many years after the war, even as the country found itself in need of their services again in the War of 1812. Approximately 15 percent of America's forces that faced the British in the War of 1812 were black. Hundreds of slaves were freed for meritorious service for their war duty. Slave owners, some out of personal attachments, some out of religious and political convictions, some out of financial considerations, continued to manumit their slaves, though in much reduced numbers, up to the Civil War.

Petitions to the courts and to the General Assembly for support of manumission of slaves overwhelmed the system. County courts did a steady business in manumitting slaves to the point that standard legal jargon was drafted to expedite the court's business and to give some legal eloquence to the common planter's request. Justifications such as "Whereas, considering liberty to be the natural and unalienable right of man" and similar revolutionary and biblical catchphrases justified slave manumissions to the courts. Examples of revolutionary manumission language are used in deeds and wills recorded throughout the late eighteenth century.

The number of court cases dealing with manumission was so large that the subject became somewhat tiresome for the judiciary. The majority of petitions to the court for manumission during this "quiescence period" of slavery received rather pro forma review. The courts seldom debated the merits of meritorious service in requests for freeing slaves. "By 1830 the laws concerning manumission had become something of a dead letter and were rather generally disregarded."[8]

Some slaves turned to the Northern states to assist with emancipations, not entirely trusting that local officials would prepare valid papers for the transaction. They used agents—trusted white friends and Northern strangers sympathetic to abolition—to carry out the transactions. Slaves would sell themselves to an agent, or their owner would do so, who in turn would then free the slave. Philadelphia was a favorite site to record manumissions and to find abolition agents who would act as a go-between, as was the case for Joseph Harding in 1792.[9]

> *John Dickins of the City of Philadelphia, Minister of the Gospel, for six pence lawful money of Pennsylvania to me in hand paid by Joseph Harding Merchant of Petersburg sell one Negro Man by the name of Plowman, one Negro man named Limehouse with one Negro woman named Senah now in the possession of my agent John Clayton of Halifax County, North Carolina.*

> *I Joseph Harding believe that God created all Men equally free. I do hereby emancipate and set free the following persons: Limehouse, a man; Ploughman a man and Sena a woman.*[10]

Planters now freed their slaves by wills and other legal documents out of personal concern and care for the individual or from a pang of moral conscience. Deathbed manumissions and wills allowed slave owners to depart life with an easy conscience. There were such manumissions prior to the revolution, but the practice really boomed in the 1780s and 1790s, after private manumission was allowed by law. Altruism did not fuel all manumissions, however. Many slave owners took advantage of the new laws to release slaves who were aged or infirm and no longer profitable.

In North Carolina in the late eighteenth century, the wholesale freeing of slaves, often in violation of laws by avoiding the courts, was so disturbing that the legislature reenacted the restrictive manumission law of 1777 in 1788 and again in 1796. Inspired by the revolutionary sentiments dominant in the 1770s and 1780s, slaves were freed for any cause and for no cause: for "goodwill," for "conscience," for "Christian charity," for the "natural rights of man." Mulattoes were frequently freed on the testimony of locals who would swear that the slave's mother or grandmother was white or Indian.

The fact that many slave owners disliked slavery or did not prosper from it can be deduced from the hundreds of slave owners who took advantage of the 1782 law of the Virginia Assembly allowing personal manumissions. The depth of their disgust with human bondage seldom appears in the legal language of the courts, but occasionally a planter braved the scorn of friends and family and gave vent to his feelings regarding slavery. In 1801 the same slave holder Baker who freed his slave Celia in 1791 in Isle of Wight disinherited "Catharine Haynes" in his will and instructed that his estate was to be managed for the benefit of his slave named Mary Simpson, perhaps his daughter.

> [F]or the advantage of Mary Simpson a Mulatto formerly my slave now free until she comes of age and capable of taking care of herself then she is to get the whole of his estate of what kind whatsoever. Furthermore, if Mary Simpson die without issue be the same lawful or unlawful he leaves the whole estate to the people call'd Quakers to be used by them for the purpose of purchasing and liberating slaves and the preference given to those who were my property—I would it were in my power to entirely banish that excreable practice . . . . 1802.[11]

George Corbin was also articulate and outraged at a system that allowed one portion of humanity to enslave another while preaching the universal freedom and liberty of mankind, even though he was one of the despised. The intense emotions of the Revolution and of Protestant Christianity apparently converted Corbin to a strongly antislavery advocate, to the point of freeing his own slaves.

> To all Christian People to whom these presents shall come, Greeting Know Ye That I George Corbin . . . for divers good Causes and Considerations me hereunto moving but, more Especially form Motives of Humanity, Justice, and Policy, and As it is Repugnant to Christianity and even common Honesty to live in Ease and Affluence by the Labour of those whom fraud and Violence have Reduced to Slavery; (altho' sanctifyed by General consent, and supported by that law of the Land) Have and by these presents do manumit and set free the following Persons.[12]

Farmers and planters occasionally freed and bequeathed land and other property to their illegitimate slave children, some of whom became prosperous in their own right. A farmer in Wilmington, North Carolina, emancipated his two mulatto sons by will but took the precaution of having his property deed approved by the state's General Assembly, not trusting the county to make a legal transfer. Another farmer in North Carolina willed a hundred acres of swampland to his "Mulatto Son Willie Abel . . . he having been free'd by the Court March term 1801."[13]

Josiah Godwin of Isle of Wight freed his servant Charles Crews with the obvious intent of rewarding him for his services, while leaving several of his slaves to various family members. It was not unusual for masters and mistresses to form a paternal bond with their servants and take special measures for their benefit.

> *I give unto my servant Charles Crews (my servant who has been faithful and honest in serving me, and is one of the most correct Men of his colour I have ever seen) $100, one cow and calf, one sow and pigs and my wearing apparel of every kind—Crews is not left to anybody.*[14]

The post-Revolution statutes allowed slaves to purchase themselves and their families out of bondage. Self-purchase was not an intent of the liberal manumission laws, and slave holders did not anticipate the large number of slaves who would manage to take advantage of the laws by buying their freedom.

There were ambitious slaves all over the South who saved enough money from hiring out to buy their way to freedom. It was not uncommon for slaves to save money from selling produce off their private plots, from working for other slave owners at night and on Sundays, and from hiring out their time to merchants and planters while paying their owner a set fee per year or per season. White slave owners respected money as nothing else and would seldom refuse to free a slave if the price was sufficient. During the leniency of the post-revolutionary era, a large proportion of blacks bought their freedom through self-purchase. Tommy Bogger suggests that as high as 36 percent of manumissions between 1790 and 1829 were by self-purchased slaves.[15]

> *Lawrence Baker of I of W has in his possession a Negro woman named Celia aged abt 42 whom I purchased of James Wills esq sheriff of I of W at the Public sale of the estate of Richard Wrenn to satisfy Thos Wrenn's exec—now in consideration of f12.1.0 current money of Va to me paid by the said Celia and which was furnished by the said Celia at the aforesaid sale being the purchase money paid for her frees her—3 Feb 91.*
>
> Petersburg Deed Book 2, 1790-1801.

> *I, Abby Smith, a free Negro woman of the town of Petersburg, purchased of Henry Randolph, Esq. of the County of Nottoway a Mulatto boy slave named Baldy (being my own son) agreeable to a bill of sale executed by the said Harrison to me bearing the date 1 April 1798, and whereas also considering liberty to be the natural and unalienable right of man, and for and in consideration of the natural love and affection I heqr my said son Have emancipated ... 4, February 1799. proved same date.*[16]
>
> Petersburg Deed Book 2, 1790-1801.

Self-hire was different from an owner hiring out his slaves. Slaves who self-hired had the permission, often the encouragement, of his/her owner to rent themselves out to the highest bidder. Slaves who were successful at renting themselves and who could make enough money to satisfy their owners fees were free to pocket whatever profits they earned. North Carolina and Virginia had numerous male and female slaves who became financially well off in the self-hire business.

Lunsford Lane of Raleigh bought himself and his family with money he earned as a messenger for the governor's office, as a maker of smoking pipes and tobacco, and as a seller of firewood. He strived to portray himself to the community as poor, recognizing that the white community resented successful blacks, free and slave. John Stanly of New Bern, a barber and farmer, bought himself and his family's freedom and that of many other slaves even as he worked slaves at his various enterprises.

Other free blacks purchased family members in order to free them and other slaves to work their farms and businesses, such as the wealthy Lydia Mangum, a Wake County free-black farmer, who owned property worth $20,000, and James Freeman, a New Hanover carpenter, who was worth $36,000 in real and personal property. By 1830 there were at least 190 free-black slaveholders in North Carolina, most owning one or two slaves, but several owning 10 or 15. Charles Mallett in Cumberland County owned 36 slaves, and Gooden Bowen in Bladen County owned 44. Pioneer historian of free blacks, John Hope Franklin, named more than 50 free blacks in North Carolina who, in 1860, owned property valued between $2,500 and $36,000.[17]

Most successful free blacks, however, labored at menial jobs and earned just enough to remain free and off the poor roles. They worked as farmers, house servants, cooks, waiters, artisans, and other menial occupations that would afford them some security and maybe a little dignity. Most, when they were fortunate, continued the occupations they held as slaves.

The 1815 *Index of Free Negroes* of Greensville County, Virginia, lists some 60 free blacks, 26 marked as "Negro," 29 recorded as "Mulatto," and 5 unlisted as to race. Of the total free-black population, 15 are "spinsters" and 37 are "planters," of which 9 owned their land. Several of the women are noted as landowners. Two of the mulatto planters, Willie Artis and Nathaniel Day, worked for Cudjoe Day, one of the free-black planters who owned land. It has yet to be proven if Cudjoe and Thomas Day are related. Only two of the total worked at a trade, one a shoemaker and the other a hatter. Of the 3 remaining, one was a hireling and 2 were house servants.[18]

The ranks of the free-black caste were also bolstered by runaway slaves who managed to find and join free-black communities, such as those that existed at Nutbush on the border of North Carolina and Virginia, and other communities in the northeast section of North Carolina. The Great Dismal Swamp was notorious for its population of runaways who made a life and a living gathering shingles, logging, building roads, driving oxen, and doing other hard-labor jobs that were not easily filled by white workers. White company owners were quick to look the other way when runaway blacks were willing to work in the mosquito and serpent congested swampland.

The population was sparse in the swampy marshland of the coastal plains, and absentee plantation owners contributed to lax slave supervision. Slaves who were fortunate enough to find these communities might hide in their protection for months or even years and eventually emerge as a free person, complete with a new name and maybe forged papers.19

The other appealing environment to runaway slaves was any town of size, such as Norfolk or Petersburg or Richmond in Virginia. North Carolina had no towns of any size—perhaps Wilmington—but Virginia's coastal cities and its capital offered ready ghettoes of African Americans which offered a support group and a social environment in which slaves could hide out and pass as freedmen.

Impact of Religion

Religion played a major role in the changing face of slavery and in the creation of a free black caste. Though most colonials were content to let the official state church handle issues of the soul in the seventeenth century, by the mid-1700s, a revolutionary way of looking at God and man's place in religion vis-à-vis the church was beginning to take root. America was to experience its own "reformation" in the eighteenth century.

The ideas of the Enlightenment and the French *philosophes* that inspired the American Revolution also fanned a shift in religious winds as colonials looked to a more personal approach to religion. The egalitarian notions of the Revolution were a much warmer match with Protestants, especially evangelicals, than with the staid Church of England. Baptists, Methodists, and Quakers stepped into the breach created by the absence of the state church, "reaping a rich harvest of human souls," as the tide of human emotion in America reversed itself and the population reached out to Protestant denominations. The emotionalism and social leveling of evangelism and revivalism caught the mood and ethos of backcountry Americans and swept the established church in their tidal wave.[20]

The revolutionary teachings of equality by evangelicals were eagerly accepted by the majority of blacks who flocked to the revivals and early churches of Baptist and Methodist exhorters and of abolitionist Quakers. The radical teachings of evangelicals revolutionized the thinking of many blacks about themselves, about their self-esteem, and about their abilities to become independent of their owners, much to the chagrin of most slave owners who worked to blunt the rebellious nature of the evangelical message.[21] John Day, brother of Thomas, experienced his initial religious awakening at a Protestant revival in Southside Virginia.

Methodists, Quakers, and Baptists made early inroads to the slave communities with their simple messages of faith and acceptance. Both creeds preached freedom and human equality, and their disciples lived up to their creeds. Preachers and missionaries worshipped with blacks and accepted blacks as preachers and "exhorters" if they received "God's call to preach." Baptists and Methodists were zealous and, as one observer noted, "remarkably warm in their religious exercises." Quakers accepted blacks as "children of God" and made no attempts to hide their determination to undermine slavery.[22]

Baptist and Methodist reformers dealt with slavery head-on. In 1787, the Virginia Methodist Conference posed the question "What shall we do for the promotion of the spiritual welfare of our colored people?" In 1789 the Virginia Baptist Convention declared slavery a "violent depredation of the rights of nature and inconsistent with a republican government." Planters supported the concept of the "unalienable rights of man" in opposition to British rule but many considered religious promotion of equality subversive and detrimental to their economic well-being.

Persecution of pioneer evangelicals by the established church and by royal government served to steel their resolve and to boost their identification with the poor, those in bondage, and other harassed minorities. The early Protestant churches were outsiders—outside the established church and the political system—and were derided by Anglicans. The early Baptists embraced their role as outcasts and threw their lot with others who were not tolerated by the establishment: slaves, other evangelicals, the poor. Separate or New Light Baptists, inspired by Shubal Stearns in the 1750s, welcomed their "nonconformist" identity, which, they believed, made them the true believers and practitioners of primitive Christianity. They were at ease with the simple folk and found little success and less patience with the "politest part of the people."[23]

Generally, the early Baptists preached against planter society and its values and against the establishment. They identified with the oppression of slaves and opposed their owners, who often refused to allow their slaves to worship with Baptist preachers and exhorters. Baptists accepted blacks, free and slave, into their congregations and made them full members of the church. Their white preachers often rode in tandem with black preachers to revivals, and some black preachers led congregations of white churches. Bishop Francis Asbury traveled in Virginia with a free black, Harry Hosier, who some considered more popular as a revivalist and exhorter than Asbury himself.[24]

Evangelism was a better fit with the casual, unfussy nature of the American frontier than the more ceremonial Anglicanism with its hierarchy and starchy rites. Protestant evangelicals expressed their religious emotions in the church, in the fields and pastures, and under vine arbors. It was not unusual for congregations to collapse on the floors of churches or on the ground during out-of-doors revivals, lose the use of their extremities, and fall to weeping and moaning. Exhorters meandered through the stricken, urging them to greater excitement and praying over the seriously prostrate.

No sects put more preachers in the field than the Baptists and Methodists did in North Carolina and Virginia. Most counties had slave and free-black preachers and exhorters, some local, others who traveled around the region, preaching to both black and to mixed audiences. Freeborn Garretson carried the gospel in the Roanoke River region across the Virginia border as early as 1777, where he once preached to five hundred whites and almost as many blacks who stood outside the preaching grounds. He then offered a second sermon for his black worshippers, for whom he would adapt his discourse "to them alone."[25]

Mixed congregations became a common and accepted practice in Virginia and North Carolina among the evangelicals during the revolutionary era. William Mulkey, a black preacher, ministered to an integrated Baptist church at Bluestone in the Meherrin Association. Jacob Bishop (1792), a black minister, replaced Thomas Armstrong (white) at Portsmouth, and the Williamsburg Baptist Church had a black preacher named Moses. Gowan Pamphlet preached at the same church in the 1780s for the Dover Association.[26]

Preachers. Until 1831 black preachers were accepted and encouraged by some plantation owners as a positive force. Blacks sometimes traveled in tandem with white preachers and delivered sermons in white churches and to mixed congregations. *(Courtesy of the Library of Congress, Prints & Photographs Division, Washington, D.C. No Use Restrictions)*

Protestant churches in Virginia and North Carolina bought a number of slave preachers and freed them for their services. Rev. Christopher McPherson, a mulatto, preached during the 1780s and 1790s in Fluvanna County. A bookkeeper and an alleged seer, he reported and prevented a slave uprising in the county, the ultimate test for a free black to make his mark with white authorities.

Ralph Freeman was licensed by the Baptist Church in Anson County, North Carolina. The man was a slave when he found his calling and was so effective in the pulpit that the church paid for his freedom and sent him on a circuit in five surrounding counties along the southern border with South Carolina. He often traveled in tandem with a white preacher named Joseph Magee, with whom he had a close relationship. Magee bequeathed his coat, his Bible, his horse, and fifty dollars to his black counterpart upon his death. Freeman's career with the church came to an end by legislative fiat in 1831 in the backlash of Nat Turner's horrific massacre in Virginia.[27]

Uncle Jack, a slave in Nottoway County, was an exceptional preacher in the area revered by blacks and whites. Rev. Dr. John Blair Smith, president of Hampden Sidney College, and other white ministers influenced the receptive slave. Jack, an African, learned his first lessons in reading from his master's children. He further educated himself by listening to white preachers and by reading the Bible and practicing his delivery. The Baptist church licensed him to preach as he developed into a powerful exhorter of Christian doctrine. He was one of a number of slave preachers who served as many whites as blacks.[28]

Preacher Jack eventually organized a large black church that was well patronized by slaves in the area. His preaching had such a positive influence in their lives that white owners often sent their unruly slaves to him for correction. Jack was so effective in the Nottoway area and of such help to the planters in the community that they purchased his freedom and gave him a house and land. Slave holders were not against supporting evangelicals when the alliance worked in their favor.

The slave preacher won greater notoriety when he debated another black preacher, name of Campbell, who espoused the New Light heresy favoring "noise" and "Spirit" over the words of the Bible. Jack apparently defeated his competition so convincingly that the other man's followers defected to Jack. Though he preached for forty years, his career was halted in 1832 by laws passed against black preachers and teachers in the wake of the Nat Turner massacre.[29]

Uncle Jack became a legend in Nottoway County and remained so for decades after his death. White writers liked to recall how the former slave never used "massa" and "missus" for *master* and *mistress* or *me* for *I* but pronounced like white folk, "contrary to the negro dialect." "The most refined and aristocratic people paid tribute to him, and he was instrumental in the conversion of many whites . . . He was invited to their houses, sat with their families, took part in their social worship, sometimes leading the prayer at the family altar."[30]

Spreading evangelism also went in the other direction. Devereux Jarratt, a traveling white Episcopal minister ordained at London, favored the Methodist movement within the church. He served Southside Virginia as minister of the Bath Parish from 1763 until his death in 1801. Worshippers praised Reverend Jarratt for his inspirational preaching, and he became a favorite of African Americans in the region. He claimed to be the first parish minister to bring "evangelical" religion to Southside and one of the first to criticize the congregation and parish ministers for drinking, dancing, and "civil mirth." Jarratt further claimed that a number of ministers were "not only wanting in seriousness, but were immoral and ignorant."[31]

John Day was one of many nonbelievers to fall under the influence of the passionate evangelicals. Following his family's immigration to North Carolina, he met with spiritual conversion at an arbor revival at Mill Pond in Warren County and was baptized into the Baptist faith at the age of twenty-three.[32]

Methodists

Methodism found its way into North Carolina through the ministry of black preachers. William Meredith was one of the pioneer ministers. He built a church on Zion Hill in the upriver port of Wilmington in 1784, only to have it burned by opposition, either racial or religious. Numerous black preachers and exhorters were molested, had their churches burned, and were tarred and feathered.

Meredith built a second church on Zion Hill that stood against the opposition and became the Methodist church of the city and a bulwark for Methodism in the state. By 1812 the church had a membership of over seven hundred blacks and almost fifty whites. By 1800 fully one-fourth of Methodists in the state were black, and by 1860 they numbered about twelve thousand.[33]

Henry Evans performed a similar feat in Fayetteville. Originally from Virginia, Evans immigrated to Stokes County in North Carolina where the local ministry licensed him to preach. The preacher also worked as a shoemaker who, at some point, decided to make his future in Charleston, South Carolina. On his journey south, he passed through Fayetteville and, struck by the lack of religious opportunities in the black communities, decided to take up his preaching there.[34]

The shoemaker threw his lot with his people in the Cape Fear River town, making shoes during the week and preaching on Sundays. He preached to such effect that he alarmed local authorities who chased him from the town's environs. Evans then preached secretly in the surrounding woods and sand hills, changing venues often to escape capture. His slave audience reacted in such a positive way to his sermons, however, that their owners changed their views about the man and began to attend his sermons themselves.

The town council lifted the ban against Evans, and his congregants erected a crude building in town for his services. As greater numbers of whites attended services, the walls of the building were knocked out, and sheds were built to accommodate the crowds of blacks and whites who worshipped. The preacher-shoemaker became an attraction for people in the area and for visitors passing through. All remarked on the power of his preaching.[35]

In 1805 the church became a member of the Methodist Episcopal Church. Evans's health began to decline, and a white minister assumed his duties in 1808. The mixed congregation built living quarters, a small shed, onto the church for the preacher, where he lived in retirement until his death in 1810. His funeral attracted a record number of people, black and white, to mourn his passing.

William Capers, the white Methodist bishop who followed Evans to Fayetteville, wrote of the black preacher that he was "most remarkable" and "pure of heart."

"Henry Evans . . . was confessedly the father of the Methodist Church, white and black, in Fayetteville, and the best preacher of his time in that quarter."[36]

Not all of the Protestant churches readily accepted evangelism. The Presbyterian Church resisted the extremes of the evangelical and revivalism movement. Some in the church warmed to the protest hymns and even fell in with the "body jerkers," but the church hierarchy practiced a religion of restraint. Howard McKnight Wilson, who wrote a history of the Lexington Presbytery, notes that a spiritual revival at Hampden-Sydney began a

> *Great Revival that enlarged into camp-meetings in Southwest Virginia, Tennessee, and Kentucky, in which bodily exercises took place without warning as one of the sensational features. An individual would fall like a log to the floor or ground "with a piercing scream" and lie like dead for hours at a time. In other cases "hundreds were flung prostrate, like a grain-field swept by a hurricane," but among Presbyterians "jerks," "groans," and "cries" were the more common manifestations of these nervous disturbances.*[37]

Church authority could not always control the impulsive responses of its congregations to the evangelical rhythms when they reacted to the verses of faith and grace written into Protestant hymns. Wilson writes that the revivals degenerated into the "Kentucky jerks" as more adherents turned toward evangelical passion. He records a sermon delivered by a Mr. Boggs that was interrupted with "bodily agitations" of the worshippers. "[O]ne of the elders rose and began to sing, and immediately the whole congregation was convulsed with various emotions and exercises; groans and sighs and cries were heard in every part, and for a while the worship was suspended."[38]

Presbyterians split over the issue of "body exercises" and "Kentucky jerks" and a more restrained service. The main church remained "free of that bigotry or superstition, pomp or parade so inconsistent with the true principles of their profession." Wilson asserts that the high standard of education was largely responsible for saving the church from the excesses of the revivalist movement. The noted black missionary and teacher, John Chavis, was schooled in the more intellectual and less demonstrative Presbyterian tradition.

"Most of the ministers gave their cautious approval to the revival but were quick to discourage any physical manifestations such as crying out in the public worship service."[39] This was the church that Thomas Day and his wife chose to join after they settled in Milton, North Carolina. The unemotional approach to religion was more in keeping with Thomas's personality, whereas his brother, John, chose the more animated evangelical churches.

Quakers

The Religious Society of Friends, or Quakers (possibly named for their propensity to "tremble at the word of God"), was the most aggressive of the protest churches in proselytizing amongst slaves. They accepted literally the revolutionary calls for liberty and freedom for all men and the biblical leveling of all people in the eyes of God.

Religious Friends came out of the protestant groupings that left the Church of England in the 1650s following the English Civil War. Like many Protestant sects, Quakers believed themselves to be the true heirs to Christianity because they strived to follow "early church" practices, especially a direct personal experience with God as captured in the description "priesthood of believers." They opposed the pomp and ceremony of the established church and the hierarchy of church officials.[40]

The Friends came to colonial America in search of souls and for security from government persecution. Their search failed in Massachusetts but found more acceptance in Rhode Island and Pennsylvania, where converts embraced their liberal agenda, even, at least in part, the governors of the colonies. Quakers were antislavery and pro-suffrage, favored prison reform, dressed plainly, swore no oaths, and espoused pacifism. Their services were unstructured and often lacked a sermon. Attendants spoke as they were moved by the spirit.

The group brought the scrutiny of the government and the Anglican Church on themselves when it overtly began to teach slaves to read and write, to give them books, and to worship with them. Quakers successfully raised money through subscriptions to establish groups within the sect to purchase slaves from willing masters. They were frequently on wrong side of colonial and state politics for their radical tenets.

> *The human race however varied in Color are Justly entitled to Freedom, and that It is the duty of Nations as well as Individuals, enjoying the blessings of freedom To remove this dishonor of Christian character from among them—But more especially in the United States where the principles of freedom as so lightly professed.*[41]

Protestants denominations marginalized the established church in America and changed the face of government and the spiritual nature of American colonists. As the protest sects claimed legitimacy and then dominance in the post-revolutionary states, the character of their doctrines shifted from outsider to status quo. They would, in short order, occupy the former position of the Anglican Church as the foundation of government and of the planter aristocracy.

As great and widespread as the religious changes were in revolutionary America, the movement would not have succeeded without the acceptance and encouragement of many prominent and lesser slave owners and planters. And part of that acceptance for some included sympathy toward emancipation of slaves. Owners were at times as susceptible as their slaves to the exciting spiritual teachings that offered freedom of will and freedom from the menacing eyebrows of priests and bishops. Some planters welcomed evangelical preachers almost as quickly as did free blacks, slaves, and farmers. All classes were drawn to the festive revivals that could attract hundreds and even, on occasion, thousands of people.

Other slave owners allowed the new religion on their plantations, and some encouraged their slaves' participation out of hope that religious moral lessons would have a positive effect on their bondsmen. Uncle Jack was perhaps as revered for his message as for his ability to calm and settle the slaves of Nottoway County. Owners applauded the biblical lessons of "slaves obey your masters" and "render unto Caesar that which is Caesar's." John Chavis preached from the slaveholders' scripture and from the perspective of the established Presbyterian church, as he was formally trained, and was widely accepted in white communities because of his conservative approach.

The Revolutionary War and the Virginia stance on religious toleration wrought a profound change in Protestant doctrine. With the weakening of the Anglican Church in America, Protestants were no longer outcasts and subversives. The new respectable revivalists won over many denizens of the merchant and planter classes during the Revolution and began to take on the trappings of a new establishment. Once Protestants bested the state church and became the new religious standard, they committed to the new social order and to its ruling interests. The former radicals quickly became the guardians of the status quo in the new nation. They acquired, according to one observer, "a taste for respectability with unbecoming ease."[42]

Between 1785 and 1797 the Baptists of Virginia expressed their uneasiness with slavery but found their post-revolutionary congregations resistant to discussions about bondage, and the church "then fell silent on the matter." Slavery was gradually moved from the "agenda of reform" of the Protestants.[43]

Cooling of revolutionary zeal

The hot winds of Protestant evangelism that rolled through the American colonies in the mid to late eighteenth century cooled noticeably during the last decade of the century. Sentiments of the "natural rights of man" and "liberty and freedom" remained sacred tenets of the middling classes and the yeomanry and even with American slaves. But the radical spirit in religion and politics waned for whites. By the 1790s the revolutionary zeal was spent, and whites left the manumission issue behind them. Slaves and free blacks, on the other hand, still felt connected to the principles of the French and American Revolutions when the issue of emancipation came to dominate America's political discourse.[44]

The issue that brought black freedom to the fore as a social and political concern in the early years of the 19th century was the rapid increase in the population of free blacks. As the number of free blacks rose, so did white fear of their freedoms and mobility. American society, colonial and national, was intended for but two races: white and black, one slave and one free. By the end of the seventeenth century, white equaled free and black meant slave. Anything in between muddied the social and political waters. "Incorporating a large number of free blacks into their society and according them the rights and privileges of free citizens went far beyond the intention of Virginia's lawmakers."[45]

Being free and black in America was a precarious life that only deteriorated as the caste grew in numbers. Freedom for most blacks outside slavery was a fragile and elusive condition, "its terms shifting with the anxiety levels of the men who ran the legislature and the local courts. In practice, periods of relatively benign neglect alternated with spells of close surveillance and sudden repression. In law, the story was one of progressive deterioration."[46]

Many questions of legal rights and social position hovered over free blacks during the colonial and national periods, but it was their color and prior enslavement that unsettled most whites. Slave owners felt that the "near-free" status of free blacks disturbed the established public order, that their pseudo freedom agitated slaves to emulate them, and that their color and connections to the slave class made them natural allies with slaves against whites. "As the whites very well realized, even if the free blacks consciously refrained from inciting the slaves to resist bondage, their very presence in a slave society posed a grave danger to the stability of the institution."[47]

> *Fear of the free Negro as a potential instigator of slave revolts was also a principal reason for the restrictions placed upon manumission in every one of the southern states during the nineteenth century.*[48]

Even so, despite white fears of slave revolts and of free blacks demanding social equality, prosperous and successful blacks emerged from the ranks of the free-black caste. These energetic souls often sidestepped the strict state laws and local ordinances that sought to control their mobility and business arrangements. They functioned much like their white counterparts and, quite often, with their encouragement and help.

Most successful free blacks fully embraced white culture or, at least, convinced the white community of their adherence to white mores and attitudes. The ultimate symbol of that acceptance was to become a slave owner. Thomas Day and his brother, John, fulfilled the requirements and met the expectations of white society even as they were kept at arm's length from social and political equality with whites. Historian Loren Schweninger writes that "prosperous free people of color were able to maintain their high economic standing in large measure because they did not pose a threat to the South's 'peculiar institution.'"[49]

Some fortunate free blacks became landowners and acquired real property, even slaves, and some of them became quite wealthy. They could negotiate contracts and sue in court. Their marriages were recognized, and their property conveyed to their heirs in the nineteenth century as it had in the seventeenth century. Thomas Day's son, Thomas Jr., managed to acquire his father's cabinetmaking shop and continue his trade at Milton in spite of the Civil War. At no time in the antebellum period was the right to own real property by free blacks seriously questioned, and those rights were defended in court cases dealing with property disputes. Property was the one area the caste was given a semblance of a chance to compete with whites; such was the sanctity of property in America.

Despite laws on the books of all colonies and later the states to restrict the movement of slaves and free blacks, exceptions were the norm everywhere; that was the nature of America's slave society. Exceptional blacks, free and slave, who possessed skills needed by struggling towns and villages and plantations, exercised considerable mobility in the eighteenth and first quarter of the nineteenth century. The Days and other skilled free blacks traveled between North Carolina and Virginia, apparently without hindrance.

Laws and statutes and ordinances often reflected merely the aspirations of white slaveholders who were the principal officeholders and who were far removed from the needs of the farmer or merchant and often ran counter to what was practiced in society at large. Or as House delegate Thomas Marshall of Fauquier County opined on the floor of the house, the 1806 law requiring freed slaves to immigrate had "never been carried into effect because its provisions were in violation of the feelings of the people."[50]

There were always exceptional free blacks—bakers, blacksmiths, barbers, maids, carpenters—people who were very useful to a particular area and who were generally well liked by most of the community's white citizens. In these cases, whites might genuinely like the individual, or at least recognized their value to the community, and made public statements in his/her behalf. There was considerable white sympathy for Thomas Day and for Lunsford Lane and John Chavis. There are hundreds of these situations recorded in court cases and in legislative petitions.

In daily life where individuals made practical decisions that affected their livelihood and their well-being, whites employed free blacks often and were not opposed to selecting them over whites if their work or service was superior. Money and quality made the difference, and Americans were no exception when it came to choosing what was best for them. "It was clear to all—even to the ideologues when they made practical, day-to-day decisions—that there were reliable and unreliable, skilled and unskilled, bright and dim people among both races, and that life abounded with situations in which it made more sense to apply that insight than to impose a simple racial test."[51]

Historian Melvin Ely has explored this paradoxical social and legal milieu that was common to all the states in the antebellum American South, but especially in the Upper South, in his detailed and intimate study of Prince Edward County, Virginia. He offers up scores of examples of ambitious and resourceful free blacks in that one county who lived, worked, and functioned well in a slave society. While whites might resent their achievements, they nonetheless sought their expertise and labor. Historian Eva Wolf makes the same point in *Almost Free*.[52]

Ely shows numerous examples of whites and free blacks associating in work and even in common social situations. He recounts daily, seemingly innocuous black-white situations, such as a fight between two white wagoners at the home of a free-black boatman, David Bartlett. The white teamsters had stopped off at Bartlett's for breakfast when they began arguing over a previous affront. One of them may have spent the night at Bartlett's. Soon it was whips and knives, with Bartlett and a well-known white innkeeper, Thomas Totty, looking on. "No one found it unusual for men black and white, well-off and humble, free and enslaved, to spend time at a free-black man's house, and for some of them . . . to eat or sleep there."[53]

Teamsters, or wagoners as they were styled then, were in the top tier of laborers. They traveled long distances and carried expensive loads and sometimes large amounts of cash. They made many personal connections with people who wanted to move freight or money, legal and illicit, from interior to town. The trade was pursued by black and white, slave and free, and the ones who proved most dependable won the customers.

Mule Driver. Most free blacks, denied an education, performed menial labor as farm hands, ditchers, loggers, servants, waiters and drovers. Their labor was often chosen over that of whites as the better quality. *(Courtesy of the Library of Congress, Prints & Photographs Division, Washington, D.C. No Use Restrictions)*

There were numerous jobs and trades that blacks (free and slave) and whites worked together and competed for: contractors, carpenters, harvesters, wagoners, boatmen, bricklayers, ditchers, and blacksmiths, among others. Free blacks often beat out whites for jobs, even at the same wage. Slave labor would sometimes best both white and free black because their labor cost about half what a freeman charged for the same work.

So how did blacks, free and slave, manage to operate stores, manage farms, perform carpentry and cabinetwork, build houses and roads and bridges, get crops to market and interact with white employers and clients, and master the other aspects of business without literacy and math?

More literate blacks existed in the South than anyone knew. Literacy was illegal, something feared by many whites and hidden by blacks, even though whites primarily taught their blacks to read and write and multiply. Slave owners and employers had numerous reasons for breaking the law, even those who opposed emancipation and favored colonization to remove free blacks. How did a slave compute the dimensions of a field task without an understanding of basic math? Or build a barn or house without the rudiments of arithmetic? It was in the best interest of the farm or the plantation to have literate workers who were capable of more complex tasks than a simple farmhand could manage.

Plantation owners and merchants could not operate without literate laborers, and not all slave owners agreed that bondsmen should be kept in ignorance to prevent their acquiring a sense of dignity. Lenient masters and mistresses saw to it that their slaves were taught to read and write and to perform basic arithmetic. Tazewell Branch, a slave shoemaker in Farmville, Virginia, was taught to read alongside his master's children, a frequent source of slave tutoring. James W. D. Bland, though born free, was taught to read by the former owner of his mother. He apprenticed as a carpenter and a cooper, trades that allowed him to support himself and a family in adulthood.[54]

For every sympathetic or accepting white of free blacks, there were many others, especially slave owners of large holdings, who wished them exiled from the country at all cost. Most slave owners thought of free blacks solely as a threat to the institution of slavery and an expense to the community.

There is irony in white criticism of free-black character and motivation, even as whites retarded those very attributes through restrictive laws. Free blacks were denied basic civil liberties, restricted in their mobility, and discouraged from education. Their status, and in many situations their very lives, were at the whim of the lowest class of white competitors and debtors. The few liberties extended blacks depended on political and economic climate, on geographic location, and on their relationship with influential whites. When the economy was bad and free blacks competed directly with whites for jobs, blacks often lost to the white competition. Outdated laws were recalled and enforced so that free blacks might well find themselves arrested and returned to a slave status or even forced into slavery for the first time.

Having forced free blacks into a social and legal ghetto, whites ridiculed their efforts to rise above poverty and join the middling classes, which is what most ambitious free blacks wanted. They wanted the material benefits of hard work and the respect of those whose lives they imitated and whose ranks they wished to join. Whites resented their aspirations to material success and blocked their attempts wherever they could.

> We reside among you and yet are strangers; natives, and yet are not citizens; surrounded by the freest people and most republican institutions in the world, and yet enjoying none of the imunities [sic] of freedom .... Though we are not slaves, we are not free.

The mobility of free blacks posed one of the most irksome freedoms to the ruling class. How did one distinguish a free black from a slave or, more annoying, from a white freeholder, since many free blacks were mulattoes of the third or fourth generation and were essentially white? Some Southern states eventually required a brand or patch that read "Free" displayed by free blacks, but the blatant nature of the badge put the institution of slavery in high relief, to the discomfort of those who had moral qualms with it, especially visitors from the North and from Europe.[55]

Arrogance was another trait that hugely annoyed whites about free blacks, especially those who had acquired some means of self-support, who were educated or articulate, and who dressed and lived well. In every case, they were "living above their station" or just being "uppity." Black pride, which may have been arrogance only to a prejudiced white, sometimes came with the independence and pride in hiring out as a slave, which often meant a large degree of self-direction and independence. Being a free black, even with the limitations of that caste, carried a definite social status and a degree of confidence.[56]

Self-esteem was a natural by-product of free-black success in a slave society, but whites loathed to see blacks "act like whites," to emulate them in speech or dress or aspiration. A society nurtured in expecting deference from a servile caste bristled at not being catered to, at blacks not moving off the sidewalk or not doffing a hat or lowering their eyes. Whites taught humility and subservience to all blacks; they expected respect from all blacks, and they complained about insolent blacks for the entirety of slavery's history in America.

> Insolence is the tyrant's ready plea ... The slightest word, or look, or action, that seems to indicate the slave's sense of any injustice that is done

*to him, is denounced as insolence and is punished with the most relenting
severity. [Humility], whether it be real or pretended . . . is esteemed by
masters, the great and crowning virtue of a slave . . . for they understand
by it, a disposition to submit . . . to kiss the foot that treads you to the
dust.*[57]

Frederick Olmsted, the renowned landscape designer of Central Park,
engaged a woman innkeeper in the 1850s near Petersburg who was free with
her opinions on race relations in Virginia. She opined that "providence had
put the servants into our hands to be looked out for" and to keep them from
wickedness. She further informed him that there were certain jobs that only
blacks would do. Her attitude toward blacks is close to the general sentiments
of whites in Virginia and the South.

> *No white man would ever do certain kinds of work (such as taking
> care of cattle, or getting water or wood to be used in the house), and if
> you should ask a white man you had hired, to do such things, he would
> get mad and tell you he wasn't a nigger.*[58]

John Quincy Adams recorded in his diary that John Calhoun of South
Carolina confided to him that he, Calhoun, could not employ a white servant
in his house for fear of his character and reputation. Manual labor was the
preserve of blacks, especially slaves. "No white person could descend to that.
And it was the best guarantee of equality among the whites."[59] As noted by
Luther Porter Jackson and others, "A standing problem with the free Negro
before the Civil War was the fact that he lived in a society intended for two
classes only—free whites and Negro slaves."[60]

> *Free Negroes stood outside the direct governance of a master, but in
> the eyes of many whites their place in society had not been significantly
> altered. They were slaves without masters.*[61]

Black on white intimacy

Interracial marriage and sexual intercourse were two areas where laws
proscribed all blacks consistently and in all regions of America. Mixing of the
races was generally taboo from the beginning of the colonies and was upheld
throughout the colonial, federal, and antebellum periods. Virginia finally
outlawed interracial marriage in 1705, and most Southern states had laws

against mixing of races in the eighteenth century. North Carolina, however, did not enact a prohibition against mixed marriages until 1838.

As with many proscriptions against free blacks, courts rarely enforced laws against mixed couples except when pressured by a vocal white majority. The very numbers of mulattoes, mixed-blood African Americans, testify to the intimate relationships between blacks and whites during slavery. Modern scholarship maintains that more mulattoes appeared in the earlier colonial period when the practice involved more white women and black men. After the Virginia act of 1782, with an easing of manumission, more black men entered the market for mulatto women, and the color scale tacked to the black side. In the nineteenth century, racial coupling was more about white men, especially white owners, and black slave women.[62]

There are numerous references to black-on-white coupling in the American colonies and in the national South. Most of the colonial references are between a black slave and a white servant woman, but one finds the occasional story of a free-black man and free white female union. One such reference occurs in *the Diary of a Journey of Moravians from Bethlehem, Pennsylvania to Bathabara in Wachovia, North Carolina, 1753.* The record tells of a meeting of Moravians with a mixed couple in the backcountry of Virginia in that year. The Moravians traveled the Great Road south on their way to a Moravian settlement near present-day Winston-Salem, North Carolina. The journal reads

> *Br. Gotlob went half a mile ahead to a Free Negro, who is the only smith in these parts, to have his horse shod. The negro and his wife, who was a Scotch woman, were very friendly to Br. Gottlob and told him that they recently come hither from Lancaster, that they had often heard Br. Nyberg preach, and also the Brn. In Philadelphia, and that they were now reading the "Berliner Reden" . . . The negro understood German well.*[63] Moravian Diary

The diarist did not comment on the rarity of the black man with the white wife or give vent to righteous indignation that the couple was guilty of blasphemy, as ministers and politicians would charge in the following century. If anything caught the notice of the Moravian, it was the intimacy and felicity of the black man with the German language.

The description of the African American is consistent with the model of colonial free blacks: educated and skilled. The black man may have been Edward Tarr, a smithy and landowner in Rockbridge County, Virginia, whose forge lay near the Great Road and whose domicile attracted an assortment of free blacks, slaves, and a "middlin'" sort of white, much to the annoyance of court officials and perhaps of white competitors.[64]

Despite the fact that Tarr was a taxpayer and a member of the Timber Ridge Presbyterian Church, the county court, under pressure from local whites, brought morals charges against his wife, Ann Moore. Tarr did not recover from the campaign against him. He sold his property at a loss and moved to Staunton in the next county, another free-black man who refused to learn his place in a slave society.[65]

Many mixed couples survived in the frontier culture, and even mixed marriages succeeded, but white society merely tolerated the practice, and interracial coupling generally fell outside the laws of colonial and national America. As always, there were exceptions to the rules. There were communities, such as across the border from Southside in North Carolina and in areas of the southeastern portion of that state, that tolerated mixed marriages and produced its quota of mulattoes.

Interracial coupling became much more of a social and political issue following the return to private manumissions in the 1780s and the increase of the free-black population thereby. By 1800 preachers and politicians denounced the practice in the public forums of church and government in language that became evermore passionate as the century wore on. If historians relied solely on early newspaper pronouncements for an assessment of mixed cohabitation, they could only conclude that such cases were rare.

In fact, mixed-race couples cohabited in many towns, especially in the larger cities of Virginia, and in certain rural communities throughout the South. Most whites in Southern towns and villages tolerated mixed couples whom they knew as neighbors and who made a contribution to the community. When free blacks of means cohabited with whites, their living arrangements generated less white hostility if their general behavior accorded with the social norms of the neighborhood and if they were well known and liked. Even the courts were cautious in their dealings with mixed-race couples, unless they were of the lowest level of society and without resources or unless their union had produced offspring likely to fall to the county to support. The courts fined, jailed, and occasionally exiled such miscreants. For couples who had resources and perhaps white friends and associates, their treatment by the courts was far more prudent.[66]

Traditional historiography of the slave states, when it dealt with the issue at all, accepted without evidence the dictum that mixed cohabitation in the South was between white male slave owners and their black female slaves. No other combination was acceptable to Southern sensibilities. Such was not the reality of slave society.

Historian Paul Heinegg, who has made an exceptional study of county documents of North Carolina and Virginia and the Upper South of the seventeenth and eighteenth centuries, found that marriage between black and white in the early colonial South was more often between a white servant woman and a black slave or a free black and that it was consensual. "Despite the efforts of the legislature [of Virginia], white servant women continued to bear children by African American fathers through the late seventeenth century and well into the eighteenth century. From the genealogies, it appears that they were the primary source of the increase in the free African American population."[67]

In a comparison of more than two hundred families from the early colonial period, the evidence documented mulattoes descending from white women and black men. In only one case was the coupling between a white male slave owner and his female black slave. The situation reversed in the nineteenth century as racial attitudes hardened and slave owners became absolute owners and assumed complete control over their charges, leaving young slave women at the mercy of their masters.[68]

As early as 1723 the General Assembly of North Carolina received complaints from planters about the "great Numbers of Free Negroes, Mulattoes, and other persons of mixt Blood, that have lately removed themselves into this Government, and that several of them have intermarried with the white inhabitants of this Province."[69] Presumably, the immigrants hailed from Virginia, where, even then, free blacks hoped to find better opportunities in the Old North state.

The complaints in North Carolina came some thirty years after the Virginia Assembly enacted a law that ordered "whatsoever English or other white man or woman being free shall intermarry with a negroe, mulatto, or Indian man or woman, bond or free, shall within three months of such marriage be banished and removed from this dominion for ever." The white assemblymen, even at this early date, were trying to protect their whiteness by forcing all nonwhites into a caste.

But the intermixing continued and would not be stayed by government decree, religious restrictions, or public disapproval. Social intimacy in the South between the races may sound like a complete contradiction, but physical closeness of the races was a condition of physical existence in the South. A century after the Moravians called on the services of a German-reading Negro blacksmith in the backcountry, the simple social intimacy between blacks and whites in Virginia as late as the 1850s astonished Frederick Olmsted and other "outsiders."

Olmsted traveled the South as a correspondent for the *New York Times* in the 1850s. His travels in the Southern states in the years leading up to the Civil War left historians with some astute insights into the social attitudes of Southerners and Northerners as well as the outlooks of blacks.

Traveling in Virginia in the 1850s, the landscape designer was shocked by the intimate company of whites and blacks. "I am struck with the close co-habitation and association of black and white—Negro women are carrying black and white babies together in their arms; black and white children are playing together (not going to school together); black and white faces are constantly thrust together out of the doors, to see the train go by."[70]

Olmsted described a family of mixed people he happened to meet on a train: a white woman, a stout black woman, and two girls, one white and one "bright and very pretty mulatto girl. They all talked and laughed together, and the girls munched confectionery out of the same paper, with a familiarity and closeness of intimacy that would have been noticed with astonishment, if not with manifest displeasure, in almost any chance company at the North."[71]

Olmsted's discomfort with the intimacy of blacks and whites in the South no doubt spoke of his upbringing in the North, where the small number of blacks rendered them little seen or heard. The journalist had little context for the social interaction between blacks and whites as it occurred in the South. Virginia, where the traveler made his observation, had a larger number of blacks than in the entirety of New England. He, in fact, had little familiarity with Southern culture in general and found himself, at various times, shocked, amazed, astonished, and angered at the "doings" of Southerners.

Frederick Olmsted was not the first Northerner or European to comment on the intimacy between black and white in the South. That intimacy, which was real enough, was not a mark of Southern racial blindness and certainly not one of social equality; it was a measure of how deep the institution of slavery was woven into the Southern social and psychic fabric. The physical intimacy and proximity was that of jailer and inmate, both imprisoned but functioning under specific rules, full of contradictions, often ignored, that served the interests of each.

That Northerners so frequently noted the personal closeness of the races in the South was at least some measure of the North's lack of understanding of Southern slave culture. White and black Southerners lived as families for generations and frequently had genuine feelings for one another, albeit the cohabitation was forced and very unequal. Not only slaves lived on white property and in white houses but free blacks as well often lived with white families to which they hired out.

In smaller households, black employees or for-hire slaves often slept in the owner's house and sometimes in the same rooms as the employer and his family. Black servants entered the rooms of white employers and owners to make morning fires and to retrieve chamber pots, even as the family slept. A young woman from New York who moved to North Carolina wrote to her family that servants were treated with kindness and a shocking familiarity.

"They are in the parlor & in your rooms & all over. The first night we spent in slaveholding states, we slept in a room without a lock—twice before we were up a waiting girl came into the room & while I was dressing in she came to look at me—she seemed perfectly at home, took up the locket with your miniatures in it & wanted to know if it was a watch."[72]

In Virginia the number of white households with live-in blacks may have been as high as 30 percent prior to 1860 and at least as high in North Carolina. In the Old North state in 1830, so many free blacks lived with white families that their white employers were required to collect the freedmen's taxes. Even after the Civil War, many free blacks and former slaves remained on the farms and in the employ of their former owners.[73]

Nanny and Child. Intimacy between blacks and whites in the antebellum period was inherent in the slave system. House servants, free and slave, lived in close familiarity with whites in the South. Nearly 30% of free blacks in North Carolina lived with white families in the early 1800s. *(Courtesy of the*

Library of Congress, Prints & Photographs Division, Washington, D.C. No Use Restrictions)

The public press often carried articles denouncing the closeness and the mixing of the races. The *Petersburg Daily Democrat* complained in 1857 that there were always "white boys hand in glove with free negroes of the lowest grade" on the streets of Petersburg.[74] Black and white fraternization in cities was a fact of life in the slave South, and most large-city newspapers made similar complaints. Four years earlier, Richmond authorities arrested "a very interesting kettle of fish, at a negro den . . . where white, yellow and black congregate to eat, drink and be merry."[75]

Henry Bibb, a slave who spent half his life trying to escape his situation, recalled that the "poor and loafering class of whites, are about on a par in point of morals with the slaves at the South. They are generally ignorant, intemperate, licentious, and profane. They associate much with slaves; are often found gambling together on the Sabbath; encouraging slaves to steal from the owners, to sell to them, corn, wheat, sheep, chickens, or any thing of the kind which they can well conceal."[76]

Whatever the complexity and ambiguity and even hostility of feelings between the races in the South, the physical proximity and closeness cannot be denied. If it was a bad marriage of cultures, it was nonetheless a marriage, sometimes of convenience, always of coercion, and it led to frequent sexual congress between the races. The social closeness was dictated by the nature of an agricultural society and by the requirements of security in a slave society. This closeness led to considerable sexual intimacy that in no way implied equality between the races, and white citizens generally acquiesced in the illicit relationships.[77]

The majority of whites who owned slaves or rented to free blacks and even shared their houses with them were restrained from intimacy by family ties and social and religious mores. Yet many planters took advantage of the availability and exposure of slave mistresses. There were sufficient numbers of mulatto children in the South to give lie to the "Southern gentleman" myth. Even then, most owner-forced contact with female slaves was denied by family and community, in keeping with slave-society taboos, even when the progeny of such unions was undeniable.[78]

Social propriety was the protective cloak donned by most philandering planters. A planter who abused his female slaves was "indebted for no inconsiderable part of his high reputation, to a very strict attention to those conventional observances which so often usurp the place of morals."[79] The roaming planter could follow his baser instincts provided he adhered publicly to the accepted social mores of the community.

Harriet Jacobs, in her harrowing tale of surviving her owner's sexual advances for years, noted that slave owners thought no slave had a right to family ties and feelings but was created solely for the benefit of the owner. Harriet herself was prevented from visiting her father's wake, though distraught with grief, in order to gather and arrange flowers for a party for her owner's wife.[80]

She tells of a young slave house girl who wanted to marry a field slave. When her mistress learned of her plans, she screamed at the girl that she would have her "peeled and pickled" if she ever mentioned the subject again. "Do you suppose that I will have you tending my children with the children of that nigger?" the owner screamed at her slave. The slave girl later had a mulatto child by the woman's husband.[81]

Most owners did not admit to feelings for blacks, especially for slaves. For slaves to treat their children humanely, even to nurture human feelings in them, "was blasphemous doctrine . . . presumptuous in [the slave parent], and dangerous to the master." Sarah Gudger, an ex-slave from North Carolina, recalled for a Federal Writers' Project interview that she was not allowed to see her mother after she died.

> One day white man come to see me. He say: "Sarah, did you know your mammy was dead?" I went to de house and say to Ole Missie: "My mother she die today. I wants to see my mother afore dey puts her away," but she look at me mean and say: "Get out of here, and get back to you work afore I wallop you good."[82]

Jacobs's memoir of her escape from slavery offers numerous examples of the intimate and contradictory nature of slave society in America. Born in Edenton, North Carolina, she was a mulatto, "a light shade of brownish yellow," and a house servant who was well treated by her mistress, to the extent of receiving a fair education from her owner. Like many slaves, Harriet was unaware of her lowly position until she was twelve years old, when her mother died. Jacobs recalls her childhood fondly, living in a "comfortable house" where she was "so fondly shielded that I never dreamed I was a piece of merchandise."[83]

Jacobs's father hired himself out by paying his owner $200 per year to allow him to pursue his carpentry on his own conditions. His daughter recalls that he was superior in his trade, so much so that white contractors hired him to supervise construction jobs, some of which were a great distance from home. The independent slave generally managed his own affairs as long as he paid his annual sum to his owner and remained sober. Jacobs recalls that because of her father's independence, he displayed emotions unseemly in a slave—audacity and insolence.[84]

House servants such as Hariett Jacobs, born into wealthy families and coddled as children, did not know the realities of slavery until the age of six or seven, sometimes later. But at some point, by reaching an age of understanding or by the death of a protective mistress or master, the pampered slave child, who often was the playmate of the owner's children and sometimes educated with them, came face-to-face with the horrors of their future lives and that of their families.

> *My mother's mistress was the daughter of my grandmother's mistress. She was the foster sister of my mother; they were both nourished at my grandmother's breast. In fact, my mother had been weaned at three months old, that the babe of the mistress might obtain sufficient food. They played together as children; and when they became women, my mother was a most faithful servant to her whiter foster sister. On her death-bed her mistress promised that her children should never suffer for any thing; and during her lifetime she kept her word.*[85]

When she was twelve, Harriet's doting mistress died. The benevolent slave owner bequeathed Harriet to the five-year-old daughter of her sister, Mary Matilda, despite her promises that she would free her slaves in her will. The mistress had been good to Harriett, teaching her to read and write and to be a lady, but her goodwill did not extend to the ultimate gift to the slave: freedom. Hence, Harriet's training and rearing ended abruptly, and she encountered an entirely new life with strange rules and values, many of them unspoken.[86]

Slaves created various stratagems for living with their debased status, one of which was songs and doggerels mocking their owners. Like Harriet's mistress, owners often promised to free their slaves upon certain conditions or at certain times, especially at their deaths, but they seldom followed through. Slave owners reneged so often on the promise of freedom that their deceit entered slave lore in the form of a rhyme:

> My old mistress promise me,
> When she die she set me free.
> She live so long her head git bald;
> She give out'n the notion of dyin' a-tall.[87]

The mother of Harriet's owner married a doctor, alias Dr. Flint in Jacobs's memoirs, but in life he was Dr. James Norcom, a prominent and respected slave owner and physician in Edenton. He became Mary Matilda's guardian and, as her stepfather, guardian of Harriet. The respected doctor had less-than-fatherly feelings toward the preteen Harriet from the beginning. He harassed the young slave girl from her first year with the family. He constantly wooed the frightened Harriet, first with promises and treats that would fester into curses and threats when the girl refused his advances. Harriet resisted for years the doctor's attempts to make her his mistress. She succeeded in her defiance of the owner by subterfuge, keeping company around her, and by the sheer moral courage of her grandmother.[88]

Blacks, even slaves, while without obvious power in the American South, found strategies and tactics that sometimes worked to their advantage and against the slave owner. On the farm or plantation, slaves knew the stratagems for slowing the work pace and for performing shoddy work without obvious effort. Malingering and faking illness showed slave defiance as they rebelled, albeit covertly, against working conditions. In urban areas, slaves occasionally employed industrial sabotage to demonstrate their anger against overseers and supervisors.

Urban blacks had some safety in numbers and public scrutiny to mute the worst impulses of slave owners. Harriet Jacobs kept herself in the company of others as much as possible to ward off Dr. Norcom's entreaties. She tried never to be caught alone if the doctor was in the vicinity. She remarked on her good fortune to have lived in a town where personal connections were close and private affairs were public business. As harsh and one-sided as slave laws and practices were, the doctor, "as a professional man, deemed it prudent to keep up some outward show of decency."[89] On an isolated plantation, she would have had less buffer between her and her owner.

Then there were blacks, even slaves, usually older ones, who, through the strength of character and moral courage, faced down abusive slave owners. Harriet's grandmother was such a slave. Her work ethic gave her a certain moral authority and supervision of the household. Her moral strength at times shamed slave owners into caution. Her cooking, some of which she sold to the public, won her community support.

Harriet claimed that Dr. Flint/Norcom feared her grandmother, who had once confronted a "white gentleman" with a pistol after he insulted one of her daughters. Her moral stance put the doctor on notice, but also, "he dreaded her scorching rebukes. Moreover, she was known and patronized by many people; and he did not wish to have his villany made public."[90]

When Dr. Flint/Norcom at last decided that he would be rid of the grandmother (Aunt Marthy in the memoirs), he arranged a private sale in order to keep the deed a secret. When the public sale opened, the grandmother, with a rare show of courage and initiative in a slave, jumped onto the public auction block and exposed the plan of the doctor. Shouts of shame rained down on the doctor, and no one bid on the grandmother except the sister, now seventy years old, of Marthy's former mistress who had shared a house with Aunt Marthy for forty years. The white sister bought Marthy for fifty dollars and then set her free.[91]

Mixed progeny of planters hurt women most, both the slave and the mistress. A black slave was forced to nurture a mulatto child who was owned by the man who forced himself on her, a man who could sell off his own child without interference by the mother. The illegitimate mixed-race child reminded the master's wife daily of her husband's sexual dalliance with his chattel. The man responsible for the violation of the slave answered to no one; he held the power in antebellum America. Who was going to tell him no? Jacobs claims that slave owners found no personal shame in siring slave children and that the entire community was complicit in the social pretense and concealment.[92]

Mary Boykin Chesnut, wife of a South Carolina slave owner, wrote in a well-noted post-Civil War diary of the demeaning nature of owner-slave sexual relations. Mrs. Chesnut was more candid and more perceptive than most Southern planters who left memoirs about their dealings with slaves. Writing about planters and their slave concubines, Mrs. Chesnut struck at the heart of the unspoken taboos and the duplicity that supported the abuse.

> *Under slavery, we live surrounded by prostitutes, yet an abandoned woman is sent out of any decent house. Who thinks any worse of a Negro or mulatto woman for being a thing we can't name? God forgive us, but ours is a monstrous system, a wrong and an iniquity! Like the patriarchs of old, our men live all in one house with their wives and their concubines; and the mulattoes one sees in every family partly resemble the white children. Any lady is ready to tell you who is the father of all the mulatto children in everybody's household but her own. Those, she seems to think, drop from the clouds.[93]*

Interracial coupling was not confined to backwater planters and unrefined slave owners. When Thomas Jefferson returned from his diplomatic mission as minister to France in 1789, the young slave who went with him to attend his daughters was already pregnant with his child. It is historically and genetically proven that Jefferson sired more than one child by a slave mistress, Sally Hemings, and that the tradition was one widely practiced in the extended Jefferson family.[94]

Moreover, residents of the area and visitors to Monticello noticed and commented on "evidence of sex across the color line on Jefferson's resident plantation." The Duc de La Rochefoucauld-Liancourt noted that slaves at Monticello had "neither in their color nor features a single trace of their [African] origin, but they are the sons of slave mothers and consequently slaves." The Comte de Volney, traveling during the summer of 1796, similarly noted slaves living at Monticello "as white as I am." Jefferson resolutely carried on a family tradition that was honored by many of the most prominent landowners, social swells and government leaders in the South.[95]

Even the esteemed Thomas Jefferson, author of the founding document of the nation, was prisoner to these social contradictions. His wife, Martha Wayles, brought to their marriage in 1772 six slaves who were her half siblings and, therefore, Jefferson's in-laws. "This was an absolute of blood, a parallel genealogical reality on in-laws not recognized in law. His marriage had thrust him deeply into the realm where people had the 'double aspect' of being both humanity and property."[96]

Blacks and whites engaged in more than work and toil in their physical proximity and interactions in most counties in Virginia and North Carolina. We find interracial couples often in court records as "fornicators" and "adulterers" because there were no laws against interracial coupling. The offense was a social, not a legal one.

Stephen Forgason, a black laborer of Prince Edward County, was indicted by a grand jury in 1828, along with his white common-law wife, for fornication. The true issue of the case was interracial cohabitation, which several white citizens of Farmville refused to ignore. Since there were no laws against interracial sex per se, fornication and adultery, which were illegal, was a legal fallback for interracial couples who offended white sensibilities.[97]

The county prosecutor in Prince Edward failed to follow up on the charge, and it went nowhere. In the 1830 census, Forgason was still living with his white lady, Susan Selbe, and an elderly white woman, probably Selbe's mother. Forgason was a grain cutter for a white planter in 1828, for whom he worked alongside white cutters, and he continued in the man's employ for years afterward at the same pay rate as the white cutters. There were no apparent repercussions against the interracial couple for all the attention they received from authorities and some disgruntled white citizens.[98]

There were at least five other interracial couples in the county mentioned in the county records. Some of them were called before the same jury that called Forgason. Their cases were dismissed as well. John Moss remained a favorite shoemaker for whites in Farmville in spite of his marriage to a white woman. James League Sr., a Revolutionary War veteran, lived with his daughter and her three mixed-race children in the same county.[99]

A similar case appeared in Charlottesville in 1822 when two whites brought charges of fornication against David Isaacs and Nancy West. Isaacs was a Jewish merchant in the firm of Cohen and Isaacs on Main Street; West was a person of color who owned a successful bakery nearby. The two lived in separate households on Main Street for at least seventeen years but sired and raised seven children who resided with the mother.

Charlottesville was a village of perhaps three hundred souls in 1820; there was no hiding the relationship between Isaacs and West, nor the fact of their children, nor the extent of their business interests. The couple apparently remained unmolested for many years though they raised a family together and operated very visible and successful companies within sight of each other. Why someone chose to bring charges against the couple in 1822 after they had raised their children and had built up successful businesses is open to conjecture. Evidence suggests that the pair had become too bold in their relationship and perhaps too successful in their businesses.[100]

The charge was brought to a grand jury that indicted the couple in 1822 on charges of fornication—*not* interracial cohabitation. Isaacs and West contested the charges and managed to stymie the county court for two years before the court, apparently flummoxed by the case, opted to send the indictment to the general court in Richmond. The lawsuit finally reached the court docket in 1826. The jurists ruled that the indictment could not be prosecuted as presented by the grand jury and sent the matter back to Albemarle County Court. In 1827 the county court dismissed all charges against Isaacs and West.[101]

There were technicalities involved in the grand jury indictment that the general court cared not to consider. The couple was not charged with breaking a specific statute but rather was implicated for living together and engaging in fornication. The General Court reasoned that if they were living together as man and wife in common, then they were not guilty of fornication. Successful cases against fornication in the antebellum South generally involved gross public displays that were offensive to the community; otherwise, the community at large was not harmed.

In fact, as Joshua Rothman has demonstrated, Isaacs and West finally moved in together as man and wife about 1819, and West moved her bakery business next to Isaacs's mercantile store, just two years before plaintiffs filed charges against them. Other free people of color resided in the same block or nearby, including another mixed-race family who rented land from Isaacs. Perhaps, as Rothman suggests, the Isaacs-West merger brought the free-black issue in town to "critical mass" and that certain whites decided that enough was enough.[102]

Free people of color, regardless of their wealth and social standing, were always subject to challenge by even the lowest class of white who might feel slighted, wronged, or resentful. West owned $7,000 worth of real property in 1850, making her the wealthiest free black in the county and a target of resentful whites. Her success would have irritated white residents, particularly if they were in the same business as West, some of whom would probably have welcomed an opportunity to remind her of her place in society.[103]

On the other hand, the case of Isaacs and West points up, as do the court cases against mixed couples in Prince Edward County, the difficulty of prosecuting interracial cohabitation, even when it was prosecuted under the guise of fornication. Isaacs and West were not average free blacks; she and Isaacs both had prominent friends and business connections in Albemarle County and in Richmond, and both were very well-to-do. They could hire lawyers. "Despite the revulsion white Virginians expressed publicly toward sex across the color line, there was very little the law could do to stop it."[104]

The more interesting question is how this mixed-race couple lived together almost forty years, bore seven children, and operated successful businesses in a small village in Virginia's slave society. A legal case like the Isaacs-West wrangle exposes in bold relief the painful ironies and ambiguities of Southern society and the fragile, murky nature of free-black life.

Public records contain many examples of cohabitation in Virginia's cities between wealthy businessmen and their bound women, even as planters made concubines of their female slaves. Robert Lumpkin, a well-known slave trader and jailer in Richmond, lived in a quasi-marriage or common-law arrangement with a slave named Mary for most of their adult lives. He sired five children by the woman, two of whom he sent North for an education, and willed his estate to her at his death.[105]

Another Richmond slave trader, Silas Omohundro, spent lavishly on his slave woman, Corinna, by whom he sired five children. He likewise freed his family at his death and willed them his estate. Hundreds of cases of mixed-race couples in the public records suggest that the human drama between blacks and whites in the South could not be contained by legal restrictions or exactly defined by law.[106]

An ex-slave, Solomon Northup, described another situation created by planters that put comely young mulatto women in difficult situations that also furthered mixing of the races. Planters not only bought young, healthy mulatto women for their own sexual pleasure but for their sons as well, to introduce them to the carnal aspects of gentry life.

> *Maria was a rather genteel looking colored girl, with a faultless form, but ignorant and extremely vain. The idea of going to New-Orleans was pleasing to her. She entertained an extravagantly high opinion of her own attractions. Assuming a haughty mien, she declared to her companions, that immediately on our arrival in New-Orleans, she had no doubt some wealthy single gentleman of good taste would purchase her at once.*[107]

Professor Genovese explains the closeness of master and slave and of blacks and whites in more general situations: the "intimacy of the Big House and of the paternalistic master-slave relationship in general manifested itself as acts of love in the best cases, sadistic violence in the worst, and ostensible seduction and imposed lust in the typical."[108] Relationships between blacks and whites in the antebellum South were seldom simple and straightforward. They often proved baffling even to the people who lived in the heart of this complex society.

"Pencillings on the Heart"—Friends of Free Blacks

The post-revolutionary decades that witnessed an explosion of private manumissions exposed many contradictions in the American caste system. While white supremacy demanded the denigration of blacks, slave and free, practical life and economy required the services and talents of skilled black workers. By the nineteenth century, whites of all levels in the South expected blacks to perform most menial labor and much of the more arduous skilled labor.

When white communities required a particular trade or skill that a trained black could fill, the denizens of the place often coalesced around the black candidate and lobbied in his/her behalf. Whites in prominent situations often argued for and petitioned for manumission of a particularly skilled slave. In the case of free blacks, white citizens lobbied their legislatures to waive immigration laws designed to remove free blacks from their home states. Whites often chose to bend and even break their own laws to accommodate their comfort and convenience by insisting on having black labor and skills on demand.

The pioneer historian Luther Porter Jackson quoted John H. Russell from his *The Free Negro in Virginia* as his source for explaining the apparent contradiction of white attitudes between free-black class versus individual blacks. Whites generally perceived free blacks as debased and worthless as a class but touted the virtues of the many individual free blacks and supported their views by petitions to the courts. Russell interviewed blacks from the antebellum period, although fifty years after the fact, about the disparate opinions by whites of free blacks during the time of slavery:

> Some of this group [of interviewees] *insisted that there were two classes of free Negroes: those who, like the many "extremely useful" and "industrious" persons just noted, were an asset to their localities, and others who were the parasites of their neighborhoods. Individuals of the first class, Russell indicates, were known as "men of color"; those of the latter class were contemptuously called "free niggers."*[109]

But there was more than white bias and whim at work in rescuing blacks from exile. Numerous town and county businessmen understood the economic consequences of eliminating such a large labor pool as the free-black laborer. Slavery distorted the work ethic as well as social standards in communities where it was the major labor source. Even lower whites absorbed the airs of landed gentry and refused to perform menial labor that was associated with slave work. Town residents eventually found themselves without a labor pool in certain critical areas, such as the fisheries industry in Westmoreland and Prince William Counties in the late 1830s.[110]

White communities in Virginia during economic slumps petitioned the legislature and the courts to waive immigration laws so that free-black labor might be brought into the state from Maryland to replenish the labor force. Residents of Accomac County petitioned the legislature in 1852 to bind all male blacks under forty-five years to hire themselves out. Culpepper County petitioned for a law that would render any contract made with a free black a lifetime servitude. The labor situation worsened to the point that Governor Henry A. Wise argued that removal of free blacks was detrimental to the state's economy because "their labor is needed in many parts of the state where they are most numerous."[111] Clearly the exile laws did not pay the dividends their authors expected.

There were also exceptional free blacks who won the respect and even friendship of whites, who then came to their aid in troubled times. Successful free blacks were not confined to the ministry, though there were many who served as preachers and ministers, like Henry Evans and Uncle Jack. Extremely few made a mark in education, like the incomparable John Chavis. More free blacks made their marks, amassed some wealth, and became men and women of note and influence in business and the skilled trades such as cabinetmaking.

Lunsford Lane was born a slave to Sherwood Haywood in 1803 in Raleigh, North Carolina, the state's capital, a town of some 3,600 people. Lane was an enterprising mechanic and entrepreneur, whose master ultimately allowed him to hire out his time for $100 to $120 per year.

LUNSFORD LANE.

Lunsford Lane. Entrepreneur, messenger for the governor's office, preacher, friend of city officials and legislators, Lunsford Lane was one of the best-known figures in Raleigh, North Carolina, in the 1820s and 1830s. Lane hired out his time to his owner, created his own business ventures, and saved enough money to buy his freedom and that of most of his family, a wife and five children. *(Courtesy of The State Archives of North Carolina)*

The clever slave, working with his father, found his first success in business as a tobacconist. He sold his tobacco and smoking accoutrements from a shed or a kiosk on the streets of Raleigh, items that included flavored pipe tobacco that caught on quickly in Raleigh and was in much demand throughout the piedmont. Lane or his father also invented an airing reed for pipe stems that cooled the smoke, another popular product among smokers. His tobacco goods were in such demand that he hired boys and men to sell them on the streets and to retail stores. Lane created markets in Chapel Hill, Fayetteville, and Salisbury, towns from forty to sixty miles from Raleigh.[112]

Lane's discretion and business reputation earned him a job as messenger for the governor's office, a measure of the confidence shown him by the governor of the state. He was a tireless worker, buying trees and making firewood, running errands for legislators when the general assembly met. Some of the prominent businessmen of the city viewed him with the same respect and hired him to chauffeur their carriages. The slave's business acumen and marketing skills made him enough money over the years that he was able to buy his freedom in 1836 for $1,000.

Lane could not be manumitted in North Carolina absent a recommendation of meritorious service, so he persuaded a wealthy merchant of the city to accompany him to New York, where he was manumitted. Perhaps forgotten by both parties, or maybe merely ignored, was the legislative act of 1826 that prohibited free blacks from reentering the state once they had left. The law required such violators to leave within twenty days or be arrested and returned to servitude for not more than ten years. Lane qualified as such a violator when he slipped quietly back into North Carolina from New York as a free man.[113]

For the next three years, he manufactured smoking pipes, sold his specialty tobacco, and operated a store and a woodyard. In 1839 the freeman was confident enough about his future to purchase his wife and six children with a note of $2,500 to their owner. He then bought a lot and house and prepared to live the life of a free-black family man.

While Lane's successes won admirers of some of Raleigh's whites, others resented his economic success and worked for his downfall. Some may have been competitors; others had heard rumors of Lane's speeches at abolitionist meetings in New York. Other antagonists needed no reason beyond that of Lane's race. His accusers made their complaints and called on the authorities to uphold the law of 1826. In 1840 Lane received notice to leave the state within twenty days. Even a bill in the legislature to exempt Lane from the ill effects of the law could not save him. The bill failed, and in 1841 Lane was forced to leave his state, his businesses, and his family.[114]

When Lane was making a great deal of money, he was aware of the dangers of displaying his wealth. Very few men, white or black, could afford a cash purchase of $1,000 (worth maybe $45,000 in current money) in the antebellum period, and with the hostility against free blacks rising every year, Lane was in a precarious position: how to earn a lot of money without showing it. So he did what all smart and industrious free blacks did: he created a sham.

> *First, I had made no display of the little property or money I possessed,*
> *but in every way I wore as much as possible the aspect of poverty. Second,*
> *I had never appeared to be even so intelligent as I really was. This all*
> *colored people at the south, free and slaves, find it peculiarly necessary to*
> *their own comfort and safety to observe.*[115]

Lane was assisted in his legal predicament by some of the leading citizens of the town, including the editor of the *Raleigh Register*, the governor's secretary, and other well-placed and affluent whites. Unable to aid him in his hometown, they helped him find friends in New England where he embarked on a lecture series and, in true Lane fashion, soon earned enough money to settle his note for his wife and children at $2,500.

In 1842 Lane wrote to the governor of North Carolina asking permission to return to the state to settle his affairs. He was granted twenty days to do so. When Lane returned to collect his family, his enemies learned of his arrival and obtained a warrant for his arrest on charges of giving abolition lectures in the North. Though the charges were dismissed, a mob would not be sated until it had tarred and feathered the enterprising Lane and sent him on his way north.[116]

A similar situation befell Isaac Hunter in Raleigh during the same years that Lunsford Lane was being harassed. Hunter was a prosperous shoemaker who had purchased his own freedom and was in the process of buying his wife and four children, when he received notice in 1840 that he must leave the state in twenty days.

Hunter had influential white friends in his corner who managed to win him a stay by the legislature after numerous testimonials in his behalf, but he received only the twenty-day reprieve. The chairman of the legislative committee that considered Hunter's petition argued for the shoemaker "as one of the surest and greatest safe guards to society, against the most awful calamity to which the free white people of the south are . . . exposed." The legislative chair, Matthew Moore, advanced the argument, accepted by many enlightened whites, that free blacks were the most effective bulwark against slave risings and rebellions. Hunter, despite his positive reputation and the support of white friends, was allowed twenty days to get his affairs in order prior to leaving the state.[117]

The "buffer" argument became standard language when a community wanted to prevent the expulsion of a valuable slave or free black. Most often the person was skilled in work critical to the economy and well-being of a community, such as a blacksmith or a tailor or a carpenter. But in some instances, the whites of a town or village wanted to keep a particular individual for the enhancement of quality of life, as in a confectioner or a washerwoman or a hostler.

Samuel Johnston worked as a servant at a tavern in Fauquier County in 1811 when thirty-eight white residents of the place petitioned the General Assembly to allow him to remain in Virginia. Johnston had bought his freedom for $500 with savings from his menial labor, which required his removal from the state. Johnston had a wife and several children still in bondage, and the freeman refused to leave them. His petitioners recommended him as an exemplary citizen and a model to other freedmen. "To the general assembly as one on whom might profitably be exercised that generosity which would afford a wise encouragement to others to behave as he has behaved, and by a like fidelity and honesty to deserve as he deserves."[118]

The petition was approved, and Johnston continued to serve at the tavern. He eventually bought his wife and children with the privilege of residence in Virginia. In 1820 his estate was worth $3,600.

There were many whites throughout the South who schooled free blacks, traded with them, and supported their petitions to the courts. Ackley White, a popular drayman in Norfolk, received notice to leave the state in 1836. White had been emancipated twelve years earlier and, according to law, was to leave the state within twelve months. The fact that it required twelve years for authorities to notice that the man remained in the community speaks to the general laxity of the immigration laws, which were not uniformly enforced until the 1850s. The laxity also points to the relatively benign attitude of many whites toward free blacks on a personal level and to the disparity between popular opinion and the politics of the issue.[119]

Sometimes all that was required to stir authorities to bring a warrant against a free black was a disgruntled white competitor or someone who felt slighted by a free-black merchant or artisan. General slave unrest or rumors of slave unrest sometimes brought unwanted notice to free blacks who remained in the state after their manumission. Or if whites in a community thought a free black was acting "above his station" or presuming too much on the white community, there were always disgruntled people in the neighborhood prepared to bring the weight of the law down on him.

Personal bias and envy were two of many forces at work against the advancement of free blacks. State laws directed at free blacks hobbled many prospective black artisans, farmers, and entrepreneurs. The laws restricted mobility, assembly, education, religious practices, and occupation of blacks. If whites thought competition too keen in a particular industry, say in freight hauling or certain tobacco work, a law would be forthcoming regulating the business to keep blacks out. Local ordinances worked in the same fashion against ambitious free-black men and women.

Christopher McPherson, a truly exceptional individual from Louisa County, Virginia, provides a case in point of local ordinances designed to frustrate free-black mobility. McPherson, the mulatto offspring of a white father and a slave mother, was educated and skilled. As a young man he became a manager to shopkeeper David Ross of Richmond, a white man who owned iron forges and other businesses. McPherson supervised eight or ten whites in his position. The man succeeded in the white world of business and eventually landed as a clerk in the United States Congress, where he met Jefferson and Madison and even shared dinner with Madison and his wife.[120]

McPherson was well known and admired by numerous prominent whites in Richmond, many of whom signed a petition attesting to his "Integrity Industry and general good conduct." In 1802 his word was accepted in court against two whites, "further evidence that 'throughout the whole course of' his life White acquaintances considered him 'one of their number.'"[121]

He returned to Richmond to clerk for the High Court of Chancery about the time that the city of Richmond Common Hall Council in 1810 disallowed blacks from being draymen and wagoners and even from hiring carriages. The Council Hall, with input no doubt from white draymen, excluded blacks from driving any vehicle "except in the capacity of maid or servant to some lady or gentleman." Apparently, some white Richmonders were concerned that black drivers were acting "above their proper stations" and called on the city to redress their grievances.

McPherson petitioned the General Assembly for redress to *his* inconvenience, pleading for himself and for his wife as infirm and at times unable to walk. Council Hall and the legislature rejected his petition. He then simply bought his own carriage and a pair of horses to convey himself and his family. While McPherson was wealthy enough and educated enough to circumvent these municipal obstacles, the great majority of free blacks had no defense against them.

McPherson, despite his unusual skills and influence, was still a black man in a slave society in which pushback against the establishment never paid dividends. This unusual, intelligent man who had contributed so much to his community and to his state, admired by so many whites, was yet at the whim of the meanest and lowest of the white working man. McPherson challenged the established order, a license few whites and no blacks were allowed. Eventually, he was shipped to the Williamsburg Lunatic Asylum, another free black who acted beyond his station.[122]

Builder and carpenter James Boon was apprenticed to a white carpenter in Franklin County, North Carolina, from the age of eighteen to twenty-one. He performed well for his master and continued to work for him after he was released from his apprenticeship. He also worked for himself and carried letters of recommendation from white men with him as he worked around Wake County and in Piedmont, North Carolina, in the 1830s and 1840s. A certificate of freedom issued by the county court in 1829 described him as "James Boon, a boy of colour who was bound to William Jones by this court [was] ordered to be liberated and set free."[123]

Boon's employers found him work, recommended him to white contractors, loaned him money, and stood bond for him. He was known as one of the best builders in the region and was recommended by many white businessmen. One white entrepreneur exclaimed that Boon's work was "executed better and with more taste than any persons within my knowledge in this section of the country."[124]

Boon worked from Raleigh to Wilmington and in between, building a strong reputation and taking letters of reference from his jobs. He worked with white laborers and slaves and free blacks and for a time owned a slave, whom he occasionally mortgaged. White businessmen were his protectors and the source of his livelihood. He married a literate slave woman and had a son by her.[125]

Boon was one of many free blacks supported by affluent and prominent whites who also developed a personal relationship with their patrons. Lunsford Lane, the successful free black in Raleigh who narrowly escaped a hanging by an anti-abolitionist mob, touched on his own conflicted feelings toward his persecutors. Lane knew some of the men who forced his exit from the state and who threatened to hang him for distributing abolitionist literature.[126]

After some discussion with his tormentors, in which the entrepreneur won over some of the mob, Lane received tar and feathers rather than a hanging. He counted the tar and feathers much the lesser punishment, joyful that he would live to see his family. During the preparations, some of his opponents stepped forward to prevent any tar from being spread on his face; others expressed their belief that he had not engaged in abolitionist activities. One of the mob returned Lane his watch, "which he had carefully kept in his hands" to protect it.[127]

The adversaries who visited the indignities of tarring on the dignified free-black man, according to Lane, all "expressed great interest in my welfare, advised me how to proceed with my business the next day, told me to stay in the place [Raleigh] as long as I wished, and with other such words of consolation they bid me good night."[128] The Raleigh mob punished Lane for his presumptions rather than for his acts.

Lane opted to be done with Raleigh and prepared to leave the following day. Before he departed the city of his birth, however, he called on his old mistress, Mrs. Haywood, "who was affected to weeping" at Lane's leaving, as was her daughter, "with tears that ceased not flowing." Mrs. Haywood released Lane's mother so that she might go north with her son. Lane's emotional attachment to his white owners and their care for him was genuine, even though nurtured in a society of perverted justice and racial bias.[129]

The free-black man called on the wife of a city judge, Mrs. Badger, who also "wept as she gave me her parting counsel." Lane explained his and their feelings thusly:

> *She and Mrs. Hogg and I had been children together, playing in the same yard, while yet none of us had learned that they were of a superior and I of a subject race. And in those infant years there were pencillings made upon the heart, which time and opposite fortunes could not all efface.*[130]

Fields (Cook), a Virginia slave, wrote a short narrative about his life growing up in slavery that expressed some of the same sentiments about childhood bonding between black and white, slave and free. Fields grew up alongside his master's son and, as a child, did not recognize his state of bondage, a sentiment expressed by other slave testimony.

> *I never knew what the yoke of oppression was in the early part of my life for the black and white children all faired alike and grew on together highfellows . . . well met untill we were nearly grown when the white boy with whom I had attached the strongest ties of affection and for whom I had often fought with as much ambition as if he had been my brother began . . . to feel some what a man and like the peafowl in the mist of a brude of chickens he began to raise his feathers and boast of the superiority which he had over me.*[131]

Fields and his white "brother" were separated when the white boy was sent to school and Fields was sent to plow. The slave was much confused over the change in his status and much hurt over the changing attitudes of his childhood friend. Though he did not speak harshly of his playmate, believing him to have been a "Christian man," the black man carried the offense with him into adulthood, despite the fact that the white boy used his school lessons to teach Fields his letters and numbers and to read.

On more than one occasion, slave and free-black women turned to white men for rescue from a particular threat, usually one of sexual molestation. Harriet Jacobs, after fighting off the advances of her guardian, Dr. Norcom, for years, at last turned to another white man to be her rescuer. Norcom decided to build a house in the country specifically for Harriet Jacobs, where he could keep her as his mistress and concubine. Having no recourse to justice in the town of Edenton, Jacobs turned to a white lawyer as a lover and a deliverer. The relationship sent the tyrannical Dr. Norcom into one of his familiar tirades, but he was, after twelve years of harassment, checkmated by the slave.[132]

Jacobs had two children by the lawyer, who professed concern for the children, but they belonged to Dr. Norcom because Harriet was his property. The doctor then used the threat of selling the children to browbeat the slave woman until, convinced that the doctor would make good on his threat, she finally escaped to a swamp where she hid out. After some months as an outlaw, Harriet eventually made her way to her grandmother's house, where she lived in desperate conditions in the attic for seven years before she was able to slip aboard a ship in 1842 that took her to Philadelphia.[133]

Few situations show the complexities of free-black relations with whites as that of Angela Barnett near Richmond. In 1792 two white men attacked Barnett over her harboring of a slave boy. A fracas ensued; one of the whites approached her with a weapon, and the woman planted an adze six inches into the man's skull.[134]

Barnett committed a capital offense that was without mitigating circumstances according to white law. Her offense was against a person, a white person, against society, and against the laws of God. How could she ever escape such a serious and heinous crime? The now criminal Barnett had worked for prominent people in Richmond and held their gratitude and esteem. Despite her crime, dozens of elite whites petitioned the governor not to hang her, and the city's mayor wrote an appeal in her behalf.

The governor refused Barnett a pardon. The jailed woman made an effort in her own behalf the next year, just eight days shy of her hanging. She wrote to the governor that she was pregnant with the child of a white man and pleaded for the life of her child. This new information moved the governor to grant a reprieve to Barnett, during which time her white patrons mounted a new campaign asserting her self-defense. In September 1793, almost one year after the murder, in extremely rare civic proceedings, Barnett was granted a full pardon for her crime.[135] Barnett's pardon was an extremely rare act of justice for a free black murderer in the antebellum period.

Whites came to the aid of free black Michael Shiner when white slavers abducted his wife in northern Virginia. The slavers sold their catch to a slave-trading firm that furnished slaves to the Deep South cotton states. The company demanded the huge sum of $10,000 bond on the family, a debt paid by six white friends of Shiner. The family was moved to the county jail and then freed.[136]

Whites made concessions to free blacks because they needed their skilled labor, but occasionally, sentiment and moral judgment also played a role. Free blacks who benefited from such white sentiments experienced a sliding scale of successes but one that would never include their most ardent wish: to be full citizens. Some, according to historian James Sidbury, "won their freedom, others managed to protect their families, others succeeded in making some money, acquiring some property or enjoying the tippling shops and gambling houses . . . Equality was not, however, a concession urban whites would make."[137]

Regardless of the esteem shown toward an individual free black or slave, whether preacher or mechanic, whether black or mulatto, and despite white praise and petitions to the legislature, free blacks had their "place," their station, their subordinate rank in antebellum society that they violated at great personal risk. Extremely few blacks had the elevated relationship with whites of the Days or John Chavis or McPherson, but even these successful individuals recognized the imperceptible clues of voice tone, eye contact, and physical deportment that kept the races separate. A eulogy to Rev. Henry Evans, one of the most highly praised blacks in North Carolina, given in remembrance by the bishop who inherited his position at the church in Fayetteville, makes the point:

> Toward the ruling class . . . Evans was unfailingly deferential, never speaking to a white but with his hat under his arm; never allowing himself to be seated in their houses . . . . "The whites are kind to me and come to hear me preach [said Evans] but I belong to my own sort and must not spoil them."[138]

The perplexity of vindictive laws against slaves and free blacks and the occasional compassionate feelings by whites toward certain black individuals occasioned the following aphorism to explain the paradox: "Southerners embraced blacks as individuals and interacted personally with them but despised the caste; Northerners accepted blacks in the abstract, as a class, but had little personal contact with them as individuals." As with many clichés, there is an element of truth in the adage.

Blacks and whites in the South lived in a society full of shadows and secrets. There were caring slave owners who employed a light hand in the supervision of their charges, and there were brutish men and women for whom slavery sparked their very worst natures. Either way, human bondage was helpful in only one direction, that of the owner. Whatever the nature of the owner, the slave could only be diminished and lessened as a human being, even those who managed to rise above their station. And white attitudes towards slavery profoundly affected white attitudes towards free blacks.

As the free-black caste grew in numbers and in strength in the labor force, they tested the old ways of genuflecting to whites, of bowing and casting down their eyes and doffing hats to white presence, as was the norm in the heydays of slavery. Whites expected free blacks to mimic slaves in their interactions with whites; free blacks expected to achieve the humanity and dignity possessed by whites.

Whites found free blacks to be a convenient scapegoat for economic and social ills. The North-South divide heated up, provided the South an especially easy target in the free black. Slavery lost some of its potency in the border states of the Upper South in the 1840s and 1850s, as free-soilers began to make inroads into those areas where free labor might compete with slavery. Southern whites were quick to blame free blacks for demanding social equality, whether free blacks sought it or not. Southern newspapers waged campaigns against the "insolence" of free blacks and their insulting "sidewalk etiquette." When white Southerners of the 1830s and 1840s were in an ugly frame of mind, they took their anger out on free blacks.

> *Southern free Negroes balanced precariously between abject slavery,*
> *which they rejected, and full freedom, which was denied them. Their*
> *world straddled one of hell's elusive boundaries.*[139]

CHAPTER THREE

Free Blacks in Southside Virginia

Free blacks lived in a legal and social milieu whose anti-black laws and customs were to some extent hidden and unwritten. To determine how free blacks functioned in a slave society, it is important fill in substantial gaps of information and to extrapolate from limited examples. Free blacks likely held as different views and opinions as did whites and educated slaves. They expressed a range of notions and positions on the important political issues of the day, especially slavery.

The attitudes of slaves and free blacks do not always convey comfortably to a twenty-first-century perspective. Black feelings and opinions are nuanced, depending on their experiences, and are often contradictory and appear to run against their self-interest. The close confines of rural Virginia did not always restrict the outlook of blacks. Their associations with whites and Northern visitors, their reading of newspapers and broadsides and their absorption of general gossip broadened the perspectives of many free blacks. The John Day family seems to have been particularly well informed of contemporary events and political discourse.

The ancestors of the Days of Southside remain hidden in the shadowy world of interracial sexual liaisons of eighteenth-century colonial America. The best that can be determined at this date is that the parents and likely the grandparents of Thomas and John Day entered the nineteenth century as free blacks already attuned to the capitalistic nature of their society. The nineteenth-century Days, who allied through marriage with another noted free-black family, succeeded financially and socially in spite of a tenuous political and social situation.

The first-recorded John Day, whom we shall call Sr., was born in 1766 and would have been old enough to appreciate and somewhat understand the seminal event of that century, the American Revolution. His future wife, Mourning Stewart, was born the same year. Both were free mulattoes.[1]

There is no record of when and how the first African American ancestor of John Day Sr. achieved freedom, but John Day was a freeman when he married Mourning Stewart circa 1795, herself a free black from a prominent and well-to-do family in Dinwiddie County. John Day's son left written record that his great-grandfather was the illegitimate son of a plantation lady of South Carolina and her black coachman to whom she "humbled herself." His great-grandmother, according to John Jr.'s account, traveled from South Carolina to a Quaker community on the Yadkin River (North Carolina) where she delivered the child. The mother left money for the boy's education and keep and returned home. That is John Jr.'s account of his lineage.

> *My father John Day a Cabinetmaker was the illegitimate grandson of an R-Day of S. Carolina whose daughter humbled herself to her coach driver. (This matter has not come to light. She was sent to the fork of the Yadkin to a Quaker's house who came with R. Day from England, where she left my [great-grand]father and money for his education . . . .) My mother was the daughter of a colored man of Dinwiddie County, VA whose name was Thomas Stewart, a medical doctor but when he obtained his education in that profession I know not.[2]*

Given the capricious nature of memories and oral tradition, especially those more than a generation removed, the entire account of the Day ancestry may be apocryphal, but it makes several very important points relative to the Day family and to free blacks of the nineteenth century. First, as Paul Heinegg has demonstrated in his studies of free-black genealogies in North Carolina and Virginia, racial mixing between white females and black males in colonial America was fairly common, evidently more so than congress between white males and black females.

The colonial pairing of black, mostly slave, men with white, mostly free, women created a distinct pattern for colonial free blacks. Children of mixed-racial pairings assumed the status of the mother, thus producing a free-black lineage, such as that of the Days of Virginia. Moreover, white mothers produced a mulatto lineage that served to muddle the planter ideal of American society, where white equaled free and black meant slave. Mulatto implied kinship with the dominant race and ruling white elite and inspired in the color caste a sense of self-esteem and superiority over their darker kin.[3]

Mr. Heinegg suggests that at least one branch of the Day family, from Southampton County, descended from Mary Day, "a white indentured servant woman of Northumberland County, Virginia, who had a child by a free African American man in 1692." That account adds another generation to the Day lineage, but the story line at least maintains the maternal Caucasian influence.[4]

If even part of John Day's account of his ancestry is accurate, the Days were free at least two generations prior to the births of John and Thomas Day of Virginia. If Heinegg is correct in his lineage of the Day genealogy, another generation of freedom accrues to their family tree. This free heritage was extremely important to the status of free blacks and was a mark of many successful businessmen and skilled artisans. Being free black served as a badge of distinction in both black and white communities in the eighteenth century and bestowed on the bearer social stature. Free status opened opportunities for work in the white community, and sometimes respect, when accompanied by strict moral behavior and a sound work ethic.

If a free black or a family of free blacks were well known in a community, as were the Days and the Stewarts, especially if they were well-off, hardworking, and of good reputation, they were relatively safe from the harshest racial humiliations and from physical brutality. If they had well-placed white friends to call on, they could go about their daily activities with a degree of certainty that their interests would not be disturbed. But the protection of a white sponsor often failed if another prominent white opposed the black interest.[5]

Harriet Jacobs recalls the rash of brutality and oppression in Edenton, North Carolina, following the Nat Turner insurrection in her book, *Incidents in the Life of a Slave Girl*. White authorities unleashed poor whites and country bullies without supervision against blacks in the town. The mobs wrecked and burned black domiciles and stole personal property from slaves and free blacks at will. They took particular delight in humiliating well-off and educated blacks. Harriet and her family fared better than most blacks when a white friend stepped between the slaves and the "captain" of the marauders to prevent their pillage of Harriet's family home.[6]

A free ancestry commonly divided blacks into social groupings of those with a long heritage of freedom and those recently manumitted. The status symbol of freedom, reminiscent of whites who traced their ancestry to European nobility, was potent in black communities before and after the Civil War. Post-bellum black social groups often defined themselves according to an antebellum free ancestry as distinct from those freed by the war.

Slaves who were free before the war perceived themselves differently from those still in bondage in 1862. Those whose ancestors were free in the eighteenth century made a distinction between their families and those more recently freed. And those who shared a white lineage considered themselves closer to the majority race and, therefore, an elect group.[7]

A North Carolina mulatto, William Kellogg, criticized the colonization movement for failing to offer a separate refuge for mixed-race people. He feared that the prejudice that existed between blacks and mulattoes in America would continue in Liberia and decided that he would prefer to remain in the hands of his "superiors" (white Americans) than fall into the hands of his "inferiors" (black Africans). Kellogg pointed out that there were "a great many mulattoes within these United State[s] who are stronger allied to the white man than they are to the Blacks."[8]

On a smaller scale, a white planter in Gates County, North Carolina, built a church, New Hope Baptist, for the exclusive use of free blacks. The church pastor was a free-black preacher named William Reid. Following the Civil War, only blacks previously free before the war were allowed admittance, "the line always being drawn between those born free and those shot free."[9] There were other churches throughout the South formed specifically for free blacks. New Bern's (North Carolina) Episcopal Church had a large Sunday school presence of the "Negro elite."

A former slave from Kentucky who spent half his life escaping from the bonds of slavery claimed that the "distinction among slaves is as marked, as the classes of society are in any aristocratic community. Some refusing to associate with others whom they deem beneath them in point of character, color, condition, or the superior importance of their respective masters."[10]

Thus, several different "societies" of blacks emerged in the American colonies during the mid-eighteenth century. After several generations of slavery, blacks born in the colonies spoke English and adopted most of American culture, its customs and traditions. They had no comprehension of African languages and knew little of African ways. They generally had plantation knowledge and skills lacking in African-born slaves and an understanding of plantation routines and expectations.

A smaller society of blacks, slave and free, managed to acquire property, real and personal, and taught their offspring the values of property. They accepted in whole the white American values of ownership and wealth and were likely to be skilled and ambitious. This grouping of blacks was well assimilated into American culture and at times held itself aloof from unskilled black labor that did not possess property. They firmly believed that "the possession of property would help them to protect their families, assert their rights in court, and secure the goodwill of whites."[11]

An even smaller group of blacks, more properly mulattoes, formed even closer bonds with white communities, at times winning their support, influence, and friendship. These slaves and free blacks spent more time in the company of whites, worked in the owners' houses, had their own businesses, and contracted work with white property owners. They too had little in common with new arrivals from Africa and rarely associated with other blacks either because of differences in property status or because of color differences.[12]

Light-complexion blacks in the eighteenth and nineteenth centuries—variously designated as mulattoes, quadroons, octoroons, and creoles—often were proud of their heritage and their relationship to the majority race. Lighter blacks frequently served as "house Negroes" and artisans and held other preferred jobs on plantations. They were more likely to be literate and to "know their numbers" (understand basic math). They might well be related to their owners and be resented by their darker fellows. Prior to the Revolution, *free black* and *mulatto* were frequently used interchangeably due to the high percentage of free blacks who were also mulatto.[13]

The gradual lightening of skin color of mulattoes who married mulattoes presented a problem of relativity for whites. At what exact point did the color line pass from black to white? The answer varied depending on the historic period and the geographical location of the question. Most of the states of the Upper South settled on four generations as the defining number. North Carolina's Immigration Act of 1826 defined free Negroes as "all free persons descended from negro ancestors, to the fourth generation inclusive, though one ancestor of each generation may have been a white person."

Richard Hildreth, a Northern farmer, wrote a novel titled *The Slave: Or, the Memoirs of Archy Moore* (1840) that dealt with the black color line. He based the book on a trip he made to Southside Virginia in the 1830s to study crop methods. His descriptions were based on his observations of slave life and slave-owner relationships on larger, wealthy plantations. His descriptions, nuanced and specific, are uncannily accurate and informed by the perspective of an outsider not beholding to the slave states.

Hildreth's protagonist, Archy Moore, is the illegitimate son of Col. Moore and a body servant to his white half brother. Archy has absorbed elitist attitudes from his mother, a favorite mistress of Col. Moore, who bore him six children, and from his own pampering as a near-white house servant and favorite of his half brother. Archy's mother is also Mrs. Moore's servant and is accorded privileges and a lifestyle that could only be envied by lesser slaves. Her son describes her life as "very careless, indolent." Archy's grandfather is Col. Randolph, scion of one the great Virginia families, officer in the Revolutionary War, planter, slave owner. His father is Col. Moore, Revolutionary War officer, planter, slave owner, a member of Virginia's "great families."[14]

Both mother and son are practically white. Archy describes his mother as being "vain of her beauty" and noted that she assumed an "air of superiority." His mother practically bequeaths a white legacy to her son, telling him on her deathbed that he had "running in [his] veins, the best blood of Virginia"—the blood, she added, of the Moores and the Randolphs. The boy is seventeen and does not yet understand that he is the property of his white father and family. "So ready are slaves to imbibe all the ridiculous prejudices of their oppressors, and themselves to add new links to the chain, which deprives them of their liberty."[15]

Moore learns to regret his haughty attitude toward the African side of his ancestry. He reflects from his mature years and regrets his attitudes toward dark field hands and other slaves who performed menial labor on the plantation. He admits that he looked down on lesser slaves, and "like most of the lighter complexioned slaves, I felt a sort of contempt for my duskier brothers in misfortune. I kept myself as much as possible at a distance from them, and scorned to associate with men a little darker than myself."[16]

"At this time, I prided myself upon my color, as much as any Virginian of them all; I thought myself of a superior caste, and would have felt it a degradation, to put myself on a level with those a few shades darker than myself. This silly pride had kept me from forming intimacies with the other servants, either male or female; for I was decidedly whiter than any of them."[17]

There were very practical reasons for free blacks to hold on to and tout their free status. As the slave states enacted increasingly draconian measures against free blacks as a class after 1790, it was essential that black freemen have proof of their status as protection against the laws and the element of whites who always stood ready to abuse the laws to punish and humiliate free blacks. "Free papers" was a valuable document that separated free blacks from slaves and gave them a common bond with whites. The documents were desired by all who would escape bondage and the most valuable thing a free black could own. "Freedom within the context of slavery gave free Negroes something to protect and transformed them into a conservative caste."[18]

The free black was on more solid footing when he or she could produce their free papers testifying to their status, but even these papers did not provide absolute sanctuary. There was a lucrative market in forgery of freedom papers, and it was common for slaves to use the papers of a friend to skirt the law. The very best insurance for free blacks against unscrupulous whites was a white sponsor who would step forward and vouch for the free man or woman.

The willingness of some free blacks to separate themselves from their caste can be explained in part by education, affluence, and status as much as color. Freed without a hint of education and possessed of few skills, the majority of blacks freed after the Revolution were ill-prepared to function in American society. As their numbers grew, they gathered in the worst urban neighborhoods, on the periphery of towns and villages, and eked out a bare subsistence.

> *Cowed, perplexed, and dispirited, they huddled together on any*
> *scant, sterile bit of land that they were fortunate enough to be possessed of,*
> *erected clusters of their frail little huts, and like oppressed, hopeless classes*
> *the world over sunk into profound listlessness and sloth. The women*
> *grew unchaste, the men dishonest, until in many minds the term "free*
> *negro" became a synonym for all that was worthless and despicable.*[19]

These groupings and sub-groupings of African Americans with their own color and social prejudices held sway when John Day Sr. labored in the cabinetmaker and carpentry trades in and around Petersburg in 1800. His sons grew up in the same muddled racial climate. The social conventions of the late eighteenth century had its influence on the Days as well as on free blacks and slaves no less than it did on the white population. The Days belonged to that smallest grouping of free blacks who were exceptions to their caste.

Petersburg, Virginia

The lives of the Stewarts and Days in the early years of the nineteenth century were played out in a three-county area of southeast Virginia: Dinwiddie, Sussex, and Greensville, a geographic area part of what was commonly called Southside, being south of the falls of the James River and stretching to the North Carolina border. The only town of any size that may have influenced their work and their outlook on the society they lived in was Petersburg, Virginia, where John Sr., possibly apprenticed. The village of Hicksford (present-day Emporia), near where the Days lived for a time and where John Sr. operated a cabinetmaking shop, was little more than a country crossroads.

John Day is listed in Dinwiddie tax records of 1800 as a "shop jointer" in Petersburg, but his urban career did not last more than several years. Petersburg was not a pretty place in 1800. A rough-and-tumble frontier town, it had the unkempt and rowdy appearance of a street urchin, caring neither for its health nor its looks. Even so, it offered a fruitful environment for the nurturing of a free-black class on a level with Norfolk and even Richmond. It was the closest city to the Days and may have been the area of John Sr.'s early journeyman work.

The rutted little backwater that became Petersburg began as a frontier fort named Fort Henry, built at the falls of the Appomattox in 1645 to protect white traders and the odd planter who had pushed up close to the Indian Line, the border between white settlers and Indians protected by the British treaty of 1644. Abraham Wood, an indentured servant immigrant turned Indian trader, first commanded the fort and kept peace between natives and colonists for years. Major Peter Jones succeeded to the command in 1675, and the site was given his name.

By the early eighteenth century, more planters than traders were traipsing along the Appomattox, looking for virgin land. The Indian Line was permanently breached in 1690 by white settlement, and 329,000 acres of virgin land that would become Dinwiddie County opened to aggressive planters who coveted the pristine woodland. To the assertive European emigrant and the second—and third-generation American, the Indian was a thwart to progress and expansion. He was, moreover, a heathen and a savage who deserved no protection by the white man's law and certainly did not deserve title to the land he refused to exploit.

Some three thousand souls shared the muddy squalor that was Petersburg in 1800, a hodgepodge of ramshackle buildings whose architectural monotony was unrelieved by a monument, a park, or even trees. No handsome public structures lined the streets, no wrought iron fences adorned house fronts, just a maze of unpainted huts and houses and lean-tos cohabiting with grogshops, taverns, warehouses, and tobacco shops, all weathered a slate gray or mousy brown.[20]

Even so, by the time of the first national census in 1790, Petersburg was Virginia's third-largest city. It had the largest percentage of blacks and the largest urban free-black population in the state. In fact, its free-black population, in percentage (10 percent), was the largest in the South, most of which resided in the black sections of Pocahontas and Blandford.

The town population was almost evenly divided between blacks and whites even from the first national census. In 1790 half the town population of 3,000 was black, though only 310 were free. But by 1810 more than a thousand of the black populace was listed as "free colored." By 1830, driven by a booming economy and an exploding population, there were 2,850 slaves and 2,032 free blacks out of a total 11,762 souls living in Petersburg, still one of the largest urban free-black populations in the Upper South.[21]

The town's focus was a central market area of trade shops and artisans and tobacco warehouses that served the surrounding plantation economy. Furniture and coach making were part of the vibrant economy, but tobacco ruled, nurtured by the Scottish companies of Spiers, Cuningham and Glassford, Leslie and Brydon, and Watson McGill & Co. Scottish firms stocked numerous stores across Southside, extended credit to tobacco farmers, and bought and moved their tobacco from the fields to Petersburg and Richmond.[22]

Horse and cattle corrals, hogpens, tanyards, and blacksmith ovens contributed their particular fragrances and clamor to the general din that kept the place awake day and night. Horses and cows slogged their way through deep mud during the wet season and added their residue to the mire. Chickens and hogs vied for slop that was pitched through open windows into streets and alleyways. Curs and mongrels fought over the same thin pickings.

Street urchins pelted tethered oxen and mules with clods of dirt, practiced their talents at lifting watch fobs, and begged for handouts. Ruffians in multipatched britches wrestled over half-smoked cigars tossed in a ditch. House girls on errands held up the hems of hand-me-down skirts from the mud while trying to hide their ankles. A threesome caterwauled a dissonant chorus of "The Girl I Left Behind Me" to a screeching fiddle bowed by a tramp in a threadbare beaver hat and a tattered black dress coat.

One merchant, on a return trip from New York, bemoaned the dilapidated appearance of the town:

> [*A*]*nd then to come to Petersburg*[,] *the coach traces breaking before we arrive—the road in ruts—the fields uncultivated—the houses tumbling down, groups of free negroes*[,] *mullatoes and whites lounging around a grog shop—the town half depopulated.*[23]

There were no parallel streets, no town center, no city plan. Streets took form as they were needed. As commerce flourished and patrons beat paths to its doors, roads and alleys were stamped out underfoot without a thought to boardwalks or even a safe shoulder. The fast pace of commerce in the first quarter of the nineteenth century democratized pedestrian traffic: planters and gentlemen rubbed elbows and jostled against drovers, artisans, merchants, dance girls, slaves, and free blacks. Dandies in hunting duds astride fine horses tore down the main street in spontaneous races, clods of mud and rocks pelting pedestrians and carriages alike.[24]

Free-black women outnumbered the men in Petersburg, as they did in all cities in Virginia. The largest number of female heads of households, seventy, were tobacco stemmers, followed by laborers. Only thirty-nine were listed as washerwomen, the leading category of female heads of households in most other cities. Freewomen worked as cooks, domestics, seamstresses, and nurses. Some of the women increased their income as concubines to white businessmen. "Many free Negro women either lived with white men or supplemented their earnings by concubinage with them . . . . The white man could involve himself in this fashion with impunity since he . . . ordinarily lost no standing in society."[25]

Petersburg was a mixture of classes and nationalities and languages. Yankees and native-born Virginians competed with immigrants from Scotland, Ireland and England for the tobacco and fur trades. There was a scattering of French and Creole and an ever-increasing population of free blacks who worked as laborers, mechanics, store and tavern keepers, servants, tobacco stemmers, and draymen. And, of course, there were slaves.

The mean streets showed off a profusion of clashing colors and styles and languages, all in the business of making a profit. But in more familiar situations the classes and nationalities kept to their own, the exception being the Caribbean French, who mingled socially with free blacks and even slaves. Foreign merchants, largely tobacco factors, chose not to mix socially and especially not to intermarry with the native-born, whom they considered ill bred. Natives scorned the immigrants as foreigners and mimicked their speech and manners. All, except the French, held blacks and Indians in contempt as inferiors.[26]

The one area in which free blacks shared space and some familiarity with whites was entertainment. Petersburg was a raucous town in the first decades of the nineteenth century and very vocal in its leisure time. Grogshops and gambling houses abounded, along with brothels and taverns. Free blacks mixed rather freely with white men in these low-class establishments, as well as in the arenas of horse racing and cockfighting. Black and mulatto women entertained white men of both the lower classes and the well-to-do.[27] John Day Sr. may have spent time in the gaming houses and taverns; the two vices followed him throughout his adult life.

Horse racing was the rage in the river town in the late eighteenth and early nineteenth centuries. The locals loved their horses and loved to put them on display. One visitor to the area claimed that no one walked when he could ride a horse. "Indeed, a man will frequently go five miles to catch a horse, to ride only one mile afterward."

The New Market Races, run in April and October, were events anticipated by high and low society every year. The town population swelled with enthusiasts from the surrounding counties and from out of state. A one-hundred-foot grandstand overlooking a one-mile oval track made up the race grounds. Ravenscroft had its own track, as did Pocahontas. Petersburg had at least two tracks, Prides Race Track on Cox Road and Raceland on the Old State Road.

Racing Billy Wynne, otherwise known as Col. William Wynne, a veteran of the War of 1812 and sheriff of the town in the 1830s, owned Raceland. Wynne's track was located at the site of an old colonial tavern called Rices Tavern. His best horse was named Timoleon, sired by the famous Sir Archy, which he sold for $4,100.00, evidence of the value of horse racing and racehorses. The races were demanding events on the horses, offering three heats of four miles, each with thirty-minute intervals between the races, an unheard-of marathon in our own age.[28]

Class distinctions blurred at the races as all levels of society joined in the festivities, placing bets, making wagers, arguing the merits of the horses and jockeys, all of whom were black. Black and white mingled freely at the tracks, though after the exhortations of the Protestant revivals, ladies were expected to remain on New Market Hill above the "promiscuous crowd." Not all of them did so. One visitor claimed that he might as well be talking to Hottentots as to the denizens of Petersburg when the races were on; so strange was the race jargon to his ears.[29]

They are excessively attached to every species of sport, gaming and dissipation, particularly horse-racing, and that most barbarous of all diversions, that peculiar species of cruelty, cockfighting.[30]

Cockfights, gambling, dancing, traveling troupes, and the theater were all popular pastimes in Petersburg, as was any patriotic celebration, such as Muster Day and the Fourth of July, as they were in all the new states. The latter was given over to almost universal inebriation, frolicking, and fights, a general "jollification" fueled by liquid spirits that on occasion required the talents of Dr. James Greenway to repair the damages.

Petersburg merchants and mechanics followed politics and financial news. They discussed the latest news of the Corps of Discovery and its expedition to the Pacific and debated the Hamilton and Jefferson sides of the national bank issue, offered theories on economic ups and downs, and argued the merits of slavery. The Burr-Hamilton duel was the talk of the town until, over time, it sank softly into the murky mire of lore. And the talk was always about tobacco: tobacco prices, tobacco factors, tobacco workers, tobacco worms, tobacco inspectors.

Petersburg joined Richmond and Lynchburg as one of the three largest tobacco-producing cities in Virginia. In 1835 there were six working tobacco factories and eight by 1840, with a workforce of almost six hundred laborers. Two of the factories alone produced an annual value worth $150,000. If the economic region of Petersburg is expanded to include the county of Dinwiddie, the number of factories would increase to twenty with an annual product value to $2,167,202.[31]

Business in Petersburg was sound enough by 1825 for town artisans to form the Petersburg Benevolent Mechanic Association (PBMA), a self-help group that promoted the business of members, made loans to them, and acted as a safety net during economic declines. The organization included mechanics and manufacturers, from tanners and coopers to printers and bricklayers, weavers and bakers to machinists and tobacconists. The association took care not to criticize slavery and was careful about allying with politics. Many of its members relied on slave labor, the use of which often "separated successful mechanics from the more middling workers."[32] The association did not accept free blacks for membership.

By the 1830s Petersburg had taken on many of the trappings of a large city, including paved streets, canals, brick buildings, factories, improved wharfs, theaters and opera, churches, railroads, and civic demands for regulating animals, people, and city trash. Industry was humming by 1835 with three cotton mills, six tobacco factories, two cottonseed mills, iron forges, pottery factories, small mercantile stores, and five railroad lines. Canals to skirt Appomattox Falls and locks to ease boat traffic into the city wharfs improved trade and opened Petersburg to a larger trade with the James River. The city would remain one of the state's largest, and its free-black population was always of a higher percentage than those of the larger cities of Richmond and Norfolk.[33]

Petersburg was an urban enclave; as such, its citizens placed a value on work and efficiency, regardless of who was doing the task. Cities offered far more opportunities for free blacks than did the countryside, which was invariably more conservative and cautious. In towns, free blacks became business owners and important assistants to white entrepreneurs, and some earned enough money to become slave owners themselves. By 1827, 69 free blacks in Petersburg owned a total of 101 slaves.[34]

Some white folks in Petersburg associated with free blacks, but they hailed mostly from the lower classes. Most free blacks in Petersburg were laborers: ditch diggers, freight loaders, tobacco haulers and twisters, bootblacks, messengers, and the like. But there were free blacks who made their marks and a nice financial situation for themselves as skilled laborers and as business owners in the hustle and bustle of the city. White businessmen entered into contracts and business arrangements, even partnerships, with free blacks but often would not walk down the street in their presence.

Most of the well-to-do free blacks in the city were industrious artisans and a few owned their own business. Free-black Robert Clark owned a livery stable, Jack McRae owned a restaurant, Phil Sewell was a teamster; all did well at their trades. Berry Bonner and Armistead Wilson operated as blacksmiths, and Thomas Scott worked as a contractor. Ambrose Bonner, Thomas Berry, and Joseph Jenkins were tobacco twisters who made good money converting raw tobacco into plugs. The tobacco warehouses and shops offered many opportunities for free blacks and slaves as twisters and cutters and packers.[35]

Barbers constituted a special category among free blacks, the trade sometimes referred to as "the birthright of the free Negro" in the vernacular of the day. Free-black barbers, often mulatto and with some education, became an elite profession, its members dubbed the "aristocracy of free blacks." It was one trade that drew a large white clientele for free blacks. Some shops catered strictly to whites, but blacks had their own shops as well.[36]

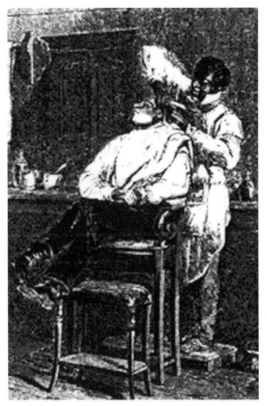

Many free blacks found work as barbers.

Free-Black Barber. Free blacks in the larger towns of the South often dominated the barbering trade, a source of good wages and sometimes of wealth. More than a few barbers belonged to the "elite" of free black communities. William Colson, a free barber in Petersburg, Virginia, earned enough money barbering to become a slave owner and partner in a shipping company that traded with Liberia. *(Courtesy of the Library of Congress, Prints & Photographs Division, Washington, D.C. No Use Restrictions)*

The operators of barbershops usually kept clean and were neat in appearance, and they worked well at the service industry, meaning in part that they knew how to engage with whites, walking that fine racial line between haughty and subservient. They were "good looking, dressed in clean white jackets and aprons, smart, quick, and attentive." In the larger towns, the trade "belonged almost exclusively" to free blacks. In Petersburg, the free black William Colson earned enough at the barbering trade to become a slave owner himself and an investor in the Liberian colonization trade.[37]

Some of Petersburg's free blacks contributed to the colonization movement of the 1830s, with several significant players residing there. The barber and slave owner William Colson was a colonizer for Liberia, as was his partner, Joseph Jenkins Roberts, a boat owner and captain. It is likely that John Day Jr. made his contacts there when he decided to try his fortunes in Africa. He sailed for Liberia on their vessel, the *Caroline*.

Roberts was one of numerous free blacks who despaired of ever being more than a slave without the title, though he was seven-eighths white and could easily pass as a white. As a young man, he joined with Colson in a trade venture to Liberia—Roberts, Colson and Company—and eventually made his life there. He and Colson shipped wood, palm oil, and ivory to America in exchange for finished goods. Roberts began his career as a boatman in his parents' boating business, which carried trade between Richmond and Petersburg, before he started his own freight business.[38]

Roberts remained a merchant and a boatman, even after he shipped to Liberia in 1829. As a settler, he brought the advantages of having wealth, his own ship *Caroline*, and a successful trading business to Liberia. He rose in the politics of the colony, became an aide to the colony's first white governor, and finally came into his own as the first president of the Republic of Liberia in 1847. In the United States, he held fewer legal rights than the most illiterate white man had. The Liberian colony counted more emigrants from Virginian than from any other state.[39]

Free-black life in early America consisted of many ironies, as is demonstrated in Southside demographics. Blacks owning blacks, men and women owning family members, husbands owning wives and children, wives owning husbands and children: it was a devil's labyrinth of technical and legal entanglements that ensnared both owners and bondsmen. An example of the complicated arrangements that ensued from black ownership of blacks is Jane Cook. Cook owned two freight boats that operated out of Petersburg, the *Democrat* and the *Experiment*. She, who was a free black, acted as an agent for her husband, who actually ran the operation. He could not own the boats because he was a slave owned by a white man.[40]

Slaves who had married, even in the "jumping the broom" sense, and who had children or other family members enslaved and who managed to acquire and save cash money, made use of the 1782 Virginian law allowing private manumission to purchase their kin and set them free. Sometimes they bought their family members outright; other times, they went through an agent or other third party. In either case, the purchase of a wife or a son or a mother, reduced to the strict legal jargon of the courts, underscored the brutal requirements of slavery and weakened the moral arguments of slaveholders for its existence.

> *I, Israel Ducourdray having in my possession and as my property a certain Mulatto woman (my wife) formerly called Sucky Ellis and her two children, to wit, Israel and Alexander, formerly held as slaves and which said Sucky and her children I purchased of Charles Duncan of Chesterfield County as per bill of sale to me dated 7 November last . . . Emancipate . . . said Sucky and her children . . . the said Sucky being my wife and the two children aforesaid considered as my Children. 2 July 1798*
>
> *I, Abby Smith, a free Negro woman of the town of Petersburg, purchased of Henry Randolph, Esq., of the County of Nottoway a Mulatto boy slave named Baldy (being my own son) agreeable to a bill of sale executed by the said Harrison to me bearing date 1 April 1798, and whereas also considering liberty to be natural and unalienable right of man, and for and in consideration of the natural love and affection I bear my said son have emancipated . . . 4 February 1799.[41]*

Isle of Wight Deed Book 2, 1790-1801

Historians continue to debate whether and how many free-black slave owners bought bondsmen, often family members, to protect them, in some case to free them, and there are numerous examples of this familial altruism. Testimony of freed slaves and their owners leave no doubt as to the generosity and affection of some black slave owners. There is also solid evidence to support the economic side of the issue, including testimony from black owners themselves who used slaves in the purely capitalistic sense of exploiting their labor.[42]

Free blacks formed an integral and important part of the Petersburg success story. Where business was the basis for economic growth, free blacks successfully competed with white workers and artisans for jobs and positions. They had not only the numbers but also the skills and the drive to make their mark on the city and to challenge the bounds of state laws and local ordinances.

Free blacks held many occupations in Petersburg, which included stonemasons, midwives, wheelwrights, potters, pilots, carpenters, caulkers, cooks, cabinetmakers, plasterers, whitewashers, butchers, bakers, barbers, fishers, and fishmongers. Most middling Virginians considered themselves above menial labor and used slave and servant labor when they could afford it. Otherwise, they hired poor whites and free-black laborers who had little choice in their means of making a living.

For all its progress, Petersburg was a sickly place in its early years, attributable to its lack of sanitation and its low elevation hard by the Appomattox River. All the white man's diseases carried by mosquitoes, fleas, flies, and rats invaded Petersburg during the damp summer months and sent the elite, wealthy planters and merchants scampering for the highlands to escape the miasma. Newspapers of the day obligingly recorded the epidemics of fevers and agues that swept through the town like a blighted fog blown by ill winds.

John Ferdinand Smyth, who traveled widely in the American colonies and after the Revolution through the states, visited Petersburg in the 1770s. His accounts are lively and strive, in their own way, to give the Americans a fair consideration, though his British bias colors his observations. Nonetheless, he bequeathed to historians a firsthand, though eccentric, description of his first encounters with the Americans and their customs, including his encounters with the obnoxious mosquito.

> The night being calm we were assaulted by great numbers of musketoes, a noxious fly, which seems to be of the species of gnats, but larger and more poisonous, leaving a hard tumor wherever they bite, with an intolerable and painful itching; they penetrate the skin, fill themselves with blood, and make their principal attacks in the night, accompanied by a small, shrill disagreeable note, the very sound of which effectually prevents you from sleep, after you have once been bit.[43]

Smyth claimed that "no child born at this place [Petersburg] ever grew to maturity . . . which is occasioned by the insalubrity of the air, and the extreme unhealthiness of the situation."

There is documentary evidence that some of the large factories in Petersburg and other large cities in the border South offered a token of care to its black employees, even its slaves. Some had a doctor on staff that was responsible for laborers; some had less-qualified personnel but nonetheless accepted the responsibility for illness and accidents. A tobacconist in Richmond "fitted up two hospitals 'in the most comfortable style'" for his workers in anticipation of a cholera epidemic.[44]

Smyth traveled widely in the South, and the intrepid traveler did occasionally find comfort and pleasure in the most unlikely places, though he was quick to offset any kind remarks with a negative comment. He found an excellent ordinary at Boyd's Tavern in Blandford, but the pleasant meal was overwhelmed by the "prodigious and incessant noise and clamour that continually assailed [his] ears from bullfrogs and insects." [45]

Ordinaries were common in the colonies and the only ready form of lodging for travelers. They were notorious for their lack of amenities, as any shed with a roof could advertise itself as an ordinary. Mr. Smyth and other visitors to the South made many rude references to colonial lodgings and noted that the American *ordinary* was used interchangeably for *tavern*, *inn*, and *public house*. They were "in reality little better than shelters from the weather; yet the worst of them is by no means deficient in charging high." Their average fare consisted of lots of hominy and hoecake and the preferred cider or brandy of the day. In Samuel Johnson's dictionary of the period, an ordinary was the "regular price of a meal" or "a place of eating established at a certain price" where diners shared a common or "ordinary" table.[46]

American ordinaries carried a certain reputation even among the natives. Commenting on the general dissipation of the ordinaries, also called "tipling houses," a lawmaker in seventeenth-century Virginia called their numbers "excessive" and claimed them to be "full of mischiefe and inconvenience by cherishing idleness and debaucheryes, in a sort of loose and careless persons who neglecting their callings misspend their times in drunkennesse."[47] The Days' father-in-law, Thomas Stewart, may have owned a tavern in Dinwiddie County.

Petersburg consisted of four separate communities: Blanford, Pocahontas (named for the famed onetime resident of the town), Ravenscroft, and Petersburg. The four consolidated in 1784 as Petersburg, even though Pocahontas was separated from the others by a bridge across the river. Pocahontas, a peninsula on the north side of the Appomattox, originated as a Native American town that was part of the Powhattan Confederacy. Pocahontas became the first and, years later, the largest free-black community in Virginia. The communities depended on the tobacco economy so heavily in the eighteenth century that they were known collectively as Nest of Tobacco Towns.

The Appomattox and James Rivers gave Petersburg its life and its trade advantage. Located just below the Appomattox Falls, the former river flowed to the James, and the James wound its way to the sea. Beginning in 1795 navigation around Petersburg was improved by construction of canals and clearing of the river of trees and debris. There were fisheries on both sides of the river, "lucrative," according to J. F. D. Smyth, their banks alive with fishermen, boatmen, laborers, and overseers. Sloops, schooners, flats, and lighters all called at the falls, but ships of burden were berthed some five to eight miles below on the James.[48]

The booming tobacco economy demanded an increasing number of slaves to plant the soil of Southside Virginia that grew the plant that fed the Petersburg warehouses. Warehouses required more slaves to store and move tobacco. Tobacco wealth brought freeholders who bought houses. Horses and carriages demanded blacksmiths. All required food and the accoutrements of town living. Tobacco fertilized the growth of Petersburg.

Tobacco was well regulated and was inspected at various towns and villages in Southside. Petersburg and Richmond had numerous warehouses that accepted tobacco for examination by government inspectors. The government inspectors issued promissory notes to tobacco sellers in various amounts ranging from five pounds to one hundred pounds. The seller might pay the inspector in tobacco (3 percent fee), but he used his promissory notes to pay his bills and to buy retail. The notes acted as a medium of exchange. Taxes, levies, and fees were all paid in tobacco.

During the late eighteenth century, tobacco along the James and Appomattox Rivers was carried in hogsheads on two large canoes lashed together with crossbeams. As many as ten hogsheads rode on the crossbeams, an average weight of five tons. After the barrels landed at Petersburg or other destinations, the canoes were separated for easier handling on the return trip. Free blacks found ready labor on the river freighters and came to dominate the bateaux business between Farmville and Petersburg. White watermen then lobbied for laws that limited free black ownership of the freight trade.

By 1810 the Appomattox was navigable inland to Farmville, and tobacco hogsheads went by bateau (bateaux, pl.), a simple flat-bottom river barge with flaring sides, some as long as sixty feet with a six—to eight-foot beam and a steering oar at one end. The all-purpose cargo boat had a draught of twelve to eighteen inches and thus could operate in very shallow water, even with a load of several tons. The bateau could carry eight to ten hogsheads of tobacco, each weighing about one thousand pounds, or sixty-five barrels of flour.[49]

The bateau normally carried a crew of three: a headman to man the oar or sweep and two boatmen to walk planks just inside the gunwales as they pushed long poles into the river bottom to move the boat upriver. Going downriver with the current, boatmen used their poles to push the boat away from the banks and to move logs and other debris while the river current carried the boat along.[50]

On return trips from Petersburg, the simple craft carried kegs of nails, bushels of coal, sacks of salt, barrels of herrings, containers of lime and seashells (to make mortar), and finished goods. The boatmen also carried letters, messages, and even money from community to community. They did a brisk trade in oysters, in home remedies, and sometimes in contraband and stolen goods. It was a fairly independent life for a slave and even for a free black.[51]

Bateaux operated up and down the Dan, the James, and the Staunton Rivers, hauling wheat, corn, flour, and tobacco. The blowing of the bateau horn, a welcome break in a routine day of labor, signaled to sellers and traders along the rivers that the vessel was approaching and to have their produce ready or, on the return trip, to come for their finished goods. Maud Clement of Pittsylvania County asserted that the Roanoke bateau was invented by Robert Rose and Anthony Rucker, but the design of the hauler and the name precedes America by many generations. They were originally used in Europe and were wielded by French fur traders in the colonial Northwest.[52]

By the mid-1830s, there were forty bateaux operating out of the small town of Farmville, with about one-third of the business owned and operated by black boatmen. Black, white, free, and slave worked as laborers on the freighters, and some owned these transport vessels that supplied Farmville with its essentials until the Civil War. The boats coming downriver entered a canal near Petersburg and then through several locks and an aqueduct before tying up in a basin at the town wharfs for unloading. James M. Venable & Co. and other tobacconists around Farmville sent thousands of hogsheads of tobacco down the Appomattox to Petersburg.[53]

Goods from the bateaux were off-loaded by black labor into warehouses at Petersburg to be reloaded and transported some six miles below the city to be loaded again onto deepwater vessels. And then down the James in ever-increasing numbers of barges, sloops, and schooners, flats and lighters filled with hogsheads of the golden weed and other produce. Ships of burden ran between Petersburg and Norfolk before they made for the open seas and the Caribbean Islands or Europe.

Yet as in other economic endeavors, when blacks as a group, slave or free, became too successful, the authorities enacted legal restraints against them. The navigation trade in Tidewater and along the rivers became so dominated by blacks that a law was enacted in 1784 to restrict the use of slaves to one-third the total of boatmen employed.[54]

Bateaux also ran the James River from Lynchburg to Richmond, the largest tobacco market in the state and the most important river transportation route. The large quantities of tobacco that traveled the James called for the building of canals alongside the river to circumvent river snags of trees and debris and the intemperance of river levels due to rains and drought. The construction of the James River and Kanawha Canal was designed to bring tobacco and produce from the interior of the state to Richmond. When completed, the canal transported freight from Buchanan at the base of the Blue Ridge Mountains directly to Shockoe Basin in Richmond. Tolls were added to each tobacco hogshead to pay for the construction of the canals, a fee that was protested by haulers and tobacco producers alike. However, the canals greatly increased trade between Lynchburg and Richmond. From 1816 to 1822, an average of sixteen thousand hogsheads of tobacco passed every year through the River Canal, or about a fourth of the state's tobacco trade.[55]

The well-known pen-and-pencil and woodcut artist David Hunter Strother (pen name Porte Crayon), who studied under Samuel Morse, traveled through Virginia and North Carolina in the 1850s, creating sketches and reporting on the locals for *Harpers Monthly* magazine. Strother recalled a trip down the James River from Lynchburg on a freight bateau when he was a young man. He described it as the most memorable experience in a memorable life of wandering America and Europe. He wrote about his visit as follows:

> *Night was the glorious time, when the boats were drawn along shore in some still cove beneath the spreading umbrage of a group of sycamores. A fleet of fifteen or twenty would sometimes be collected at the same spot. The awnings were hoisted, fires lighted, and supper dispatched in true boatman-like style. The sly whisky-jug was passed about, banjoes and fiddles were drawn from their hiding places, the dusky improvisatore took his seat on the bow of the boat and poured forth his wild recitative, while the leathern lungs of fifty choristers made the dim shores echo with the refrain.*[56]

Crayon enjoyed the rough lifestyle of rural America. He often tested himself against narrow mountain passes and roads, dared to explore mountain caves, chanced himself upon makeshift bridges across roiling rivers. After a very middle-class childhood in Martinsburg, Virginia (now West Virginia), Crayon found America's out-of-the-way places as something rustic and exotic, artifacts from a simpler time before the comings and goings of steam engines on rails and steam-powered mills and factories. He wrote many articles for *Harpers Monthly*, describing the quirks and peculiarities of the rural folk as perceived by city folk. He was one of the country's first "color writers."

The artist was intrigued by individual blacks, and while he exhibited the bias and prejudice of Southern customs, he gave verbal descriptions and pencil sketches of many blacks that are much more thoughtful than the usual stereotypes offered in most publications. And their music and dancing struck him as particularly intriguing.

Crayon described the music and singing as "thoroughly African," meaning it was unintelligible to his ears, and alluded to the themes of the songs as sometimes humorous, sometimes sad, and taken from the drudgeries of plantation life.

> *The melodies were wild and plaintive, occasionally mingled with strange, uncouth cadences, that carried the imagination forcibly to the banks of the Gambia, or to an encampment of rollicking Mandingoes.*[57]

The singing often led to an "antic dance," with all joining in until the partying became so riotous that the captain of the boat would order all to bed. Fence rails laid across the bateau, under cover of awnings, made a bed for the crew. Some spread blankets or rough hides over the tobacco hogsheads for an improvised place of rest. The boats rocked gently to the roll of the current as small campfires flickered under the bluffs like distant lanterns.

Slaves were tutored in European music and musical instruments to play for the soirees of their owners, but the banjo (also called the banjor or banjur) was popular with blacks at slave dances and parties. The stringed music box adapted a similar African instrument made of a reed for the neck and a gourd for the body and strung with wire or catgut. As Mr. Strother testified, whites found the music "alien" to their ears, something altogether different from those performed by slaves when they played at the parties of planters.

Another informant on slave music and dance in Prince Edward County is Dr. William B. Smith, who recorded his impressions of a beer dance in 1838. His interpretation of the banjo music played by slaves is especially insightful and surprising, coming from a planter and slave owner, a class not noted for giving praise to their bondsmen even when they deserved it. But in his description of the banjo music he heard at a neighbor's farm, Smith recognized something even rarer and deeper than the melody; he found a human quality in the music that is seldom allowed light of day in the reports and opinions of white slave owners in the antebellum South.

> *Although I am of the opinion that persimmon beer is not intoxicating, yet I have witnessed great glee, and highly pleasurable sensation produced in our slaves, over a jug-gourd of beer; but I ascribe this reverie or pleasurable hilarity to the wild notes of the "banjor," which give zest to the beer. There is an indescribable something in the tones of this rude instrument, that strikes the most delicate and refined ear with pleasing emotion; the uninterrupted twang or vibration of its strings, produces a sound as it dies away, that borders on the sublime. I never could account for its wonderful effect on a well-organized ear, capable of distinguishing and appreciating agreeable sounds; unless it be admitted, that concord and discord are so completely blended as to produce perfect harmony. This opinion, however absurd it may seem at first view, is not without its supporters. Pope says, "all discord is harmony not understood."*[58]
>
> Farmers' Register

The doctor was a well-read and articulate man; his library apparently included Alexander Pope. He was certainly familiar with the banjo and its music as performed by slaves. He found something in the music that Mr.

Strother could not hear, or at least, could not appreciate, possibly the primitive beginnings of syncopation that distinguished New Orleans ragtime and jazz in the first decades of the next century.

Dr. Smith heard more in the expert banjo playing than most whites admitted to hearing. The overall scene is so striking and so delighted the observer that it should be told in full. The exotic vista of color, language, song, and dance—a "rare sport," he termed it—"Virginia slaves, dancing jigs and clapping 'juber' over a barrel of persimmon beer" inspired the poet in Dr. Smith.

Incidentally, John Ferdinand Smyth wrote in the previous century of Virginians using ripe persimmons as a base for beer. The persimmons were kneaded into a pasty dough with wheat bran and baked in an oven: "Of these they brew a fermented liquor, which is called persimmon beer. This serves for their common drink, and is tolerably pleasant and wholesome."[59]

Meanwhile, the dance near Farmville in 1838 was preceded by ritual and song. "The Ball was opened with great ceremony by singing a song known to our Virginia slaves by the name of 'who zen-John, who za.'"

> *Old black bull come down de hollow,*
> *He shake IT tail, you hear him bellow;*
> *When he bellow he jar de river,*
> *He paw de earth, he make it quiver.*
>
> *Who-zen John, who-za.*

"Then was a sky rocket thrown out, as a prelude to the general exhibition, and will give the reader some idea of what is to follow. Those who could not get seats in the house, took their stand outside, peeping in the door and through the logs, making remarks on the dancers; and here I will observe, that there was a complete Babel jargon, a confusion of tongues!

"Here the banjo man was seated on the beer barrel, in an old chair. A long white cow-tail, queued with red ribbon, ornamented his head, and hung gracefully down his back; over this he wore a three-cocked hat, decorated with peacock feathers, a rose cockade, a bunch of ripe persimmons, and to cap the climax, three pods of red pepper as a top-knot. *Trumming* his banjor, grinning with ludicrous gesticulations and playing off his wild notes to the company. Before him stood two athletic blacks, with open mouth and pearl white teeth, clapping *Juber* to the notes of the banjor; the forth black man held in his right hand a jug gourd of persimmon beer, and in his left, a dipper or water-gourd, to serve the company; while two black women were employed in filling the fire-place, six feet square, with larded persimmon dough. The rest of the company, male and female, were dancers, except a little squat wench, who held the torch light. I had never seen Juber clapped to the banjor before, and you may suppose I looked upon such a novel scene with some degree of surprise. Indeed I contemplated the dancing group, with sensations of wonder and astonishment! The clappers rested the right foot on the heel, and its clap on the floor was in perfect unison with the notes of the banjor, and the palms of the hands on the corresponding extremities; while the dancers were all jigging it away in the merriest possible gaiety of heart, having the most ludricuous [*sic*] twists, wry jerks, and flexible contortions of the body and limbs that human imagination can devine."[60]

Farmers' Register

Our intrepid traveler, Mr. Smyth, had witnessed very similar dances a generation earlier in Virginia and noted that slaves sometimes traveled six or seven miles at night after a day in the fields to attend "a negroe dance, in which he performs with astonishing agility, and the most vigorous exertions, keeping time and cadence, most exactly, with the music of the banjor (a large hollow instrument with three strings), and a quaqua (somewhat resembling a drum), until he exhausts himself."[61]

Planters and merchants of the upper crust in America were generally reserved men who held closely to standards of dress and conduct. One simply did not cavort or perform spontaneous movements. Rigid deportment, for men and women, exemplified a lifestyle of restraint, in movement, dress, music, and dancing. The Euro-American planter class considered moderation and self-control the mark of the lady and the gentleman; carefree movement and careless language were the marks of the lowly classes. Hence, the planter mocked and belittled the speech, gestures, and emotional spontaneity of his slaves.

Clapping, patting, or slapping "juba" or "juber" is a reference found throughout nineteenth-century Southern letters, diaries, and newspaper articles on slave music and dance, whether secular or spiritual. The reference is to the percussive sounds made on the body with hands and feet to beat out a rhythm. Musicologist Dena Epstein, in *Sinful Tunes and Spirituals*, claims that the earliest reference in American literature to "patting juba" is found in ex-slave Henry Bibb's autobiography, circa 1820s.[62]

Epstein describes the movement as "striking the hands on the knees, then striking the hands together, then striking the right shoulder with one hand, the left with the other—all the while keeping time with the feet, and singing." Other references include more complicated movements and involve slapping the thigh and the head. Though there is no mention of the "dance" in seventeenth—and eighteenth-century American literature, she recognizes the rhythmic movements as a "staple element in African music." Descriptions of "body slapping" to keep time were made by numerous travelers to Africa beginning in the seventeenth century. European traveler Richard Jobson noted Africans clapping hands to keep time in 1621, one of the earliest images recorded.[63]

Bibb, the onetime slave, mentioned "pat[ting] juber" in an indictment of slave owners who resisted religious instruction for their slaves for fear that it was "incendiary." Sabbath school and even preaching could lead to education of slaves, a thing abhorred by many planters as the fertile soil of slave insurrection. Religious meetings of any kind gave bondsmen and women a taste of dignity and self-worth, a slippery slope that might lead to insolence and resistance.[64]

Bibb wrote that owners who feared religious instruction encouraged their slaves instead to take to the woods to gamble, drink, and fight. "When they [slave owners] wish to have a little sport of that kind, they go among the slaves and give them whiskey, to see them dance, 'pat juber,' sing and play the banjo. Then get them to wrestling, fighting, jumping, running foot races, and butting each other like sheep."[65]

A more technical description of patting juba was made by Beverly Tucker, the Virginian jurist and novelist, in a letter to Edgar Allan Poe in 1835. In his description of the antics of a slave dance he had witnessed, Tucker gave this report:

> *The beat is capriciously irregular; there is no attempt to keep time to all the notes, but then it comes so pat & so distinct that the cadence is never lost . . . . Such irregularities are like rests and grace notes. They must be so managed as neither to hasten or retard the beat. The time of the bar must be the same, no matter how many notes are in it.*[66]

Most white people perceived the singing, dancing, and even worshiping of blacks as so much "antics" peculiar to slaves, the sort of things a child would do. Very few observers understood the generations of African culture that coursed through the veins of slaves patting juba, singing, and dancing or the spiritual nature of the chanting and humming and intoning that accompanied their dances. Whites knew simply that slave "antics" were foreign to their own ways, that they were African in nature and were therefore "backward" and illiterate.

Joel Walker Sweeney was a white banjo player from Appomattox Court House who used the banjo in minstrel shows in the 1830s and by the 1840s was traveling to Europe with his group, the Virginia Minstrels. Some identify him as the first white man to play the banjo onstage. Appomattox Court House was less than a day's ride from most areas of Prince Edward County. The geographical proximity raises interesting issues of cultural cross-fertilization in antebellum Southern music.

The Days and Stewarts in the Countryside

John Day Sr. may have found his honed his craft in the relatively urban atmosphere of Petersburg, and the city may have influenced his attitudes, but he spent most of his adult life in the rural environs of Dinwiddie, Greensville, and Sussex Counties, farming and cabinetmaking. The Land Tax Book of Greensville County documents John Day Sr. and Thomas Stewart as early as 1782. In that year, John Day owned 140 acres of land, and Thomas Stewart owned 114 acres in Sussex County. The records show that the two men owned their land through the 1790s.

Dinwiddie's population, including Petersburg, at the first national census was 4,800 whites and 7,895 blacks, 561 of whom were free. Neighboring Greensville County was smaller yet with 2,500 whites and 3,832 blacks, only 212 of whom were free. Those numbers would explode over the following three decades. It is instructive that there were only 283 voters in Dinwiddie County, a period when voting rights were tied to property holding and taxes.

The Day and Stewart families united through the marriage of John Day Sr. to Mourning Stewart, daughter of Thomas Stewart, in 1795 or 1796. The Stewarts appear in numerous county government records, and family members began the new century as landowners. The Stewart sons—Armstead, Charles, John, and Thomas—had land recorded in the 1820 county land book, 80 acres each on Walker Road in Dinwiddie County, as did their mother, Winny (150 acres). Thomas, the family patriarch, who is noted more than once with the appellation of "Dr." or "Doc." by his name, is listed in the Virginia Tax Payers of 1782-1787 in Dinwiddie County as a poll with 17 slaves.[67]

Stewart farmed (probably tobacco), maybe acted as the local doctor, and for a period, may have owned a tavern. The Virginia census of 1800 lists Thomas Stewart as "Stewart, Thomas Doc." and records that he owned eleven slaves and held an ordinary license. Stewart may have contributed to the patriot cause in the Revolutionary War. Virginia war records document that a Thomas Stewart supplied 3,251 pounds of beef and 4 bushels of oats to the Virginian rebels and received payment for the transaction after the war. The transaction was recorded in *The Court's Valuation of Property Impressed for the Use of the Public in Greensville County, Virginia, During the Latter Period of the Revolutionary War*.[68]

Stewart was an ambitious, competent, and accomplished man in the Southside tri-counties who fully participated in the slave-owning economy and society in which he achieved success. At his death, Stewart willed to his wife, Winny, his "mantion," four servants (slaves), a stage wagon, furniture, and farm animals. He left to John Day Jr., his grandson, a girl named Thody and emancipated nineteen other slaves.[69]

Day paid taxes in Greensville County in 1795-1796 on a slave and in 1797-1799 on two tithables. He paid taxes in Dinwiddie County in 1800-1802 and in Greensville County in 1787 and 1803-1804. He leased a farm in Sussex County in 1807 and lost it in 1810. During 1813 through 1817, he returned to the cabinetmakers' trade and was listed in the Dinwiddie County tax records for those years, though he rented farm properties as well. John Jr. recalled, many years later, that during these years, his "father had become intemperate; sold his pretty little plantation [in Sussex County], moved into Dinwiddie County, and was living in a rented house."[70]

Carpenters, blacksmiths, bakers, and other skilled and unskilled laborers were in demand as Petersburg grew haphazardly into a full-blown city. When the economy dipped, as it did often in the mercurial boom of the young town, or when his fortunes were at low ebb, Day would return to the country and take up farming. He seemed to have been adept at finding farms to rent; he worked at several in Dinwiddie County and owned one "pretty little plantation" in Sussex County. He was equally adept at losing them.

The Days and Stewarts lived and worked over the years in small communities that also influenced their behavior and aspirations: the community of Jarratt, near John Day's Sussex County farm and near where John Jr. attended school; the Great Creek/Reedy Creek area in Dinwiddie, where the Stewarts farmed; the Three Creek (sometimes Three Creeks) area, where Thomas Stewart may have operated an ordinary; and the Scottsville area of Dinwiddie County, where John Jr. worked and lost a shop to an accidental fire.

In their country homes, the Days and the Stewarts lived a lifestyle far above that of the majority of the population, considerably above that of most whites. They were more affluent, better educated, and more skilled than perhaps 80 to 90 percent of the population. Furthermore, they were well-spoken, had considerable white associations, and were near white themselves, if John Jr. may be taken as representative of the family.

The men and women who most influenced the lives and careers of Thomas and John Day were often white and usually of some social standing in the community. White connection to free blacks, especially to free mulattoes, was not unusual, and the ties frequently were familial, even if it they were not sanctioned by law. Mulattoes generally ranked higher in the black community, especially if they had a few years of formal education.

One of the earliest influences in the life of the young John Day was Edward Whitehorne (also Whitehorn), a white farmer who lived fifteen miles southwest of the Sussex Courthouse, probably in the vicinity of the community of Jarratt. John Jr. boarded with the Whitehornes at the age of eight or nine, spent his time with the Whitehorne children, and attended school with them under a teacher or tutor named Jonathan Bailey.[71]

Greensville County Land Books show the principal players in the young John Day's life living within five miles of one another in the southwest corner of Sussex County. John Day Sr.'s farm in 1815 stood eleven miles southwest of the county courthouse. Edward Whitehorne's farm was fifteen miles southwest of the courthouse. Nathaniel Chambliss lived ten miles southwest of the courthouse. Jonathan Bailey lived fifteen miles southwest of the courthouse. Thomas Stewart's farm lay thirteen miles southwest of the courthouse on Walker Road.[72]

The five years between 1805 and 1810, when John Jr. attended school and boarded with the Whitehornes, may well be the most important in the formation of his character and his future career choices. In a very autobiographical letter written when he was fifty years of age, Day recalls his schooling and his introduction to religion at the Whitehorne home as the formative events of his youth.

Respectability, John Jr. explained, was the essential trait of his family that gained himself and his brother Thomas a chance at an education in Southside Virginia, an education at a white school, no less, at a time when the formal schooling of free blacks was illegal and frowned on by most whites. He noted in the letter that, though respected in the community, his parents were not religious and that he had no knowledge of religion until he boarded with the Whitehornes. It was there that he learned that he had "an immortal part which would stand before an Eternal God, to be judged according to my conduct here." He wrote that the subject affected him "seriously."[73]

In the same letter, Day recalled his teachers, Jonathan Bailey and William Northcross, and a preacher, Nathaniel Chambliss, minister of High Hills Chapel. All the aforementioned lived in the area just north of Hicksford and east of Jarratt, just over the line in Sussex County. Day returned to the Jarratt area in 1816, where he visited a camp meeting and experienced a personal religious conversion. "I saw as I never saw before. I felt as I never felt before ... My heart melted, my soul bowed down, my life in review passed before me; and with what bitterness of soul did I look back on 12 years of misspent life."[74]

Though it would be another four years before Day was baptized into the faith, he clearly made his commitment at the revival meeting in Sussex County in 1816. Even leaving room for embellishment that thirty passing years and the learning and teaching of the Bible might have instilled in the missionary, his memory of the religious experience of his youth seems especially strong.

The notion of people of color having close friendships with whites in the nineteenth century strikes an off note, but the reality seems to be that laws and official attitudes toward blacks in general and especially toward free blacks were considerably harsher than that of the people who lived and worked with them daily.

The majority of whites, the poorer classes and artisans, who resented the competition for jobs and who needed a class of people below them to disparage, generally opposed the class of free blacks as a whole but would admit to individual exceptions. So would the upper classes who viewed free blacks as a threat to the docility of slavery and who resented them for their assumption of dignity beyond their station.

The general public stance on free blacks varied according to the person and to circumstance. There were many white individuals, such as the Whitehornes and the Northcrosses of Sussex County, who boarded mulattoes and went to school and to church with them, taught them and preached to them. Race relations in Virginia and North Carolina transcended law when the individual person or act called for it.[75]

In fact, about 25 percent of free blacks in Virginia in 1830 actually lived in white households or on the property with whites for whom they worked. Free servants, waiters, washerwomen, farm laborers, and nurses lived much as they had as slaves; that is, they lived with and cared for their white employers but for wages and other means of support. That amounted to about eight thousand free blacks who lived on intimate terms with whites in Virginia, as counted by the 1830 census.[76]

To recall the testimony of Frederick Olmsted in 1853 on the intimacy of whites and blacks in Southside Virginia: "I saw squads of negro and white boys together, pitching pennies and firing crackers in complete fraternization. The white boys manifested no superiority, or assumption of it, over the dark ones."[77]

The racially biased laws of Virginia against blacks expressed the wishes of the upper class of citizens who had power and influence within the establishment, those who could reach legislators or were legislators and caused laws to be passed that favored their station. Legislators were drawn from the slave-owning class. Their laws did not necessarily reflect the feelings and opinions of the working people in town and country who lived with and knew free blacks as individuals, as helpers and laborers for white families.

Some whites championed the increase of free blacks or, at least, of keeping productive free blacks in the state, in the belief that they could be taught and trained to be contributing members of society. Progressive whites argued that exceptional free blacks should not be punished because of the apathy and illiteracy of the majority of their brothers and sisters. Even the most liberal-minded white compassion, however, did not extend to anything approaching social or political parity. White supremacy was a hard-and-fast canon in the white "rule of law."

Even so, whites continued to rescue free blacks from expulsion from the state in the first decades of the nineteenth century. Though Southern immigration acts had been the law of the land since the late seventeenth century, laws that required blacks freed from slavery to leave the state, the acts were mostly honored in the breach. These laws were tweaked and amended from time to time to fit the temper of the moment.

Laws notwithstanding, whites generally interpreted these immigration acts casually unless racial relations were strained by some event or when a white with a grudge or offended sensibility chose to make a case. Otherwise, any black, free or slave, who was of economic importance to the community, and some who had won the trust and friendship of whites, might have his/her expulsion petitioned by white supporters and reversed by the legislature or the courts.[78]

The case of Randale Evans illustrates the flexibility of immigration laws on free blacks. Evans, a confectioner in Winchester, was the subject of a petition by his white patrons after he purchased freedom for himself and his family and, by law, could not remain in the state. The petitioners sought to keep Evans in the state after his manumission with the argument that "[c]onfectionary is a source of great convenience and utility to our citizens." Evans operated his successful confectionary shop in Winchester for many years thereafter, the community's sweet tooth overruling the threat of free black corruption of the slaves.[79]

Such cases were numerous throughout the South, and many of them went to the courts with often mundane petitions from whites who asked for various waivers of the law to allow important manumitted slaves to remain in the state. For the baking of cookies and pastries to assume such importance to a white community suggests the casual attitude of the community toward state immigration laws. Certainly it suggests that the community had strong feelings for its confectioner.[80]

In the 1830s, Arthur Lee, a blacksmith who purchased his own freedom and that of his family with money from hiring out, had 145 white signers who petitioned the court in 1835 in his behalf to let him remain in the state. His petition was successful and he was allowed to remain in Virginia, a case of a much needed free black skill winning over the community and the court. Isaac Atkins of Isle of Wight bought his own freedom and was supported by white petitioners to remain in Virginia, as was John, a sawyer, whose services were "much required," and Solomon, a gardener, and Isaac, a farm manager. All had the support of their white community leaders in petitions to the courts and the legislature to waive the immigration laws against them.[81]

White residents wanted to keep Ben Cooper, who was a coarse shoemaker, carpenter, and cooper. Billy Williamson, a farmer in Campbell County, had fifty-seven white signatures on his petition to the court. Harriet Cook, a washerwoman of Leesburg, had almost one hundred signatures on her petition, which included seven justices of peace, five ex-justices, sixteen merchants, six lawyers, and the postmaster. This case most likely was *not* about dirty clothes but about affection for the likable Cook.[82]

Petitions to waive the exile of manumitted free blacks became so commonplace in the nineteenth century that any well-connected freed black who had the respect and sympathy of his community might have a petition presented to the legislature. The language of petitions often made clear that the pleas represented not necessarily the interest of the threatened freedman or woman but the interests of the white community, which would suffer the loss.

An 1842 petition from the citizens of Essex County, Virginia, addressed the General Assembly for Ben, a freed black, with the following plea:

> *We would be glad if he could be permitted to remain with us and have his freedom, as he is a well disposed person and a very useful man in many respects. He is a good carpenter, a good cooper, a coarse shoemaker, a good hand at almost everything that is useful to us farmers.*[83]

Fortune Thomas, a free-black woman of Halifax, was singular in her community for her creation of pastries, cakes, tarts, and candies. When the threat of expulsion loomed over Thomas, white citizens of the town petitioned the court to waive the law for her, insisting that "no party or wedding can well be given without great inconvenience should her shop be broken up and discontinued."[84]

Ackley White's customers, who were white, raised a hue and cry in 1824 and petitioned the General Assembly to exempt their drayman from the law. And it was done. Many free blacks in Virginia and across the South successfully defied state statutes that called for their exit from the state after manumission. So many cases before the courts were successfully petitioned that the requests for exemption and the court permission were, at times, almost routine.[85]

The Day and Stewart families of Southside benefited from these white sentiments and had the advantage of strong white support. Throughout their careers, white civic leaders and businessmen responded positively to the career moves of John and Thomas Day, came to their aid financially, and petitioned the legislature when necessary.

The surname Day in court and census records throughout the eighteenth and nineteenth centuries often denotes free-black landowners who lived along the North Carolina and Virginia borders. In 1810 the Days showed up on the North Carolina side of the border in Person, Caswell, Granville, Warren, and Northampton Counties, a total of thirteen families. On the Virginia side of the border in the same year, they were evident in Halifax, Mecklenburg, Dinwiddie, Sussex, and Greensville Counties, with forty-six recorded families. Most of the Day genealogies originated in Virginia, first in Tidewater and then in Southside.[86]

In most cases the records show that the Days of these counties were free blacks, usually mulatto, often landowners, and mostly taxpayers. George Day was a free-black seaman from Northampton County and a taxable in the 1787 tax records. Winnifred Day of the same county registered her children in St. Stephen Parish as "free born Mulattoes." Ann Day of Caswell County (North Carolina) bound her son George, "of color," to Samuel Winstead in 1780. Rachael Day headed a household of seven "free colored" in Person County, North Carolina, in the 1780s. Jesse Day was head of household of ten "other free" in 1810 and five "free colored" in Orange County, North Carolina, in 1820.[87]

By 1790 large concentrations of free blacks lived on the Eastern Shore of Virginia, in Southside, below the James River, and in the northeastern portion of North Carolina. "This was a pattern of settlement similar to that of newly freed white servants. Land was available in Southside Virginia and in the northeastern part of North Carolina at prices former servants [free blacks] could afford."[88]

Southside from an Outsider's View

The counties of Dinwiddie, Greensville, and Sussex at the close of the eighteenth century were flat, treeless swaths of land sparsely populated by planters who required several hundred acres to make a successful and profitable tobacco crop.

Tobacco was the principal crop of the region for generations, a commodity used as a trade good, a barter item, and as a legal currency on the issue of warehouse inspection notes. The yellow plant inherited from American natives created many wealthy planters and factors, who in turn helped sustain urban merchants and nurtured the slave trade within the country. Free blacks found their places in the hierarchy of tobacco economy as workers and owners.

As previously noted, fifty-nine free blacks listed as "Negro" and "Mulatto" in the 1815 census in Greensville County, all appeared as "planters" or farmers, with the exception of a "hatter," a shoemaker, a house servant, and a "hireling." Nine of those planters owned their property; the others worked for other free-black farmers. Sixteen of the free blacks of the county were "spinsters," one of whom owned her land. [89]

Corn was the food crop used to feed planters, slaves, horses, and hogs. On market day, drummers crowded the courthouse square at Hicks Ford and Petersburg to sell their tobacco and cotton, trade horses, swap and barter hogs and corn. Deerskin, raccoon, otter, and beaver brought in from the backcountry were always in demand and brought good prices. Slave and free alike took advantage of the carnival atmosphere and the loosening of social restraints on market day to engage in social intercourse denied them in the humdrum routines of farming life.

The countryside of Southside was generally poor. There were a few grand estates in the counties in the eighteenth century, especially around Petersburg, but they were exceptions. The norm for the countryside was described by one John Ferdinand Smyth, the English soldier-adventurer who traveled through the colonies in the 1770s. On his way to Halifax, North Carolina, Smyth was usually critical of the accommodations he found, describing one "inn" in Southside where he spent a sleepless night as "a mansion of misery, a shell of a house where a young white overseer and five or six slaves all lived and slept in one room."[90]

Smyth dismissed this particular "mansion" as a "poor apology of a house." The structure had no inside lathe or plaster and neither ceiling nor loft. The land consisted of about fifty acres planted in corn. There were no outbuildings or fruit trees, as was common on most large farms. Cider was the common drink of the day, and any "plantation" worth the name had fruit trees. Hogs rooted beneath the house which swarmed with fleas and mosquitoes. The overseer and slaves were shucking corn in the one-room house during the night, and their singing kept their visitor awake and caused him to complain.[91]

> The houses are almost all of wood, covered with the same, the roof with shingles, the sides and ends with thin boards, and not always lathed and plastered within; only those of the better sort are finished in that manner and painted on the outside. The chimneys are sometimes of brick, but more commonly of wood, coated on the inside with clay. The windows of the best sort have glass in them; the rest have none, and only wooden shutters.[92]

Another of the intrepid traveler's common complaints was about country food, especially that offered in ordinaries, which he found boring and unappealing. He described hoecake as Indian corn ground into meal, kneaded into dough, and baked on a hot, broad iron hoe. He found it "extremely harsh and unpleasant." Hominy, however, an "Indian corn, freed from the husk, boiled whole, along with a small proportion of a large kind of French beans, until it becomes almost a pulp," he pronounced very agreeable. Hoecake and hominy were standard fare at Southern taverns and inns. At Stewart's Ordinary on his route to Hick's Ford, Mr. Smyth sampled "toasted Indian hoecake and excellent cyder," a rare praise of tavern food in the region from the proper Englishman.[93]

Smyth was equally critical of the land and of the primitive agricultural methods sometimes employed by the colonists. Many Virginia planters failed to practice even rudimentary care for their land. Soil was so cheap and plentiful that it proved easier to use up the fertile topsoil and move on to new areas. Increasingly, as the eighteenth century closed on the American colonies, these voracious planters of Virginia pushed harder toward the Indian lands along the Appomattox into present-day Dinwiddie County. These produced an abundant tobacco crop and made large strides toward building inland markets and transportation routes to inland ports.

Fertile soil was abundant in Southside Virginia, even in the early eighteenth century, before tobacco farmers exhausted the soil with their lackadaisical husbandry. Planters found virgin land so cheap that it was easier for them to slash and burn than to cultivate, rotate and nourish the soil. So burn they did, huge forests of longleaf pine and swamp cypress and upland hardwoods. What forest was not burned was girdled with an ax and left to die. Wasted forest land was not plowed; tobacco seedbeds were laid out between stumps in the dark topsoil, as had been the method since John Rolfe planted the first tobacco bed in 1612.

Slaves covered the beds with straw to protect them from wind and cold until they were mature enough to be planted. They attacked the soil with hoe and mattock, never plowed it. The tobacco beds remained on the safe side from wandering animals by split-rail fences called worm fences, stacks of split trees laid in a zigzag fashion. The lopsided pattern of the fences made them a metaphor for drunkenness among the colonials: an unsteady drinker might be accused of "making Virginia fences." An average farm of 350 acres would make a decent living for a tobacco farmer in the region south of the James.[94]

Tobacco preparation and harvesting was year-round work. Laying the initial seedbeds was just the beginning of a year of hoeing, replanting, weeding, and draining the fields if there was too much rain. Mature plants required constant supervision for bugs, worms, and "tobacco flies." They had to be "suckered" at the appropriate time and watched until the stalks were cut and transported to barns in September or October. Then the weed required hanging and drying in tobacco houses, after which the leaves were stripped and tied into bundles before being pressed into hogsheads for shipping. Tobacco leached the soil of nutrients after years of growth of the single staple, and planters were ready to move on to new land.[95]

The traveling Brit was quick to point out the destruction of tobacco growing. One might travel Southside for miles through blackened wastes of skeletal trees that had been girdled with axes or tomahawks. The trees required years to completely die off, but the planter did not wait. He dug holes and tamped his little tobacco plants into the ground under the spindly branches of dying trees. Within several years, no one was safe while the trees lingered, dropping their limbs and branches with the sharp crack of a rifle report, sometimes entire trees crashing to the ground, taking with them whatever person or animal happened to be in the way.[96]

Eventually, the trees died completely and were cut into logs that made up a great series of bonfires. The fires were enormous, and their light could be seen for miles. Often, standing healthy trees caught fire, and acres of virgin timber and grassland would burn for days. Such was the abundance of forests in colonial America that no care or thought was given to conservation. The huge fires would rage until stopped by a river or a heavy rain.[97]

Smyth was not the only European or Northern traveler to report harshly on conditions in Virginia. The cotton broker Richard Rawlins and other travelers to the South found poverty and neglect in its villages and towns. Rawlins pointed out the contrast between the stunning natural beauty of the Shenandoah Valley with the unwholesome air of its small hamlets, the results of a slave economy that freed many whites from menial labor.

> *Neglect is visible to even the unobservant eye all along this beautiful valley . . . Slavery and its effects . . . are written on every village we pass through. The wooden houses are unpainted and rickety, and utterly destitute of neat and cleanly appearance. No little garden ornaments to the front, which comes at once upon the street by ill-constructed stairs.*[98]

For all his grumbling about Americans, Smyth was at times astonished at their generosity. He cited an example of planters and farmers who owned orchards, allowing anyone, complete strangers traveling by their farms, "even a negroe," to help themselves to as many apples and peaches as they wanted—without permission. And "if the proprietor should see him, he is not in the least offended, but makes him perfectly welcome, and assists him in choosing out the finest fruit."[99]

What Smyth witnessed in part was the incredible abundance of produce that was often available on Virginia farms and in the wilds. He exclaimed that "the finest peaches imaginable are so abundant, that the inhabitants daily feed their hogs with them during the season." The noble Englishman could not shake off his British-class roots, and he found it difficult to travel and lodge amongst the great underclasses of America. Their customs, even when benevolent, ruffled his "proper" English upbringing.

CHAPTER FOUR

The Days Move to North Carolina

John Day Sr. struck out again in 1817 to improve his fortunes, but this time, he left the state for Warren County, North Carolina, just across the border from Southside Virginia. We do not know what led him there, but he left his eldest son, John Jr., to take care of his debts. John Day Sr. was still in Warren County in 1820 when he was listed in the census as a head of household of five "free colored," most likely family members.

Many of Virginia's urban free blacks found a home in North Carolina in the late eighteenth and early nineteenth centuries, and a large number of them hailed from Southside and even from Petersburg. They were welcomed in several of the northern border counties that bound North Carolina and Virginia. Most were farmers, others were artisans, such as John Day, who may have apprenticed in Petersburg in the cabinetmaking trade. In any case, free blacks in the 1790s and early 1800s found North Carolina more accommodating to their caste than Virginia.[1]

It was not unusual for blacks to cross state lines, either on business for themselves in the case of free blacks, or for their owners in the case of slaves. Virginia and North Carolina had extensive shared business interests carried on by the several wagon roads and railroads crossing the border from Southside. Much of the produce and tobacco from the northern tier and the northeastern counties of North Carolina moved north to Virginia, especially to Petersburg and Norfolk. The Petersburg-Weldon Railroad greatly increased that trade in the 1830s.

Personal travel for blacks across the state lines went unhindered. John Chavis traveled extensively in the two states before 1830 as a free minister. The

Days moved into North Carolina without any record or mention of hardship. Any black traveling with a white to vouch for him/her made the transition between the states with little fuss. But the highest traffic across the borders was likely those free and slave blacks who took advantage of the frontier conditions of the area to come and go as they chose. Travelers along the few roads connecting the two states commented frequently about the distance between settlements, ordinaries, and towns. "In some cases their coming was doubtless surreptitious, but usually, by selecting a quiet period, and settling in a favorable neighborhood, they ran little or no risk of having the law enforced against them."[2]

The Days' immigration to North Carolina in 1817 would be a permanent departure from their home state. Whether the family moved as a unit or in separate journeys, they were together in 1819 when the census was taken. Whether they took official leave of Virginia and made a documented entry into North Carolina or simply crossed the border in a concealed wooded area, John Jr. does not bother to mention in his letters. He does make a point of saying that he walked to North Carolina "on [his] two feet" to get his father's tools.

One historian suggests that John Day Sr. followed a former Petersburg cabinetmaker to Warrenton. Thomas Reynolds had a cabinet/carpentry shop in Petersburg, perhaps one of the ten shops identified there between 1780 and 1800. Reynolds removed himself and his business to Warrenton in the first quarter of the nineteenth century, possibly after the disastrous fire in 1815 that leveled the greater part of commercial Petersburg. He employed black workers in his shop, though their names remain unknown.[3]

The Reynolds shop in Warrenton was a large one, advertising mahogany sideboards, secretaries, and bureaus. The owner worked apprentices from New York, Philadelphia, and Richmond. If John Day went to work for Reynolds in Warrenton, it may suggest that Mr. Day was trained by Reynolds in Petersburg.

There was a tradition of heavy traffic of free blacks along the two borders, most of it moving south into North Carolina. Many free blacks were in flight from Virginia's increasingly repressive black codes that singled them out for punishment. The political and social "liberalism" of the revolutionary era shown toward blacks had faded by the second decade of the nineteenth century, as the generation that remembered the fight for independence from Britain was dying off. Likewise, slavery was proving itself a profitable labor system, and the price of slaves was increasing. A more mercenary and unforgiving spirit stalked the South, just as Thomas Jefferson described it in 1821.[4]

On the more lenient side, North Carolina was one of the last states in the South to disfranchise free blacks. Its free-black population was allowed to carry firearms until 1840 despite reports of slave risings and plots hatched by Denmark Vesey, a free-black "exhorter" of Charleston, South Carolina. Vesey allegedly planned a general slave uprising, for which he was hanged in 1822. Other risings and reported conspiracies, including the horrific massacre by Nat Turner, fed Southern paranoia and encouraged legislators to pass increasingly rigid laws against free blacks but North Carolina, for its own reasons, often lagged behind.

Nat Turner—1831

One of the most violent slave uprisings in the slave states occurred in Southampton County, Virginia, on the North Carolina border in 1831. The young leader of a massacre of whites was a literate slave who was a devout exhorter in the Baptist faith. Nat Turner was also something of a seer who reported visions and signs from God and who claimed that his attack on whites was directed and commanded by God. The two most visible signs to him were solar eclipses that occurred in February and again in August of 1831. Turner read the latter eclipse as his signal to move against slave owners in his neighborhood. A messianic personality was a defining mark of Turner and of other slave insurrectionists.

Turner's ragtag group of some seventy slaves and free blacks attacked slave-owning whites, killing indiscriminately men, women, and children in Southampton County. To mute the sounds of their violence, the killers used knives, hatches, and axes—rather than guns—and gave no quarter to the homesteads that were selected for attack. The rampage blazed for two days before militia and white farm owners put the group to flight in an aftermath of fifty-five murdered white people.

Sixty to seventy blacks were captured during the roundup, of which forty-five slaves were tried. Fifteen members of the group were acquitted, twelve were sold out of state, and eighteen were hanged, including Turner. Untold numbers of blacks were beaten, tortured, and killed by whites seeking revenge.

Nat Turner was the nightmare that slave owners had predicted and feared since the seventeenth century, when planters gradually hobbled the second generation of Africans in America by legal statute. It is telling that for all the speeches and threats from slave holders and politicians about slave uprisings, there was not a single slave revolt during the almost 200 years of colonial rule. The Turner massacre not only frightened Virginians but turned most Southerners into die-hard defenders of slavery while voices for moderation on the issue were silenced.

After Turner, Virginians increasingly chose removal of free blacks as the answer to lull their slaves into docility. Its colonization program was one of the most active in the country during the 1830s and 1840s. Virginia authorities decided on three tactics that would prevent future uprisings: prevent preaching and teaching by blacks, enact even more restrictive laws against slave mobility, and remove free blacks from the state.

The new limitations on free blacks, some of which were adopted by neighboring North Carolina, went hard on some of the most noted men in the caste, including John Chavis and many other noted preachers and exhorters and teachers. A onetime slave named Fields Cook recalled the repercussions of Turner's massacre in the Richmond area.

> [W]hen I was a boy about the time of Nat Turners insurrection who had better never been born than to have left such a curse upon his nation . . . I was living in the country and we poor colored people could not sleep at nights for the guns and swords being stuck in at our windows and doors to know who was here and what their business was and if they had a pass port and so forth and at that time a colored person was not to be seen with a book in his hand . . . many a poor fellow burned his books for fear.[5]

Black mobility and education were hard-hit by the tidal fallout from the Turner massacre. Some regions forbade the meeting of any blacks in public places, forbade gatherings for church and funerals, forbade visiting of family and friends at farms. Black preachers were prevented from offering their sermons in public, even to white audiences. Loyal ministers such as Ralph Freeman and John Chavis of North Carolina and Preacher Jack of Nottoway County in Virginia were cut off from their missions and from their income. Whites who tended to educate their slaves for a more efficient labor force halted the practice. Though black preachers in North Carolina lost their licenses, free blacks still had mobility and less restriction on their movements than those of Virginia or South Carolina.[6]

White mob and vigilante revenge erupted all across the South. Any slave disturbance evoked new restrictive laws, but they were often preceded by mob action in the towns and villages whose white populace felt most threatened. In and around Edenton, North Carolina, authorities called in country bullies and poor whites to terrorize blacks on the premise that some might sympathize with Nat Turner.

The vigilantes invaded houses and cabins inhabited by blacks, slave and free, on the pretext of looking for seditious literature. Once released, with the blessings of white authority, the mobs wrecked black houses and cabins without discretion and stole anything of value. They took personal writings and letters from the ransacked homes, though they could not read, and burned them or delivered them to white slave owners. Jewelry and fine linens were confiscated on the theory that blacks could not afford such finery, so they must have been stolen. Slaves were rounded up in groups to be whipped and locked in jail, "unless they happened to be protected by some influential white person."[7] The mobs also burned and wrecked black churches.

Harriet Jacobs has written that nothing annoyed poor whites so much "as to see colored people living in comfort and respectability . . . [They] exulted in such a chance to exercise a little brief authority [as vigilantes], and to show their subserviency to the slaveholders; not reflecting that the power which trampled on the colored people also kept them [poor whites] in poverty, ignorance, and moral degradation."[8]

The mob violence would eventually burn itself out, and the rowdies would fade away into the country or into the slums of town. Occasionally, as happened in Edenton, mob bloodlust would boil beyond control, and whites and their houses would fall to the rage of the impassioned crowds. Then slaveholders and town and county authorities would be forced to take action against their own vigilantes and send them away.

The Southern psyche never recovered from Nat Turner. Southerners, slaveholders and nonslaveholders alike, bonded together increasingly in their paranoia of slave revolts and Northern abolitionism. The entire South took up the narrative of resistance to Northern aggression against the Southern way of life.

In spite of slave risings and conspiracies and rumors of rebellion, the border Carolina counties remained welcome territory for free blacks because they contained a large population of freedmen already. Their numbers in Northampton, Bertie, Halifax, Hertford, Craven, and Granville counties, along and near the Virginia border, amounted to about 5 percent of the population. By 1810 Halifax County in North Carolina counted 18 percent of its population in free blacks, an unprecedented representation.[9]

These residents of the border counties maintained good relations with free blacks and Indians as far back as the early colonial period. In 1762 and 1763 prominent whites in the area, recognizing the positive economic impact of their black neighbors, petitioned the colonial assembly to rescind a discriminating tax against free blacks. Fifty-four white citizens of Granville, Northampton, and Edgecombe counties signed the 1763 petition that lauded their "Free Negro & Mulatto" neighbors as "persons of Probity & good Demeanor [who] cheerfully contribute toward the Discharge of every public Duty injoined by law."[10]

During the colonial and early national period, at least one member of most of the African American families in the border counties owned land, which suggests that they were free and implies that they were mulatto and were people of some means. Landownership by blacks often helped make for a closer relationship with whites. North Carolina white attitudes in these border counties contrived for a few free blacks to vote in the 1701 North Carolina General Assembly elections.[11]

Some of the northern counties bordering Virginia at times had sufficient numbers to hold the balance of power between whites in an election. These few free blacks, in the border counties and in other North Carolina counties, held onto the elective franchise until they were disfranchised at the 1835 Constitutional Convention.[12]

Contemporary observers as late as the 1830s remarked that free blacks voted in state elections and participated in the contest for a new constitution in 1835, in which they lost the right to vote. One Judge Buxton claimed that "the opposing candidates, for the nonce oblivious of social distinction and intent only on catching votes, hobnobbed with the free men [free blacks] and swung corners all with dusky damsels at election balls."[13]

Roger Shugg, who wrote an article titled "Negro Voting in the Antebellum South," states that there were, at one time before the Civil War, "300 colored voters in Halifax County and 150 in Hertford County." Fifty free blacks cast votes in Chowan County, and another seventy-five did so in Pasquotank County.[14] Free blacks lost their right to vote in Granville County, according to county lore, by their consistent loyalty to Robert Potter, a notorious politician and a roughneck who "disgraced himself by committing a brutal mayhem upon two of his wife's relatives."[15]

Some of the free blacks in the area were major landholders, the results of colonial manumissions from the earliest freed slaves in Virginia who became landowners there. The Chavis clan in North Carolina, for a notable example, derived from eighteenth-century free-black Virginians who immigrated to the border counties of Halifax, Warren, Vance, Person, and Orange. In North Carolina, the name signified free-black landowners, several of whom achieved some degree of notoriety. William Chavis ("Negro") of the Virginia Chavis families was in Col. William Eaton's Granville County (North Carolina) Regiment in 1754. He owned one thousand acres, eight slaves, and a lodging house frequented by whites. His son, Philip Chavis, owned one thousand acres and traveled to properties in Northampton and Robeson counties and lived for a time in Craven County, South Carolina.[16]

The Presbyterian minister John Chavis owned property in Raleigh and near Nutbush in Granville County, North Carolina. He was an acquaintance of one of the state's prominent legislators, the Honorable Willie P. Mangum, whom he had no compunction of lecturing about national politics. In a letter to Congressman Mangum, the Reverend John Chavis reminded his friend in 1832, "Tell them if I am Black I am free born American and a revolutionary soldier and therefore ought not to be thrown entirely out of the scale of notice."[17]

Chavis had a lengthy correspondence with the congressman for several years. His letters reveal several unusual conditions regarding relations between some free blacks and their white communities in the late eighteenth and early nineteenth centuries. One was that a free black corresponded as an equal with his congressman. Free blacks, as a rule, stayed away from politics, considering it the province of white folks. In the main, they could not vote or run for office, so there was no advantage involving themselves in politics. Such was not the case in several of the border counties, where several hundred free blacks were voters in the late eighteenth and early decades of the nineteenth century.

For a free black to speak as an equal to a white man—and, in addition, to a man of the political and social stature of Senator Mangum—bespeaks of a confidence and ease that is extremely rare in a Negro of the period. It says much about how Chavis was reared and his complete educational and religious immersion at Washington Academy and perhaps at Princeton. Chavis understood the political and social repression of his race, but he placed himself, by virtue of his education and his acceptance of white attitudes, outside the social restrictions of most free blacks.

Chavis insisted on a degree of respect from whites for being "born free," in spite of the fact that he was born black. "Born Free" was a badge of pride for decades in the South, both prior to and after the Civil War. Chavis used the claim to enhance his status with Mangum, to make a point with the congressman, even though Mangum was well acquainted with Chavis and his achievements and well knew he was freeborn.

In addition, the black freeman gently chided his friend that he was a soldier of the American Revolution. Documents reveal that Chavis was a "batman" in the war to an American officer and likely received a bounty warrant for his service. The minister was proud of his service and wore the experience as a badge of honor. "Lexington Presbytery was also concerned for the spiritual welfare of the Negroes and licensed John Chavis, a full-blooded Negro veteran of the Revolutionary War, to work among the people of his race."[18]

Other successful free blacks hailing from Virginia moved deeper into the heart of Carolina. Though not a border county, Dobbs County, farther south and east in North Carolina, counted Edward Carter (black) as its fourth-largest landowner in 1780. He held 23,292 acres in the 1790 census and headed a household with "8 other free," including a white woman and twenty slaves. John Gibson, Gideon Gibson, and Gideon Chavis, all free blacks, married daughters of prosperous white North Carolina farmers before moving eventually to South Carolina.[19]

Many families of the border counties traced their heritage to eighteenth-century Virginia families. Bass, Bunch, Chavis, Gibson, and Cumbo families owned more than a thousand acres on both sides of the Virginia-Carolina border. They became prominent families in North Carolina, and all traced their lineage to colonial Virginia. The Carters, Copes, Driggers, George, and Johnston families of Craven County, North Carolina, hailed from Northampton, Virginia. The Jefferies of Greensville County, Virginia, immigrated to Orange County, North Carolina. They were mulattoes, landowners, and veterans of the Revolution. Jacob and Drury Jefferies of Southside Virginia moved into North Carolina and served a year in the military, and a John Jefferies enlisted as a volunteer in the war. The Jefferies were neighbors of the Days in Virginia and again in North Carolina. The Days were aware of some of these prosperous free blacks in North Carolina and may have been lured to the Old North state by word of mouth.

> *The family histories of over 80% of those counted as 'all other free persons' in the 1790-1810 federal census for North Carolina indicate that they were descendants of African Americans who were free in Virginia during the colonial period.*[20]

The historian David Dodge conducted a random survey of blacks in the late nineteenth century, seeking in particular people from the border counties. He found a consensus that prior to the Civil War, free blacks in that region migrated from Virginia "about sixty or eighty years ago, and that they were unhindered. Here they found cheaper lands, and laws, in their execution at least, more lenient, as well as a social attitude less hostile than in aristocratic Virginia."[21]

This pride in their colonial roots continues in North Carolina and Virginia today. The author interviewed an elderly black woman in Jefferson County, North Carolina, in the 1970s who informed him, without provocation and much to his embarrassment, that she did not "issue" from any of "them sot-free [Negroes]; we came here free from Virginia."

J. F. Smyth wrote of his time in the border counties of North Carolina in the 1780s and met many of the prominent planters of the area. He spent some time in the little village of Nutbush, just west of Halifax, where he met the irrepressible Nathaniel Henderson, lawyer and associate chief judge, and speculator in Indian lands. Smyth called Henderson one of "the most singular and extraordinary persons and excentric [*sic*] geniuses in America, and perhaps in the world." High praise from a man who found the general population of eastern North Carolina to be some of the lowest and dirtiest people he had ever met.[22]

Nutbush was a community on the great road between Virginia and North Carolina, near Taylor's Ferry, one of the busiest ferries on the Roanoke River. Nutbush Creek in present-day Vance County was named by William Byrd's dividing line survey party because of the abundance of hazelnuts in the area. The community contained a number of free blacks, including, for a time, the Reverend John Chavis, who may have owned property there. Biblical scholar C. Eric Lincoln has stated, without citation, that Chavis was born in Nutbush.[23]

What is more arresting about Smyth's visit in Nutbush is that he met Henderson and some other notables at the home of a lawyer named Williams, "who is said to be, and is very much like a mulattoe." If Smyth is accurate in his assessment, the observation gives heft to the argument that free blacks in northeastern North Carolina had more social status than those in Virginia and perhaps even a modicum of political influence. The Days would have found the locale appealing.

Free Black. Many free blacks strived for the same values and wanted the same rewards as whites: freedom, dignity, and an opportunity for economic success. Many of them achieved those goals despite a national culture that discouraged their progress. *(Courtesy of the Library of Congress, Prints & Photographs Division, Washington, D.C. No Use Restrictions)*

The border counties of North Carolina welcomed free blacks as late as the 1830s, a decade when all Southern states had stripped free blacks of whatever rights they had managed to cling to after the Revolution. A Halifax County newspaper, the *Roanoke Advocate* (editor: Edmund B. Freeman), began its New Year's edition in 1832 with a defense of certain prominent free blacks in the county.

> [W]e sincerely trust that the Legislature will be guided by a temperate and humane policy, and that all laws affecting the rights of this class of citizens ... will at the same time be moderated by a spirit of compassionate forebearance. It cannot be denied that free negroes, taken in mass, are dissolute and abandoned—yet there are some individuals among them, sober, industrious and intelligent—many are good citizens; and that they are sometimes good voters we have the best proofs ....
> We do think that too much prejudice is excited against this class of our population.... That it is a desideratum to get rid of free negroes, en masse, is most true, because for the most part, they are idle and debased—but, at the same time, there is a class of white skinned citizens, equally low and abandoned, whose absence would be little regretted.[24]
>
> *Roanoke Advocate*

Thus, North Carolina would have been an attractive choice for a family of educated, ambitious free blacks who were looking for larger opportunities. At the same time, John Day Sr. may have exhausted his options in Southside Virginia by failing to make his rent payments. By 1817 the patriarch had sold his last farm and lived on several rented properties, trying to eke out a living in a country depleted by aggressive tobacco farming. A local legislator of the period claimed that Greensville County was "one of the least fertile tracts of country in the southern part of the State." Surrounding counties were in a similar state of soil exhaustion.

If the Days needed other reasons to migrate to the state of North Carolina, the legislature of Virginia offered yet another in 1816. The state delivered an official insult to the free-black caste when its assembly passed a resolution requesting the U. S. government to locate a place on the northern Pacific coast where Virginia free blacks might be settled outside the boundaries of the states and territories of the United States. This is the same year the American Colonization Society formally organized in Washington, DC. In its first meeting, Senator Henry Clay of Kentucky called for the removal of the "pernicious, if not dangerous," community of free blacks from America.

Petersburg, where Day Sr. trained and worked in the carpentry trades, might have been an option for the Days to pursue the cabinetmaking trade, but the city suffered a disastrous fire in 1815 that consumed some five hundred structures, about two-thirds of the commercial area. Numerous artisans left the city, either ruined by the conflagration or unwilling to wait for the city to rebuild. Petersburg bounded back from the catastrophe, but not soon enough to entice the Days to wage their future there, if they were so inclined.[25]

Many artisans, especially cabinetmakers, made tracks for North Carolina even before the catastrophic fire. Historian Jonathan Prown at Williamsburg has counted at least eleven cabinetmakers that left Petersburg after 1800 and "followed the trade routes into North Carolina, primarily Hillsborough, Raleigh, Halifax, Warrenton and other smaller towns that were not yet fully incorporated into the national economy."[26] There is evidence that Thomas may have spent time in Hillsborough, North Carolina, before moving on to Milton. A newspaper ad for Day furniture appeared in Hillsborough in the early 1820s.

Whomever John Day Sr. worked for in Warrenton, he left his oldest son to carry on in Virginia and to cover certain debts he had made and to handle some other family business. This was not the first time Day Sr. had taken to the road to find work or to remove himself from difficult business, and perhaps, personal situations. John Jr. wrote, years later, that his father "had become intemperate; sold his pretty little plantation [in Sussex County], moved to Dinwiddie County, and was living in a rented house."[27]

In fact, John Day rented several farms from 1807 until his departure from the state in 1817. He did not always have his family with him. The cabinetmaker worked at various times for Robert Gyne, James Wilson, and James Spicely, all of Dinwiddie County. He was listed as a cabinetmaker in Dinwiddie during those years. It was not unusual for artisans to move back and forth from farming to a mechanics trade, depending on the economy. But as Day Jr. noted in a letter, his father was also dealing with some personal problems of alcoholism and possibly gambling.

When John Sr. fell on hard times, he did not hesitate to call on his eldest son to assume his debts. John Jr. explained the reason his father left him in Virginia: "In 1817 my father went over to North Carolina and left me in Dinwiddie to pay a debt he owed to Mr. John Bolling. I carried on a little cabinetmaking business in a village in that part of the county called Scottsville, paid my father's debt, and was likely to do well in the world's estimation."[28]

What is remarkable about Day's recollection in his letters is that he does not dwell on the social and legal obstacles to free-black success; he does not vent about his problems with his father or even with whites. Instead, he takes responsibility for his father's errors and for his own without excuses. Most of all, he recalled his formative years with a confidence and self-assuredness in himself and his abilities to make his own way in a world that publicly denigrated his race and worked to undermine his economic and personal success.

John Day's lack of complaint does not suggest that his upbringing in Southside Virginia was without racial incidents toward his family. Day grew to manhood surrounded by harsh laws against free blacks and brutal treatment. His lack of rancor suggests how completely the Days were enveloped by the social and economic structure of their day and of how easily John Jr.'s attitudes approximated those of whites. If he and his family were insulated from daily insults and humiliations suffered by free blacks as a caste, it was by virtue of their light skin, their wealth, and their connections to whites.

John Jr. was no shrinking violet in his formative years, his late teens, and early twenties. He ran at times with a raucous crowd that had money and enjoyed the pastimes of drinking and gambling, just as his father had done to excess. John Jr. recalled that, in 1817, he came close to embracing the sporting life and following the negligent path of his father:

> [A]ssociating myself with . . . young white men, who were fond
> of playing cards,[I] contracted that habit. J. L. Scott a merchant and a
> friend of mine came into my shop to see me and I frankly told him that if
> I continued in that place that I should ruin myself.[29]

Once again, John Day Jr. casually mentioned, in his letters to Rev. J. B. Taylor, his social relations with whites in Southside, the sort of personal black-white association that so captivated Frederick Olmsted some thirty-five years later. He was comfortable in the company of whites in part because of his association with them in his rearing, in his schooling, and in his business relationships. His light complexion certainly played its part in negotiating the color line.

John Jr. had the fortitude, the work ethic, and the basic moral values to remove himself from what he knew to be the debasing social company of white rowdies. He moved to the village of Scottsville outside Petersburg, where he set himself up in the cabinetmaking business. A drunken journeyman in the shop caused a disastrous fire that destroyed Day's business, including all his tools. At every station of Day's early career, a close acquaintance befriended him and helped him recover and begin again. But Day's fortitude is what carried him through many social and business obstacles and attracted moneyed whites to his success. Though the neighbors in the village offered to set him up again in business, the young Day abandoned Virginia and walked to North Carolina, where he joined his family in Warrenton.

> *I would not accept any thing but a coat and hat of my friend J. L. Scott. I went on my feet to Warren County, North Carolina and got in possession of my father's tools, borrowed money off a gentleman, and commenced work there.*[30]

John Day Jr., even though a free mulatto, never lacked friends, including many whites, and seldom had a problem borrowing money from them. At times he lived with whites and used their names to promote his personal career when it mattered. Even in his adopted home in North Carolina, without the family and community connections he had nurtured in Southside Virginia, the young cabinetmaker found financial backing for his business ventures "off a gentleman" (certainly a white man). Yet he was a self-respecting man who carried his own weight and did not accept help casually. He held to the values of the white elite of Virginia: personal responsibility, respect for authority, care for his family, and a strict work ethic.[31]

North Carolina was not a state held in high regard by its neighbors. In the early decades of the nineteenth century, the state was frequently referred to as the Ireland of America and the Second Nazareth for its poverty. It held the distinction of having the lowest per capita in wealth and income in the nation, a low standard of living, and a reputation of "extreme backwardness." Its economic position resulted from a poor geography and a small-farm economy of subsistent farmers. It had no deepwater ports because the maritime sandbars of the Outer Banks kept deepwater vessels away. Hence, no Charleston or Norfolk or Baltimore rose on its coastline. The state's maritime trade tended to be coastwise and to the Caribbean Islands in small sloops and schooners.[32]

The state's reactionary politics ensured its backward orientation. An oligarchy of Eastern planters who passed their political power from father to son ruled the legislature. The state seldom mounted a genuine two-party election, and local government generally rested in the hands of county courts and appointed magistrates who looked after the interests of the landed gentry and plantation aristocracy.

Politicians and state and local government represented landed interests. The voting population supported the status quo and in fact exhibited some indigenous pride in its lack of sophistication and education. State voters repudiated internal improvements (roads, railroads, canals), state support for education, and expansion of the electorate. By 1840 one-third of the adult white population was illiterate. If one adds blacks and youth to the equation, more than one-half of the population could neither read nor write. It has been calculated that by 1820 some four hundred thousand North Carolinians were living in other states. Many of those immigrants were the young, the educated, and the ambitious, just the caliber of citizen needed to move the state from its "Rip van Winkle" isolation.[33]

Thomas and John Day, despite their handicap of being "free coloreds," were entrepreneurs of the caliber needed by the state: reputable artisans and businessmen with capital who would open shops, hire labor, and produce goods. Affluent towns such as Warrenton and Hillsborough welcomed artisans and businessmen of the Day caliber, choosing to emphasize their talents and overlook their ancestry. If the brothers were free blacks, they were also skilled, educated, and acculturated.

John Jr. was a cabinetmaker by trade, but he was equally serious about and more committed to his spiritual life. Within three years after moving to North Carolina, the artisan took a momentous and fateful step that would chart the course of his adult life. At the age of twenty-three, in October 1820, John Day Jr. was baptized into the Baptist faith by Reverend Walker at a Methodist church at Mill Pond in Warren County. The church was under the regular guidance of the Methodist minister, Mr. Godwin, and it was that clergyman who first put Day in the pulpit and who later sponsored his license to preach in 1821. It was at that church that Day perhaps felt the first serious sense of making his mark in the world.[34]

According to Day's own writings, he moved that same year to Milton, North Carolina, not in search of a career in cabinetmaking but at the behest of Reverend Godwin in search of a religious mentor named the Reverend Abner Clopton.

> He [Reverend Godwin] *frequently mentioned the subject* [of preaching] *to me but on the first Sunday in June 1821 came to me and took me by the arm and conveyed me into the pulpit saying to me: You are going to Milton and I want you to have license before you go . . . . In July following I removed to Milton, Caswell County, NC where I became acquainted with Rev. Abner Clopton.*[35]

John Day was in store for some "old light" mentoring under Elder Clopton, one of the most morose riders on the spiritual circuit. Though born in Pittsylvania County, Virginia, in 1784, Clopton spent many of his formative years in North Carolina. He studied at Bannister Academy and a private school in Guilford County, North Carolina, holy ground to the Friends Society that began their work in the fertile piedmont of the Old North State.[36]

Clopton studied at the University of North Carolina in Chapel Hill, graduating with AB and AM degrees. While studying at the academic village, he married, separated from, and divorced a wife in 1809, highly unusual for its time. He then studied for a brief period under a Dr. Rice of Halifax County before moving to Philadelphia in 1811 for medical study, during which time he was struck by a mysterious and debilitating illness that sent him to bed for weeks.

The studious Clopton returned to Chapel Hill to take up the study of medicine that was interrupted in Philadelphia. He worked as a tutor to pay his way. While at Chapel Hill, he was felled again by the mysterious illness in 1815 and again in 1817. At the time he was a member of the church of John Roberts. He began "exhorting" in 1816.

Exhorting was the colloquial term assigned to evangelical preachers who brought "heat" to their sermons, so different from and opposed by the established churches that relied on ritual and catechism and gave the minister complete control of the service. The "heat," on the other hand, called forth vocal and bodily passion, including but not limited to shouting, vigorous gesticulating, striding the pulpit, and generally giving emotionally arousing, loud, and even threatening sermons.

Described by the Reverend Jeremiah Jeter as "irritable" and "melancholy," Clopton began his career as an "open communionist," taking communion with Presbyterians and accepting anyone into his congregations who showed interest in his sermons. In an unusual arrangement, he once placed himself under the authority of the Orange Presbytery, the same organization that nurtured the Reverend John Chavis. Some of Clopton's more orthodox brethren eventually brought him around to the less generous "strict communion" persuasion that demanded strict adherence to evangelical precepts that precluded formal association with Presbyterians.[37]

Reverend Jeter described Christianity as "a religion of self-denial, mortification, and godly sorrow." Reverend Clopton worked overtime to conform to that severe monastic description, one he gradually accepted and eventually achieved. He prayed and meditated three times every day. He read the Bible unceasingly, wrestled with his "unworthiness," and demanded strict adherence from his congregation. His naturally irritable temperament often flared into heated anger with those who opposed him, and he struggled for control of his feelings and opinions for years.[38]

The austere minister traveled and preached widely in North Carolina and Virginia. His associates and his congregations revered him. His biographer noted that the exhorter "always manifested a peculiar anxiety to afford the colored part of his congregation, ample room and comfortable seats, at the house of the Lord."[39]

Elder Clopton was called to Milton, North Carolina, to head the Milton Female Academy in 1820. As indicated above, John Jr. soon followed him there the next year, sent by his Warren County minister, Rev. Godwin, to be tutored by the seasoned Clopton for missionary work. Day immediately rented a house and a shop for his cabinetmaking business.

Most early Protestant and evangelical preachers performed their services without salary or fees. Notables such as Clopton, who earned a living by teaching or as school headmasters or other professions, were exceptions. Neophytes such as John Day, and even established ministers, had to pay their own way from whatever work they could find. John Day was far ahead of the average preacher in that he was well educated and was a skilled artisan who managed a decent living wherever he set up shop.

John Jr. was certainly committed to his spiritual journey and, especially, to his preparation for missionary work, but he also had familial obligations and the need to make a living. He had returned to his home territory in Greensville County in 1821 to marry Polly Wickham. Hence, his first efforts in the village of Milton were to find a house for his family and then a shop for his work. The cabinetmaker may have rented both for his first year, but by 1823 he was sufficiently solvent to purchase fifteen and one-half acres on the Stamps Ferry Road to the Dan River.[40] A deed made in 1824 makes reference to a lot on Liberty Street of one and one-half acres in Milton "on which John Day resides."[41]

The village of Milton stood on a pretty knoll overlooking the Dan River, which coursed out of southwest Virginia due east along the border with North Carolina until it emptied into the Roanoke River. The main road through town was the road between Hillsborough, once the colonial capital of North Carolina, and Danville, Virginia, destined to be the last capital of the Confederacy. By the time John Day moved there, the town had bout fifteen houses, a female academy, a church, a dry-goods shop, several artisan shops, and some tobacco warehouses.

John Day was about twenty-four years of age when he moved to Milton. He worked in Milton for three-plus years making furniture and simultaneously studied for missionary service at the feet of the ill-humored Clopton. At some point in his tenure there, definitely by 1823, Thomas Day joined his brother in the furniture business in Milton.

Thomas may have been working his way to Milton as early as 1821. He received mail at the Hillsborough post office in Orange County, bordering Caswell County, in 1821 and in 1823 ran the following advertisement in the *Hillsborough Recorder,* Feb. 23, 1823:

Thomas Day, Cabinetmaker, Returns his thanks to his friends and the public for the patronage he has received and wishes to inform them that he intends continuing his business at his old stand.[42].

Whatever the exact location of Day's "old stand," he was confident that his clients and potential customers were well acquainted with it enough so that directions were not required. Thomas was only twenty-two years old when he first advertised his cabinetmaking business in Hillsborough, but he was apparently old enough to operate on his own terms in the furniture business, or equally likely, he operated in partnership with his older brother. Thomas also advertised his furniture in Milton in 1823, by which time he was almost certainly working with his brother.

John Jr. may have remained in Milton had it not been for some dramatic changes in the career of his mentor, Abner Clopton. The same year that Day bought property on the Stamps Ferry Road, Reverend Clopton was called to Charlotte County, Virginia, to pastor Ash Camp, Chaney's Chapel, and Mossingford Baptists churches, leaving the young aspiring missionary without his spiritual mentor.

Day had it in mind to become a missionary to Haiti, sometimes an alternative to Liberia for free blacks who sought immigration as an answer to American racism. Day had sought out Clopton initially because of the minister's interest in the Haiti missionary field. John Day's spiritual quest suffered a major blow with the exit of Clopton from Milton.

Day remained in Milton just long enough to dispose of his properties. In January 1824, he sold the fifteen and one-half acres he had purchased the previous year to George Claughton for $200, making $50 on the transaction. In November 1824, he sold his home and property on Liberty Street to Thomas McGehee of Person County. The suddenness of the move, timed with the departure of Reverend Clopton and the sale of his property in Milton, suggests that John Jr. considered his missionary career more important than his cabinetmaking.[43]

In 1825 John Day took his leave of the town and returned to Virginia to find another sponsor for his missionary work in Haiti. Business issues of either his father or his father-in-law interrupted his plans, forcing Day to remain in Virginia longer than he planned. He appears in the 1830 census in Hicksford with four children and two slaves, indicating that he was there in 1829 when the census was taken.

John Day was undoubtedly disappointed in the interruption of his plans for a missionary career to Haiti when Clopton left Milton. Worse yet for his missionary plans was a personal feud that occurred within the High Hills Baptist Church in Sussex County that may have put an end to his Haiti plans.

The disruption affected Day greatly and caused him to leave his chosen church and move to the town of his youth, Hicksford.

JOHN DAY (1797-1859). John Day Jr. first moved to Milton, North Carolina, in pursuit of his calling to missionary work under the mentoring of Rev. Abner Clopton. Day opened a cabinetmaking business to sustain his family while he learned at the arm of the white minister who headed the Milton Female Academy. *(Courtesy of Library of Congress, Prints & Photographs Division, Washington, D.C. No Use Restrictions)*

Arminianism had divided the evangelical movement since its beginnings. Named for the teachings of sixteenth-century professor Jacobus Arminius at the University of Leyden, Holland, the Arminius doctrine sparked a revolt against the predestination dogma of Calvinism, which the author of Arminianism described as "repugnant to all the instincts of his soul." The Arminian doctrine divided Holland and Calvinists into opposing religious camps. The Arminians were called Remonstrants, meaning "those opposed."

Arminianism likewise divided English Protestants when the creed migrated across the Channel and the American colonists when it crossed the Atlantic. In American Methodism, the divide separated those who leaned toward "free grace" or "free will" in the acceptance of salvation verses those who subscribed to the "elect of the few" strict predestination of Calvinism. All the Protestant sects and later their churches had Arminian adherents who, on occasion, caused their churches to split into separate camps of the faithful, including the Baptists, known for its many sects.[44]

Day found a similar division in his own church when he returned to Virginia from Milton. He leaned to the "free will" side of the fight that also favored abolition, placing him at odds with members of his church. Much had changed in the political climate since Day left for North Carolina some eight years earlier. By 1825 the Protestant churches were no longer the bastions of the antislavery movement. As they evolved from a fringe religious movement in the mid-eighteenth century (estimated to four thousand members in 1775) to established churches in competition with the state church in the last years of the 1790s (estimated at thirty-seven thousand by 1790), the Protestant churches assumed their own dogma and ritual and became increasingly conservative, especially after the Revolution which greatly weakened the established church. With the exception of the Society of Friends, Protestant denominations by the 1790s began to find biblical sanction for slavery. They increasingly bowed to the leanings and demands of their new congregations that included slave owners.[45]

Orthodoxy was a serious issue with Protestant churches in colonial America and during the federal and antebellum eras. Even when the colonists ousted the established church, the various Protestant denominations proved aggressive in attempting to replace it as the dominant American church. Doctrine was priority and interpretation took on overriding importance. People who differed with the prevailing orthodoxy were excommunicated.

One R. Snead, pastor of Black Creek Baptist Church in Hanover County, Virginia, was excommunicated for his Arminianism. A church associate explained Snead's sins thusly: "He was really a double-minded man, who was unstable in all his ways; some-times he would be a Quaker; sometimes a Pedo-Baptist . . . . He was alternately a Calvinist, an Arminian and a Universalist. When excommunicated for his principles (for his morals were correct), he would return after some time and make such apparently sincere concessions that it would seem uncharitable not to excuse him."[46]

Day was accused of being an Arminian, and though he was not excommunicated from his church, the charge put him under suspicion and contributed to a troubled climate in the church. The dispute may well have ended his efforts to become a licensed missionary for the church to Haiti and turned his attention to missionary efforts in Liberia. He talked years later about the dispute in letters to his friend Rev. J. B. Taylor.

> *Disappointed in my hope of being a missionary to heathen[,] in my expectation of going to Haiti, called an Armenian[,] I felt little esteemd among the Baptists, suffered great religious declension. Scarcely ever preached, scarcely ever communed with the church.*[47]

The disagreement was a major wound to John Day's moral soul and to his pride; it left a scar that would not heal. In a eulogy to Day in 1859, the Reverend Edward Blyden of the Southern Baptist Convention mentioned the interruption of Day's theological studies as a "circumstance to which, even down to the day of his death, he frequently referred with expressions of unmingled regret."[48]

Licensed or not, Day was determined to leave the country and make his name in missionary work. His personal and religious contacts at last brought him the mission he had sought for many years. In 1830 Day, after divesting himself of his real estate, gathered his family, wife and four children, and made the voyage to Africa, where he lived out his personal mission of ministering to the "blighted heathens."

The Mood of the South Darkens

John Day appears to have been a more conflicted man than his brother, Thomas. He struggled from a young age with his spiritual self and with his place in Southern society. He was enticed by a vocation that drew support and praise from white men of influence but was sensitive to white attitudes toward him and his family. Thomas seems to have had more composure when dealing with the racial attitudes of his community and to have been more accepting of the inequalities in society.

Even exceptional free blacks of influence and affluence were never far from the harsh repercussions of white reactions to black resistance, imagined and real. A publication in 1829 may have impacted John Day's plans to immigrate to Africa. On the eve of the new decade, a free black from Wilmington, North Carolina, David Walker, wrote an *Appeal to the Colored Citizens of the World*. Published in 1829 from Boston, where he had immigrated and joined antislavery forces, Walker's *Appeal* swept through the South like a firestorm.

Walker was born to a free mother and a slave father in Wilmington, where he observed the corporal punishment and emotional degradation of slaves and free blacks. He lived for a time in Charleston, South Carolina, where he was immersed in African Methodist Episcopal Church activism, the same environment that produced Denmark Vesey.

Walker was literate and armed with a direct, aggressive writing style that attacked slave owners on their own terms, presenting his polemic in the structure of the United States Constitution. He compared American slavery to that of Egypt, Greece, India, and Israel and found American slavery to be more savage and demeaning under the rule of "Christian" whites than that of any other nation in history. He ridiculed the premise of the nation calling itself Christian while owning humans and for speaking of Turks and Indians as barbarous. Christian and democratic America was the epitome of hypocrisy, according to the *Appeal*.

Walker amassed religious, political, philosophical, and historical arguments against the "peculiar institution," using many of the same arguments that proslavery proponents used as apologies. The orator and agitator gave particular attention to Thomas Jefferson, who Walker thought, as author of the Declaration of Independence and the Statute of Virginia for Religious Freedom and defender the "unalienable rights of man," should be held responsible for his commentaries that touted the inferiority of the Negro. "I say, that unless we refute Mr. Jefferson's arguments respecting us, we will only establish them."[49]

Walker's *Appeal* was the most militant tract written to date against the institution of slavery. It called on slaves to throw off their "groveling" servility and to use whatever means necessary to achieve freedom. The pamphlet struck fear and hatred in the hearts of Southerners, so sharp was its attack on the very moral basis of their society. Many Northerners, even some abolitionists, condemned the rebellious and revolutionary tone of the tract. Boston's mayor, speaking for his fair city, regarded the article with "disapprobation and abhorrence" and "absolute detestation." But he balked at the Savannah mayor's call for Walker and his printer to be delivered to Savannah for trial and for a federal law prohibiting the publication of such material in the future.

The *Appeal* brought beatings and lynchings to blacks in the South who even uttered the name of Walker or talked about his pamphlet. The audacious pamphlet led to drastic actions in Southern cities: mailbags were searched, black seamen were not allowed to leave ship at some Southern ports, and slave cabins and villages were searched and wrecked. The State of Georgia offered a ten-thousand-dollar reward for the delivery of Walker or a thousand-dollar reward for the man who killed him.

Walker's *Appeal* was the opening shot in the militant antislavery movement. The following year, William Lloyd Garrison published his antislavery newspaper, the *Liberator*, devoted to marshalling forces against the "peculiar institution." Prominent names joined Garrison in his antislavery efforts, including Arthur and Lewis Tappan and Frederick Douglass. In 1833 they formed the American Antislavery Society, a political and moral crusade against slavery that attracted thousands of followers, including many women, who were, however, excluded from the society.

The rise of antislavery activity in the North generated more violence in the South, including threats of retaliation and secession, the burning of abolitionist literature, the whipping and even hanging of any blacks found with such literature or even suspected of having such articles. Free blacks came in for the lion's share of the newly increased hatred and hostility, the favored "whipping boy" in the South henceforth to the Civil War.

By 1836 Congress had received so many antislavery petitions from abolitionists that the U. S. House voted for a gag rule that prevented the body from discussing or debating the issue of slavery. The following year, one of the prominent abolitionist editors, Elijah Lovejoy, was murdered for his anti-slavery views in Alton, Illinois. A Presbyterian minister and journalist, the abolitionist had three printing shops burned in St. Louis before moving across the river into the free state of Illinois. The move did not save him. His new press warehouse was burned by a proslavery mob, and Lovejoy was shot dead.

By 1840 women had forced their way into the antislavery movement. Shunned by the American Antislavery Society, women called their own conventions in the late 1830s and formed their own strategies and tactics. Lydia Maria Child, Elizabeth Cady Stanton, and Sojourner Truth took to the church and civic circuits to persuade people of the evils of slavery. Their crusade overlapped with feminist and temperance issues that would cause a schism in the abolitionist movement. But women found their antebellum voice in the cause of abolition.

Colonization

A major debate over slavery flowed through the revolutionary currents of mid-eighteenth-century America and carried over well into the nineteenth. In black and white American communities, there was always a murmuring background in social and political talk over the rights and wrongs of slave ownership. One element of the dialogue was black colonization, plots and plans to move free blacks en masse out of the United States into western American territory or to Africa or Haiti.

Most whites supported black colonization as the least harmful and most efficient means of ridding the country of unwanted blacks, especially free blacks whom many whites considered subversive threats to the institution of slavery. A small minority of whites and most blacks and abolitionists interpreted colonization as a ploy to deny blacks freedom and to rid America of what colonizers termed the "Negro problem" in America. Some abolitionists favored colonization as a last resort and as the only possible solution to the country's unsolvable racial dilemma. These people had abandoned hope of finding justice in a race-based society.

The black majority, however, agreed with most white abolitionists in denouncing colonization. They saw the plot for what it was: a means of ridding the country of free blacks. Most blacks, slave and free, viewed themselves as Americans, felt a pride in their country, and could not imagine living in a foreign country. Many blacks intuited the contradiction at the heart of the colonization: that America would rid itself of an unwanted free-black caste while holding those same blacks up to Africa as models of achievement to be emulated. They viewed the proposed forced immigration as punishment for black people not completely under white control.[50]

A small minority of blacks, however, supported colonization as the only alternative to finding freedom and dignity for blacks, even if it meant forsaking their country. These supporters believed that the white majority would never accept blacks as equals or allow them any social status short of second-class citizenship. The leadership of this minority tended to be free, educated, experienced, well-traveled, and relatively well—off. Men like John Jenkins and Colston Waring of Petersburg and John Day of Hicksford had the means and the status to create options for themselves.

Colonization as a concept had been tossed about for years in the backwash of the liberalism of the American and French Revolutions and the evangelical movements that spread across Europe and North America. Britain established a trial colony in West Africa at Sierra Leone in 1787 for resettlement of slaves, but it failed from lack of planning, lack of capital, and hostilities from the indigenous population. Africans did not necessarily welcome their American relatives with open arms.

The first American to make a concerted effort to colonize in Africa was a free black named Prince Hall, an active abolitionist of Boston who championed education for black children and equal rights for free blacks. He helped establish a black Freemason hall that was chartered by the Mother Grand Lodge of England. Hall became its grand master and held the office until his untimely death in 1807.[51]

Hall tried to integrate Boston politics, Freemasonry, and schools. When those efforts failed, he petitioned the Massachusetts General Court for support to "return" seventy-three "African blacks" to Africa due to the "disagreeable and disadvantageous circumstances" of free blacks in Massachusetts. The abolitionist argued not only that blacks would never receive equality in America and he employed the very arguments used by American patriots when they were rebelling against England: "taxation without representation" and the natural rights of man. In truth, America's slave society was a fundamental deceit in the nation's political underpinning and in its founding documents.[52]

Prince Hall never won over Boston's white or black communities to his cause, and he died in 1807 having never seen Africa. Whites chose not to see the inherent contradictions of slavery and free-black restrictions, and free blacks had no interest in moving to an alien land away from their families and property.

Paul Cuffee (1759-1817), also of Massachusetts, was the next free black to make a serious effort at colonizing American blacks in Africa. Cuffee, a free black with Indian heritage (his mother was Indian), had advantages that Prince Hall lacked. He was a sea captain and thus had the means to move colonists to Africa by his own resources. He was also a businessman and trader who wanted to incorporate colonizing into his shipping business, thus underwriting immigration and perhaps making a profit in the process.[53]

Cuffee taught himself to read and write and the basics of maritime building. He signed onto a whaling ship and began a maritime career that would bring him a huge estate. He became an aggressive businessman and honed a sharp and deep political instinct. In 1779 he and a brother built their first small open boats with which they traded coastwise along the Atlantic until they had capital to build larger and larger boats and then ships, from a 69-ton schooner to a 268-ton ship. Cuffee ultimately became one of the wealthiest free blacks in the United States from his many enterprises.[54]

Cuffee was a Quaker who often spoke at the Meeting House, of which he was a donor to its building. He was concerned with education for black children and for equal rights, and he spoke often and in public for his beliefs. He petitioned the council of his county to forego taxes on free blacks who were not allowed the vote. The petition failed, but in 1783, in part because of his efforts, all free males in the state were enfranchised.

The wealthy mariner was attracted to the colonizing effort as a businessman and as a Quaker who believed in a moral duty to help uplift African Americans. Encouraged by the African Institution of Philadelphia, Cuffee made a fact-finding visit to Sierra Leone in 1811 and organized the Friendly Society of Sierra Leone with some of the leading black businessmen of that colony. The aim of the group was to encourage industry and prosperity based on trade among the free people.

The impending war with Britain in 1812 interrupted Cuffee's return to the United States. US Customs seized his ship, and the mariner was forced to travel to Washington to plead his case directly to Secretary of the Treasury

Albert Gallatin and President James Madison. The president, eager to learn about Sierra Leone, was impressed with Cuffee's mission. He ordered Cuffee's ship and cargo released.

Cuffee began a speaking tour in Baltimore, Philadelphia, and New York to solicit free blacks to immigrate to Sierra Leone and to build support for the African Institution and the Friendly Society at Sierra Leone. Cuffee, unlike so many immigrating free blacks, had practical plans for putting his immigrants to work so that they could become self-sustaining. Finally, with the end of the war, he sailed in 1815 with thirty-eight colonists for Africa and arrived in February 1816 with farming tools and parts for a grist mill.[55]

Cuffee returned to America in 1816 and worked with Congress and the African Institution to finance a colonization plan, but he received little financial help. He died in 1817, leaving an estate of $20,000 and his dream for an African home for American blacks based on commercial trade with the United States unfulfilled.

Northern blacks were not the only ones interested in opening Africa to American blacks as a refuge for freedoms denied them at home. Lott Cary was born a slave in Charles City County, Virginia, in 1780. By 1804 he worked in a Richmond tobacco warehouse, where he was to make his mark as a man of influence. Cary apparently ran with a rough bunch of men because he built a reputation as a drinker and profaner.

Somewhere, somehow, Cary was attracted to the First Baptist Church in Richmond, an illiterate slave baptized in 1807 by church elder John Courtney, and the church association turned his life around. He studied under the church's care and learned to read the Bible. He not only mastered his language arts but demonstrated proficiency for preaching and exhorting. The reformed Cary was sent into Richmond's black districts and into surrounding counties to minister to his people.[56]

Literacy brought him advancement in his work, where he was promoted to supervisor and was allowed the small perks doled out to enterprising blacks. Favored workers at Cary's level were permitted to collect the scraps of tobacco from the warehouse floor, following a sale, and to sell it for their own profit. The man's work ethic and sobriety won him friends among warehouse personnel and even local merchants, who helped him in his businesses.

By 1813 the slave was earning $800 per year at the tobacco warehouse, speculating in tobacco, farming, and preaching. He had saved enough money to purchase himself and two of his children outright for $850. Cary prospered financially and used his money well. He continued to advance in his religious studies and found help and encouragement from church members. At some point in his spiritual life, Cary chose to devote himself to missionary work.

He agreed with the concept and aims of black colonization and assumed a leadership role in forming the Richmond African Missionary Society.[57]

Lott Cary was praised highly by the members of the First Baptist Church of Richmond and by the board members of the American Colonization Society and the Baptist General Convention. Cary teamed up with a fellow black church member Collin Teague, and the two traveled about Richmond in tandem, preaching and exhorting. Teague was also a preacher, though illiterate, but with the "keenest of penetration as almost any man," according to one of his sponsors. Teague was a competent saddle and harness maker who had put enough money by to purchase his wife and children for $1,300. At some point, the two men decided to sail for Africa as missionaries.

The sponsors of the two men described them as both about forty years old who had been preaching about ten years and who were "accustomed to speaking in public." Both their wives were Baptists, "their children, amiable and docile, have been to school considerably." The board of the Baptist General Convention took supervision over the instructions of both men in 1820 and prepared them for a year in missionary work.

Cary and Teague were publicly ordained and "set apart as missionaries to Africa, in the First Baptist Church in Richmond, of which church they were both members." Cary gave a final sermon in the church that, according to one minister, was "entirely clear of the senseless rant too common with many pious colored preachers." It was described by one communicant as a sermon that "contained many touches of the true sublime."[58]

The Convention Board sent a warning in a letter to the two missionaries, surely without any sense of irony, that they must be prepared to "bear with prejudices" in Africa, meaning the un-Christian rituals and customs of the natives. It is likely that Cary was far beyond his advisors in spiritual sensitivity to alien faiths. He revealed his personal faith and a surprisingly modern take on Christian ethics when he wrote that

> *no complexion or condition is thrown beyond the pale of devine benevolence, for in Christ Jesus "there is neither Greek, nor Jew, barbarian, Scythian, bond nor free."*[59]

The new missionaries and their families shipped from Norfolk in February 1821 on the brig *Nautilus* and arrived at Freetown, Sierra Leone, on March 13 after forty-four days at sea. Cary and Teague had to fund their own and their families' passage to Africa. The Virginians learned quickly that the promises made by the colonization board and the board of missions fell far short of expectations. America's first Baptist missionary to Africa did not fare any better with the indigenous powers. Freetown authorities rejected Lott and his entourage because the Colonization Society had neglected to buy land for their settlement.

Religious and philanthropic groups occasionally sponsored vessels and mariners who captured slave ships and their cargo. Rather than transport the Africans to America, the American benevolent groups preferred to plant them in a free colony such as Liberia or Sierra Leone. Black American colonial leaders in Africa such as Cary and Teague and John Day were at times straddled with the added burden of caring for these unfortunates of the slave trade. The Colonization Society in Sierra Leone held slaves that it needed to settle, so it rented land to accommodate the entire lot, Cary and company and the homeless slaves all thrown together.

Cary, Teague, and their families worked as common laborers until money could be raised to buy some land for their colony. Cary was a resourceful and determined man. Rather than surrender to adverse fortunes, he immediately learned the cooperage trade to support himself and his family.

Meantime, Cary worked at his mission to convert Africans when he could. He established a mission among the Mandingoes and preached his mission wherever he went. He lost his wife to disease in the first year, a tragedy that beset many of the American pioneers to Africa. In 1822 the society finally found some land at Cape Montserrado, to which the colonists moved. The natives at the Cape immediately went to war against the Americans.[60]

In 1824 a ship arrived with 105 emigrants. They all died within a month. Cary became, out of necessity, the medical doctor to his colony. When "recaptives" were sent to the colony, he found a way to assimilate them. He established a secular school and a Sunday school. He experimented with growing rice, coffee, and other crops. He exercised freely the intellectual potential that he could not use in America.

The humiliations and social rejection Cary faced in America offered him, who had known many years of hard times there, a standard against which to take a measure of his life in Africa. Even as one of the promoted and supported free blacks in the South, he lived in emotional and intellectual incarceration, unable to speak his mind freely or to offer his opinions on any matter of substance. He once recalled his battles with the natives at Cape Montserrado and wrote that "there never has been an hour, or a minute, no, not even when the balls were flying around my head, when I could wish myself again in America."[61]

Cary was made vice-agent of the colony in 1826, and when the colonial agent died in 1828, Cary stepped in as interim presiding officer of the colony. It was an unusual and exciting life for a black man born into slavery, an adventure created by the inexplicable convergence of the vanity of white Protestant missionary zeal and the innate desire for personal freedom of a black slave. Cary knew what he wanted, even if his yearning for freedom was tempered by his own need to serve his race. He wrote of his feelings with a directness and insight:

> *I am an African, and in this country* [America], *however meritorious my conduct, and respectable my character, I cannot receive the credit due to either. I wish to go to a country where I shall be estimated by my merits, not by my complexion; and I feel bound to labor for my suffering race.*[62]

Virginia free blacks were divided over the rewards of colonization. Some stood with and some against Northern free blacks, most of whom opposed the removal scheme. There were educated and ambitious free blacks in Virginia who accepted as fate and fact that they would never rise to full citizenship in America, would never be recognized for their talents and achievements, would never have the rights and privileges accorded whites. These folks saw Liberia as a proving ground for their abilities and an alternative to second-class citizenship status in America. Some cloaked their wish to migrate in religious and missionary language, but extant letters from free blacks who made it to Liberia place freedom at the top of their list of reasons for going to Africa.

> *Free black Virginians of property and local standing felt a need to escape the narrow, restricted lives to which even the most successful of them were consigned but did not believe that moving north would improve their circumstances or resolve their identity problem.*[63]

Northern free blacks and especially abolitionists refused to accept that blacks could not walk proudly in the future with full citizenship and recognition of their many feats and triumphs. Their campaign was for education, the vote and freedom to compete with whites for jobs and professional positions.

> *Color was always the essence of the "imperfect connection" of free blacks with full citizenship, but free mulatto families thought, until the end of the Revolutionary Era, that this barrier might be overcome by further admixture, piety, commercial success, and exemplary behavior.*[64]

White Efforts for Colonization

The colonization effort would never make significant headway, however, without the power, prestige, and money of whites. Prominent white men of note began to sign on to the effort about the time of Cuffee's last trip to Sierra

Leone. The Reverend Robert Findley of New Jersey, a relation to several prominent families, joined with some other notables, including Francis Scott Key, to form the American Colonization Society in 1816.

The Presbyterian Findley had been casting about for a humanitarian project worthy of his talents and his status when he crossed paths with Paul Cuffee. It was to Findley's benefit to attach his crusade to an African American who had knowledge of and experience with the Sierra project and one who proselytized for the venture. Cuffee gave Findley legitimacy.

Findley's message to his sponsors and supporters, mostly white, was that colonization would help clear the United States of the undesirable free-black caste as well as unproductive old and decrepit blacks who were a liability to planters and county governments alike. There were numerous promises to the public that colonization of free blacks would lead the way to a gradual end of the slave economy, that colonization for free blacks was a precondition to ending slavery. The legal name of the organization telegraphed the true motivation behind the efforts: The American Society for Colonizing the Free People of Color in the United States.[65]

The makeup of the board of directors of the ACS could hardly have been more biased. Findley himself spoke often, if privately, in rude terms about free blacks and the need to rid the nation of them. Elias Caldwell, secretary for the society, lamented that "the more you cultivate their minds [free blacks], the more miserable you make them." Both men would have denied inherent racism in their views.[66]

There was a humanitarian appeal in colonization aimed at those of a more sensitive nature and religious bent along the lines that colonization would benefit "benighted" Africa by bringing it "partially civilized and Christianized immigrants." These became the buzzwords whenever supporters of black removal spoke in public or argued in ordinaries and pulpits. The pitch was to put a humane and benevolent coloring to a dark scheme of deportation of "free" Americans.

The drive for colonization was by necessity ambiguous in order to appeal to the abolitionists of the North and to the slaveholders of the South, a large order for the men hoping to bring the opposing political extremes in America together. There were abolitionists who accepted that black and white communities in America would never unite, that there would always be a separate path for the races. For those people, a free but separate colony or country of blacks was a second choice, but one that was preferable to slavery.[67]

Virginia colonization leaders assumed a major role in free-black removal schemes. More blacks from the state immigrated to Liberia than from any other. And Virginia sponsored more ACS auxiliary chapters which donated more money to colonization efforts than any other state. The rhetoric of the

ACS Southern chapters tried to soften that clang of hypocrisy in its appeals by wrapping its goals in Christianity and humanism, the same old bromides slave owners had been spooning out for generations: "American slavery saved thousands of condemned African souls; Better a slave in America than a free heathen in the Land of Darkness." Virginia ACS argued that colonization would free the American Negro and bring Christian enlightenment to a benighted Africa.

Significant for its clustered meanings, African colonization was but one among various theories and practices that permitted white Virginians to live with the intensifying contradictions of slavery and liberty.[68]

Findley cloaked his colonization sermons with a humanizing message in public, but in private, he found a more candid voice that spoke for the sentiment of most whites: he described *free blacks* as "unfavorable to our industry and morals" and feared the "intermixture" of the races. Free-black economic competition and miscegenation were standard threats used by proslavery factions against free blacks, slogans guaranteed to put the majority of whites in a bellicose mood.[69]

The makeup of the board of directors of the ACS were men of prominence. White men. Most of its spokesmen used the same ambiguous language as Findley in public while expressing harsh anti-black sentiments in private. Despite its alliance with religious organizations and churches and the attempts to put a humanitarian slant on the project, the ACS and its goals were certifiably racist. The rational for its aims was as perverse as the religious credo that a slave African in America was better off than a free heathen in Africa.[70]

In a memorial to Congress in search of financial support, the society's draft spelled out the free-black menace: "This immediate species of population cannot be incorporated so as to render the Body Politic homogenous . . . which must be [the] essential consideration of every form of government . . . . [The free black was an] imperfect connection, just raised from the abyss of slavery, but not to the level of freedom, suspended between degradation and honor."[71]

The State of Maryland enacted legislation in 1831 that publicly exposed the colonization scheme again for what it was, if anyone had doubts about the true nature of the plan. The law imposed a tax to support the transportation of blacks to Liberia. The tax, however, would be levied on the counties in proportion to the number of free blacks within their borders, another burden on free blacks sold to the public as a humane effort to support colonization.[72]

But it was the ACS presiding officer Henry Clay—speaker of the House of Representatives, slaveholder, and planter—who put the ultimate political spin on the tortuous rationale of the society.

> *Can there be a nobler cause than that which, whilst it preposes to rid our country of a useless and pernicious, if not dangerous part of its population, contemplates the spreading of the arts of civilized life, and the possible redemption from ignorance and barbarism of a benighted quarter of the globe.*[73]

Mr. Clay weaved a colorful tapestry with his promises of free-black colonization, well aware that he was courting sympathetic company with his sentiments. Thomas Jefferson, James Madison, James Monroe, Samuel Adams, John Marshall, Stephen Douglas, and the presidents of Harvard, Yale, and Princeton found themselves to some degree in agreement with the remarks and sentiments expressed by the president of the society.[74]

The voyage to Africa was in a deep sense a reversal of the African diaspora: leaving the homeland, the middle passage back "home," the battle for survival in a strange land, the dealing with an "uncivilized" population, and the creation of a new form of government. The scenario pleased whites and offered them an uplifting narrative that they were emancipating American slaves *and* bringing a semblance of civilization to Africa. Some black emigrants bought into the white rationale, but their ability to speak truthfully to American press or authorities was still very circumscribed so that their true motives only can be guessed at.

The society made scant progress immediately after its founding but attracted a larger following in the late 1820s and early 1830s as white attitudes against free blacks became more visceral and widespread. Free blacks became more vocal in their opposition to colonization as they parsed the words and noted the actions of politicians who spoke about the deportation of their caste. William Jay, the jurist and abolitionist, cogently described the fault line in the rationale of the ACS officers and their comments about the purposes of the American Colonization Society:

> *There is no single principle of duty or policy recognized in it, and the members may, without inconsistency, be Christians or Infidels; they may be the friends or enemies of slavery, and may be activated by kindness or hatred toward free people of color.*[75]

The majority of free blacks and slaves who had opinions on the subject of colonization wanted no part of the scheme concocted by whites. They considered America their country as much as it belonged to whites: "We claim *this country, the place of our birth, and not Africa,* as our mother country, and all attempts to send us to Africa we consider gratuitous and uncalled for." Few

American slaves in the early 1800s knew anything about Africa, its language, or its culture. Most had known only American life, where they had lived out their lives, raised families, and carried memories of their parents and grandparents.

Blacks in all the major cities along the eastern seaboard echoed the sentiments issuing from free-black communities. One of Baltimore's prominent black educators, William Watkins, articulated the anger and resentment of blacks against the white scheme: "We had rather die in Maryland under the pressure of unrighteous and cruel laws, than be driven, like cattle, to the pestilential clime of Liberia, where grievous privation, inevitable disease, and premature death, await us in all their horrors."[76]

Free blacks from Providence, Rhode Island, sent the following message: "Here we were born—here we will live by the help of the Almighty—and here we will die, and let our bones lie with our fathers." Free blacks and slaves considered America their country as much as whites. By 1860, of the 262,000 free blacks in the Southern slave states, a mere 4,300 chose to sail for Liberia.

Much less criticism against the American Colonization Society came from free blacks in the South, especially from the Deep South, where the numbers of city blacks were too small to afford protection against reprisals from white authorities and rivals. Moreover, a few moneyed and educated free blacks in the South sided with white planters in their views of ACS goals, as well as on some slavery, religious, and economic issues. But the scheme of black colonization ultimately failed because free blacks thought of themselves first as Virginians and Americans.

In a preliminary report on the Eighth Census, 1860, statistician Joseph Kennedy wrote that the "total number of colored emigrants sent to Liberia from 1820 to 1856 inclusive, is stated at 9,502, of whom 3,676 were free born." Manumitted blacks leaving for Liberia by 1850 were estimated at 1 for every 3,181 slaves in America; in 1860 the ratio had fallen to 1 to 6,309 slaves. From another perspective, freed blacks leaving the United States equaled in numbers those who escaped their owners annually: 1 to 3,165 in 1850 and 1 to 5,000 in 1860. Clearly, colonization efforts failed woefully to achieve its purpose.[77]

John Day was one of the few free blacks to choose Liberia in search of an opportunity to reach his personal potential that he could not achieve in America. Day's actions ran contrary to black sentiments regarding Liberia and colonization, especially free-black thoughts on the subject. John and his brother Thomas, at various times, assumed positions on slave society and the North-South divide that seem to run counter to their interests. They were essentially victims of a brutal and unjust economic and social system that willfully drafted laws to harm and constrain their class. The Days, however, and some other free blacks of their status considered themselves members, albeit tenuous ones, of the elite planter and professional classes and often acted and spoke in that capacity.

John and Thomas acquitted themselves as the equal of white men except in the exercise of civic rights. By their actions and words, they often found themselves siding with the planter class in such areas as education, politics, economics, and religion. And throughout their careers, whites often treated them as colleagues. On more than one occasion, whites came to their defense, praised their character, advanced them money, chose them to represent white institutions, and even passed a state law to help Thomas out of a legal challenge.

The brothers also held a typical Southern planter perspective and bias about the North. As John Day wrote in one of his lengthy letters from Liberia,

> there are many good, and excellent men in the northern states, yet there is among many such a mysterious reserve, such a distance between their sentiment and action that I can not feel with them ... They astound the South with their professed desire to free, and elevate the colored race, while in practice they do atrocity.[78]

John and Thomas made disparaging remarks on other occasions about Northerners. The question is whether they were playing to their Southern audience or making heartfelt statements. In one of his letters to the secretary of the Foreign Missionary Board, John Day disagreed, humorously, with his superior about where to find literate men to serve in Liberia. Day pointed out that he was never "farther north than Philadelphia; there I found a Methodist bishop [Allen] who had barely sense enough to ride a goose to mill." Richard Allen was a Methodist bishop who founded the first independent black denomination in America, the African Methodist Episcopal Church, in 1816. On the other hand, Day claimed to have found "several well read, gentlemanly men" among the colored Masons of the South.[79]

Other blacks in the South, free and slave, voiced a prejudice against the Northerners. Frederick Law Olmsted noted several cases of Southern blacks telling him of their bitter experiences in the North. In one situation, a slave owner asked his slave to buy himself because he had cost the owner in medical bills and had made no money for him. The slave did as he was asked, borrowing money from his family to buy his freedom. He went to Philadelphia but was soon back in Virginia with a report that only runaways were aided in the North; free blacks could find little work.[80]

Olmsted cited another case concerning a slave who returned from New York because "niggers were not treated well there." By the 1850s when Olmsted relayed these interviews, most whites, North and South, held free blacks in low regard. The caste had become a scapegoat for all the South's problems, and the North was not exempt from exploiting the class for its own political ends.

Frances Anne Kemble, an English actress who traveled in America in the 1830s, pointed to Northern racism and its hypocrisy in a travel memoir. She noted in her *Journal* that, while the majority of blacks in the North were not slaves, "they are pariahs, debarred from every fellowship save with their own despised race, scorned by the lowest white ruffian in your streets, not tolerated even by the foreign menials in your kitchen."[81]

John Jr., a man designated by the state as a "free colored," once explained his reason for serving as a missionary with the proslavery Southern Baptist Convention rather than the antislavery Northern Board as having to do with pensions, claiming that the Northern Board did not provide benefits for the children or widows of its colored missionaries. Reverend Day continued, in a salute to the land that enslaved his ancestors, "The work I call yours [the Southern Baptist Convention], as I felt it should be the glory of the South; to be able to prove themselves, the Greatest benefactor of the negro race."[82]

Ironically, after Day's death, the Southern Baptist Convention ignored repeated pleadings from Mrs. Day and a last letter from Rev. John Day seeking help from the board for his wife in her widowhood.

The Days recognized the racism in America and the unequal treatment free blacks received at the hands of white authorities and of whites, but they were protected from the harsher aspects of the system. This "permanent marginalization" of free blacks sent some educated and skilled American free blacks like John Day to Liberia before the civil upheaval in America. They certainly recognized the brutalizing and pernicious effects of slavery and spoke to its lasting damage. In a letter to the Southern Baptist Convention requesting colored missionaries, John Day warned against sending former slaves to fill the job:

> *Only in very rare instances, should men be taken who were ever under the blighting influence of slavery . . . grown up under the withering influence of oppression. The effect of which follows them through life, disqualifying them for generous and noble action.*[83]

John Day Jr. put himself into a very challenging situation in Liberia. A man of some wealth and much dignity, he chose to prove himself in a land of direst poverty and want; a man of peace, he was often tested by indigenous tribes hostile to the mission of Liberia. He put himself in the care of people who, similar to those who moved against him at High Hills Baptist Church in Sussex, were guided by dogma and would not hesitate to enforce their will on their hirelings. The loss of his wife and children to disease shortly after arriving in Africa testifies to the enormity of the task he chose.

The Reverend Day relied on personal strength in Liberia to steel him to the very harsh obstacles to missionary work in Africa, both from the foreign environment and from the bureaucracy of the SBC. Nonetheless, he proved inventive in overcoming the constant shortcomings of the SBC with regards to resources for the far flung missionary outpost and in dealing with hostile native people. Day had talents of management that aided his building of a church and secular schools. In addition to converting many natives to the Baptist faith, he opened a school that prepared several Africans for future government and church careers, and he sat for a time on the Liberian Supreme Court as a lawmaker.

John Day Jr. had deep convictions that at critical periods of his life caused him pain and trouble. His adherence to strong beliefs and his loyalty to his religious creed and conscience often worked to his detriment. But his determined faith and his strong work ethic earned him admiration from many influential men of the ruling elite, men who assisted him at critical points in his life. He held to the same personal standards in Liberia, where he faced greater challenges than ever in America.

The careers of John Day, Paul Cuffee and Lott Cary demonstrate the talent and creative energy of free blacks when unleashed from restrictive laws and customs. These three men had an impact on their American communities despite social stigma and legal acts that hobbled their ambitions. Freed in Africa to rely on their skills and abilities, Day and Cary wrought profound change in bringing education and trade skills to a small corner of the African continent.

CHAPTER FIVE

"To Wear a Free and Easy Expression"

Thomas Day was making his own mark in Milton in the furniture industry as his brother John wrestled with his spiritual calling. By 1827 he had purchased his own property on Main Street adjacent to the former Bell Tavern lot. The aspiring entrepreneur paid $550 for the property that came with thirty-two-foot road frontage. He also advertised in the local newspaper about his business:

> *THOMAS DAY, CABINET MAKER, Returns his thanks for the patronage he has Received, and wishes to inform his friends and the public that he has on hand, And intends keeping, a handsome supply of Mahogoney, Walnut and Stained FURNITURE, the most fashionable and common BED STEADS, & which he would be glad to sell very low. All orders in his line, in Repairing, Varnishing, & will be thankfully received and punctuallo attended to.*[1]
>
> *Milton Gazette and Roanoke Advertiser*, March 1, 1827

The migrant furniture maker did well in his new home. The following year, he added another few feet to his property with a purchase from Dr. Willie Jones. In 1836 he would buy a second lot adjacent to the property for $525. Ultimately, Day would own one of the premier properties in Milton, the former Union Tavern, and a farm outside the town. Day made a positive impression on influential whites wherever he lived, whether they were businessmen or government officials. He communicated equally with tobacco farmers and university presidents, bank officers and governors.

Union Tavern. Thomas Day announced his standing in the town of Milton with his purchase of Union Tavern, a prominent two-story brick inn on the main road between Danville, Virginia, and Hillsborough, North Carolina. The cabinetmaker added a large shop/factory to the rear of the house where, by the 1840s, he worked a dozen artisans, black and white, and operated steam-powered saws. *(Courtesy of The State Archives of North Carolina)*

Day's leverage with North Carolina authorities was his industry, and his contacts with prominent whites in the area created a broad support for his ambitions. The fact that so many prominent whites were prepared to sign their names to a legislative petition in his behalf after he had lived in their community for only six years speaks loudly for the cabinetmaker's abilities and his ease with the white community.

The community of Milton and the larger county area that arranged to have a petition presented to the North Carolina General Assembly was not directly for Thomas Day but for the woman he had married in Halifax, Virginia. It was Aquilla Wilson who was exempted from the legal act against immigration of free blacks into North Carolina even if the intent was to accommodate the cabinetmaker. The light was on Thomas Day, however, the man who brought a valuable skill and created a valuable product and opened jobs in Milton that was praised in the wording of the petition:

> *That Thomas Day, a free man of color, an inhabitant of this town, a cabinet maker by trade, a first rate workman, a remarkably sober, steady and industrious man, a high minded, good and valuable citizen, possessing a valuable property in this town, did, on the 6th day of January last, intermarry with Aquilla Wilson, a free woman of color of good family and character, a resident of Halifax in the State of Virginia . . .* [2]
>
> NC House Journal, 1830-1831

The inconsistency of harsh state laws and the rabid newspaper and broadside attacks on the free black cast on the one side, and the effusive praise that marked the content of most such citizen petitions to waive those laws in favor of valuable blacks on the other, characterize the contradictory and complex racial and legal dynamics of the South's slave culture. Black laws directed at free people of color were also conveniently ignored and deliberately circumvented when enforcement went against white interests.

Thomas Day benefited from the contacts he made with influential Carolinians and Virginians. He traveled throughout piedmont North Carolina and Southside Virginia putting up furniture and house interiors and making acquaintances with planters and merchants and with town and village officeholders. His travels covered wide swaths of central piedmont North Carolina and Virginia. He also carried on wholesale trade with regional businesses and hired and partnered with local builders and carpenters. He was a large-property owner and in 1834 bought stock in the state bank that located in Milton that year.

Numerous individuals in the county, including the state's attorney general, Romulus Saunders, supported the Milton petition in Day's behalf. Local county officials, magistrates, tobacco planters, and businessmen—most anyone who had business dealings with Thomas Day was inclined to support his residence in the small river town with large ambitions. Regional planters had already put Day to work crafting furniture for them and building mantels and stairs and newels in their homes. All knew him as a "free man of color of very fair character, an excellent mechanic, industrious, honest and sober in his habits."[3]

Romulus Saunders and the surrounding planters—the Hairston and Donohos and Angles and Hunts—knew John Day as a businessman in Milton and the owner of a slave woman. Thomas likewise used slave labor in his shops and on his farm in later years. Saunders would have been reassured by Day's status as a prominent businessman and stockholder in the state bank, but the most important aspect of his behavior to his white supporters may have been his status as a slaveholder. Nothing put the slaveholding class at ease with a free black as knowing that he/she approved or participated in the slave culture and presented it no threat.[4]

The paradox of free blacks owning slaves is a serious issue for historians and social scientists who, on the whole, abhor and reject the concept of slavery. The issue has bothered this writer enormously for years and he is no closer to a satisfying explanation. An easy position is to argue that black slave owners made life easier for black slaves. The assumption will not hold up under close scrutiny: there were black slave owners with a heavy hand and others with a lighter hand, the same as with white owners. The reader and student will make his/her own resolution with the issue.

Aquilla Wilson Day and Thomas Day had two sons and a daughter. Aquilla was a partner in his business ventures (she owned a farm in her own name), and a companion in his religious and social life. In 1841 Thomas and Aquilla joined the Milton Presbyterian Church, just a block away from their residence, as full-fledged and equal members. According to the records of the church, "Mr. Thomas Day & his wife Aquilla Day offered themselves as Candidates for Church membership after a Conversation on experimental religion which was intirely [*sic*] Satisfactory. They were recommended into full Communion."[5]

Day and his wife participated fully in church affairs, even to holding church session meetings in their home, a rare event unless the host was a ruling elder in the church. Prominent county men—silversmith M. P. Huntington and town merchant John Wilson—attended the meetings at Day's home. Day built and installed the pews for the church and attended services there with his family and some of his servants.[6]

During his almost forty years in Milton, Day built up a remarkable furniture business in North Carolina and Virginia. He carried a standard line of furniture in his shop for walk-in trade and also built fine customized furniture for merchants and planters who could afford it. Records document his work for the Hunts and Donohos of Milton, the Roans and Hatchetts of Yanceyville, and the Hairstons of Virginia, all well-to-do and prominent planters of the Dan River Valley. In the early 1850s, he filled several orders of custom furniture for North Carolina governor David S. Reid.

Part of the appeal of Day's furniture was that he fashioned it after the high urban styles of the period: furniture made at Petersburg, Baltimore, and Philadelphia. Examples of his work from the 1840s and 1850s, and there are many pieces still in use, suggest that he worked from pattern books of the day, such as John Hall's *The Cabinet Makers' Assistant* (1840) and the models of John Henry Belter, a New York manufacturer who used laminated wood for fancy curves in his baroque and rococo revival ornamentation.

Those who could afford the stylish furniture patronized Thomas Day.[7] Collectors from North Carolina to Virginia and from New York to California own examples of Day's furniture today. There is a large permanent collection in the North Carolina Museum of History at Raleigh.

Thomas Day Desk. Day made every variety of home furniture, including bureaus, sideboards, armoires, dining tables and chairs, sofas, and bedsteads. He also crafted interior architectural details such as mantels, newel posts, molding, and stairways. *(Courtesy of The State Archives of North Carolina)*

Thomas Day was more than a cabinetmaker. He was also a builder-contractor who designed and supervised the building of mantles, stairs, newel posts, room trim, and window and door framing throughout piedmont North Carolina and Virginia. In 1847 his superior work for the planters and merchants in piedmont North Carolina earned him a prized contract with the University of North Carolina to furnish library shelving for the Philanthropic and Dialectic Societies, debating clubs at the school.

The work was put to bid, and though Day's bid was a third higher than a local firm, university president David Swain opted to give the work to Day. Swain may have lobbied the university board for the higher contract. He asked that Day keep the amount of his bid undisclosed. "For my justification to them [the societies] and to the Trustees," Swain wrote Day, "I must rely upon the superior manner in which I expect you to execute the work."[8]

Day worked on the room furnishings at the university for over a year. The quality of his work may be judged from additional work orders he received from the university. His original contract later expanded to include seating, rostrums, curtains, and blinds. He negotiated some of the work directly with the president of the societies.

Progress on the projects, however, was not smooth. Day missed his deadline to complete the work more than once, and the correspondence between him and President Swain and with Philanthropic president John D. Mallett reveals frustration from all parties. Day's aggravation was with his suppliers of material, sometimes from as far away as Baltimore and Philadelphia, and with being rushed by his employers. On one occasion, a drought lowered the water levels so as to prevent his shipments from reaching Milton.

While at work on the university contracts, Day bought one of the finest properties in Milton, the two-story brick Union Tavern, formerly the Yellow Tavern, on the Hillsborough-Danville road. He used the former tavern as a residence and built a twenty-by-seventy-five-foot-frame building onto the rear of the brick house for his cabinet shop. The house and shop contained two stoves, five chimneys, and twelve fireplaces, a steam-powered saw, and the usual equipment necessary for cabinetry and carpentry work.

Day began his cabinetry business as a traditional eighteenth-century cabinetmaker and created much of his solid-wood furniture by hand. By the 1830s he presided over a preindustrial factory. He worked several to a dozen artisans, jointers, and turners who put furniture together in assembled pieces. By the 1840s his shop hummed with steam-powered saws that could produce laminates and veneer. Day became an entrepreneur who supervised craftsmen and journeymen, upholsterers, and cabinetmakers.

By 1850 Thomas Day owned one of the largest cabinetmaking businesses in North Carolina. If the census of that year is to be trusted, Day owned almost a fourth of the state's capital investment in carpentry and building and produced about a tenth of the state's total cabinetry output. The census shows a capital investment of $5,800 and an annual product value of $5,700. Day had seventy thousand feet of lumber in stock and operated with steam-powered saws. He had a workforce of twelve, five of whom were white journeymen and laborers. Three of his cabinetmakers and two of his laborers were born in Virginia, perhaps an indication of his continued ties to his home community.[9]

On at least one occasion, Day hired cabinetmakers from the Moravian community of Salem, North Carolina, a disciplined settlement of Moravian Protestants with a valued reputation for their crafts, record keeping, and municipal organization. According to the diary of Augustus G. Fogle, who apprenticed under Jacob Siewers, his boss and another hired hand went to Milton in 1838, when "work was slack," and "hired to Thomas Day a colored man, who ran a large furniture shop."[10] Apparently Day had other contacts with the Moravians. On one occasion his daughter took piano lessons in the settlement.

Day and his wife also owned farms outside Milton. The 1850 census credited Day with 140 acres of improved land and another 130 acres of unimproved land worth $1,350. Aquilla is listed separately with 125 improved acres and 175 unimproved acres with a cash value of $800. Both owned horses, cattle, cows, hogs, and sheep and hundreds of bushels of crops: wheat, corn, potatoes, and oats, as well as butter, flax, beeswax, and tobacco (5,100 lbs.).[11]

Even as Day acquired property and succeeded at his profession and made himself and his family a comfortable place in the small town of Milton, dark clouds of a personal and business nature hovered over his success. Some of those concerns can be gleaned from letters exchanged between Day and his daughter, who attended a progressive Northern school, Wesleyan Academy, in Wilbraham, Massachusetts.

It is unusual to uncover uncensored writings between black family members or between black friends from the slave era. Fortunately, copies of letters between Thomas Day and the three children he sent to school at Wesleyan Academy between 1847 and 1851 survived. The letters, preserved by Day's descendants, first appeared in *Negro History Bulletin* in 1950.

Wesleyan Academy, likely the first coeducational school in America, had strong ties to the Underground Railroad. The school was progressive, even radical, on the slavery issue. Mary Ann, Devereux, and Thomas Jr. matriculated in the North at a time when the slavery issue dominated national politics. Absorbing the progressive political sentiments of Wilbraham, Mary Ann came to abhor the slave South and expressed a very different perspective of her home and of her family than did her father.

Tutor and Student: Successful free blacks at the economic level of Thomas Day placed a high value on education, expecting that schooling would lift them out of their social caste and earn them equal treatment before the courts. *(Courtesy of the Library of Congress, Prints & Photographs Division, Washington, D.C. No Use Restrictions)*

Thomas Day surely knew the Wesleyan attitude toward slavery, yet he appeared impatient with his daughter's condemnation of the slave system. At other times, he almost agreed with her negative assessments of Milton and the South and sounded wistful about a better future for his family. In his correspondence with his children, Day was always the concerned father, fretful over his children's manners, habits, and welfare.

In one especially lengthy letter to his daughter, Day addressed several concerns that are universal for parents, writing as a father to a daughter and as a man who knew his place in the world and who feared his children's heedless acts and their lack of understanding of the threats facing them as adults. Day emerges from these letters as a stern but yielding father striving to instill moral values and a work ethic in his children.

In one case, father and daughter disagreed about the behavior of Mary Ann's brother Devereux. She apparently had written in a letter to her mother, explaining that her brother Devereux was "depraved" as a result of being raised in "a shop of the meanest of God's avocation" (her father's shop) and in the "Oppressive South."

In reply, Day defended his trade and business with force and reiterated his opinion of his son's character. He wrote that Devereux was "the worst boy I ever had to manage in my life" and that his "habits as Example among boys is crude." In this letter, Day seemed to accept his life and lot in North Carolina.

> *I see you labor under a great mistake as to the Causes of his [Devereux's] depravity. in your letter to your mother you say it is not to be wondered at that D should be so depraved when you consider he has been raised in a shop of the meanest of God's avocation & that on the illusion that being born in the oppressive South has had a Miserable influence on our Family. You Greatly mistake the character of the shop and hands. There is not a more respectable house of the kind in my knolege and no hands as laborers have a higher credit than ours. Devereux I am sorry to know was the worst boy I ever had to manage in my life; in most of his wais he was not so publick in some of his follies as some others but his habits as Example among boys is crude.*
>
> *The meaning of your letter seems to make some complaints on the country and place of your birth . . . it pleased the Lord to create Adam & Eve in Eden & it also pleased the Lord to permit you to be born in Milton & the best thing you can do will be to improve the privileges before you. To make yourself acquainted with useful learning & Embrace all possible opportunities for spiritual and Temporal knowledge. As to the place you was born or the place you die concern yourself but little compared to improvements of your time and talent as God has given you and will require of you.*
>
> *The Boys has riddled out their money very foolishly—Children should Ever mind to be prompt to their promises, when you promise any thing never fail to comply or render some reason in time why you cannot comply. This is a Great fault with Devereux he promises fairly but complies badly, and He complains there is no Confidence cherished in him by his parents but he dont look at the Reasons.*[12]

In another portion of the letter to his daughter in 1851, Day commented of his time in Milton: "I am perfectly satisfied as regards Milton—I came here to stay four years & am here 7 time 4. I love the place no better nor worse than the first day I came into it—My Mother & Many other unavoidable incomberances has held me here and I am as busy as you Ever see an Old fellow trying to work my way out."[13]

Day was concerned not with his children's material welfare but with their spiritual and emotional health. He wanted his daughter to acquire the confidence of a mature female, one who would feel at ease in society and feel free with her talents.

> *No doubt my great concirn at this time & will be is to get some sootable place for you and your Brothers—us all—to settle down—I want you to be in some place where your turn of feelings & manners can be well met with associates. & I fully Expect to affect my purpose if I live long Enough . . . . I want you to learn music well—to learn all other Branches well that you have taken—learn to walk well—to stand Erect—learn to feel free & to feel well & easy—learn to wear a free and & Easy Expression—and never forget the Modesty and Gentle cartion* [caution] *so necessary in a Lady to give her an independent and unquestionable Caracter.*
>
> *I intend to get you a Piano and am in hopes you will learn to play on the Guitar so to amuse yourself while traveling perhaps on the Broad Ocean . . . Nothing new in Milton worth attention—when you come home you must expect cool Comfort so far as human intercourse is concerned—There is nothing here but to make a little money & that but little to induce us to stay here.*[14]
>
> *From your Affectionate Father Thos Day*

Day has lofty plans for his daughter's future; he is determined that she will live the life of a refined lady. Even so, he warns in the same breath that she can expect little interaction with the Milton community. Because of the lack of educated people to talk to? Or, because the community does not interact with the Day family? Milton and North Carolina was not the same accepting place that it was when the Day brothers arrived there in the 1820s. The South was moving toward a civil war, and free blacks increasingly were accused of siding with abolitionists. What white would have been happy at the prospect of Days children being educated at Wilbraham?

Day noted that Mrs. Wilson, Aquilla's mother, took the stage for Cincinnati the previous week and that his own mother, Mourning Stewart Day, "continues quite childish or insane but no great matter." Then he closed with a harsh statement citing his father as an example of people who are foolish with their time and their talents.

> *My Father Died after 66 years* [of] *Health & Great strengths the poorest man to his chance I know. He lived poor. He never failed to take his Hives before his honey matured.*[15]

Even as Day built a solid reputation and created one of the largest furniture businesses in the state, the economic climate of the 1850s darkened, money tightened, and unemployment rose. As passions flared, free blacks came in for random and vicious criticism as instigators of slave restlessness and supporters of Northern abolitionism. They increasingly became scapegoats for economic setbacks and racial unrest. The 1850s were not good years for free blacks, and the Panic of 1857 sounded a death knell to many black-owned businesses.

The economic panic of 1857 was brought on by the collapse of the Ohio Life Insurance and Trust Company (through embezzlement) and by the end of the Crimean War. Ohio Life's fall brought down other branches of the extended company and other financial companies, eventually resulting in a financial panic. The end of the Crimean War returned farmers to the fields in Europe and led to a corresponding fall of agriculture prices in America.

The financial collapse was deep. It affected real estate and retail markets and led to unemployment riots. Thomas Day's successful cabinetry and woodworking business was not immune to the financial free fall. Day had business arrangements as far north as New York that failed, leaving him without supplies and material. Local accounts fell off too; the late 1850s was a convenient time for debtors to ignore their bills, especially those owed to black businessmen. We can be almost certain that Day's financial difficulties were not due to a decline in the quality of his work. Even in the dark days of economic depression, the *Raleigh Register* lauded Day's reputation as an exceptional furniture maker. "We doubt very much whether there is a superior artist to Mr. Day in the southern country [the South], certainly not in this state," the newspaper reported.[16]

Day's personal health slipped in the late 1850s. History does not record his ailments, but some of his correspondence alludes to his illness. In a letter to former governor and client David Reid, Day wrote in 1858 that his health had hindered his efforts in the business and that he was "[v]ery much disappointed in getting work put up . . . I do hope you enjoy your prosperous and happy Arrangements with more cirtinty than my afflictions allows me."[17]

That same year, Day's business went into receivership, with his longtime friend and business client Dabney Terry appointed trustee for his property. His house and shop, tools and steam engines, two rental properties, wagons and vehicles, teams and harnesses, and six slaves fell to the supervision of the court. Thomas Day Jr. signed a note for his father's indebtedness and accepted the property under the trusteeship of Charles D. Hill. By 1861 Thomas Day's body lay in a grave in or near his adopted town of Milton. Thomas Jr. worked the cabinetmaking shop through the Civil War and into Reconstruction. He and his wife sold the property in 1871 and moved to Asheville, North Carolina.

The Raleigh Corporation Land & Building Association and Thomas Day Jr. and his wife, Annie, signed a property deed to Day's former shop and home, and the property conveyed to Raleigh Corporation on January 29, 1870. Thomas Jr. and his family moved to Asheville, N. C. A contract was made to William F. Farley on September 25, 1871, the property "lately occupied by Day as a residence & cabinet shop."[18]

There is a strong oral tradition in Milton and in Caswell County, North Carolina, that Thomas Day negotiated a seat in the main sanctuary of the church for himself and his wife by building pews for the church. The tale began in the early twentieth century and was repeated so many times in newspaper and magazine articles that it carried the weight of fact. The story reflects the bias in the region as late as the 1970s when Milton's "local historian" related the same erroneous tale to the author.

It was the custom in the twentieth century in Day's adopted town for the locals to refer to him as Tom Day. Referencing a black by his/her first name, as one would a child, denied blacks their dignity and was the standard form of address to blacks in the South, both ante—and postbellum. In Day's case, however, the name Tom was never used in the historical records. Business and social colleagues, in the records, invariably use Mr. Day as the form of address, indicating his status in the community as a social equal, even if legal realities would occasionally intrude on Day's comfortable life in the little backwater village of Milton.

Thomas Day and his wife did not come before the officers of the Milton Presbyterian Church with hat in hand. In fact, church officers held business sessions in the Day home, said meetings recorded in church minutes, an event of some rarity unless the host was a ruling elder in the church. Some of the town's most prominent citizens, including noted silversmith M. P. Huntington and the wealthy merchant John Wilson, with whom Day carried on a robust wholesale business, attended these meetings. Colleagues addressed him as "Mr. Day" at the sessions and he was so listed in the recorded minutes of the church.[19] The Milton Presbyterian Church still stands a block from the former home and shop of Thomas Day, and the pews remain in use.

The several magazine and newspaper articles written about Day in the twentieth century seem to have followed the example of the white "informants" in Milton who insisted on referring to Mr. Day as Tom. The media repeated the error and continued to use the diminutive term in newspaper and magazine articles into the 1970s.[20]

The legends about Day circulated during the first half of the twentieth century are outlandish; they range from Day's immigration from Jamaica to his birth in Milton, to his education and apprenticeship in the Northern states. These tales were written mostly by "color writers" who used the "older citizens" of Milton as sources. The stories are a jumble of folklore about Day mixed with a large dose of early-twentieth-century racial prejudice.[21]

The Museum of Early Southern Decorative Arts (MESDA) at Old Salem mounted an exhibit of Day's furniture in 1991. It was a modest exhibit that drew a modest amount of press that included *The News & Observer* of Raleigh and *The Caswell Messenger* from Yanceyville, North Carolina. A state representative read a paper at the opening of the exhibit provided by Milton's "local historian" in which the same old tales and lore written about Day in the 1930s and the 1950s were repeated. *The Messenger* article included an alleged photograph of Mr. Day in a coat and tie of obvious post-Civil War vintage, a fashion of some twenty years after Day's death.[22]

The accuracy about the lives of Thomas Day and his family was never so much the concern of twentieth-century North Carolina partisans as was their need to have Day conform to their perceptions of how a free-black citizen would have been treated during slavery. There was a need to put Day "in his place," to separate him from full citizenship and from white interaction. The concept of the Days occupying a standing of equality in the local church or in the business community did not square with twentieth-century Caswell County racial conceits or with its social and political traditions. Yet behind the paternalism of the rural white folk of Caswell County, there is a discernable pride in Thomas Day and his legacy to the county.

The successful professional careers of prominent free blacks like John and Thomas Day, officially designated "men of color," raise many questions about the disparity between the official and legal attitudes toward free blacks in antebellum America and the acceptance of some free blacks by prominent whites and their place in "white" society. How did free people of color navigate the "hidden laws" of the dominant culture? What mental and psychological adjustments were required to accommodate a society of such enshrined contradictions?

Free blacks and even slaves, as individuals, had always found friendship and even love and intimacy with some whites. Many whites in the South "compartmentalized" certain blacks from the generally accepted perceptions of the race as shiftless and lazy and inferior to whites. In many cases, the intimacy of adolescence between black and white children influenced adult feelings toward certain blacks. Religious and even political scruples inclined some whites to approach the racial divide with a semblance of evenhandedness.

On the other side, some blacks made exceptions for certain whites, made a decision to trust them with personal feelings and information, depended on them for support in a business, even when the social climate frowned on such partnerships.

Historian Leonard Curry wrote that urban free blacks in the first half of the nineteenth century aspired to the white equivalent of the American dream: freedom, economic success, and personal improvement. Successful free blacks wanted what the Constitution promised: life, liberty, and the pursuit of happiness. As a free people, they did not understand why they could not have equitable laws. There were white people who were much more forgiving and accepting than their laws and their politics would suggest, white people who encouraged free blacks in their aspirations of personal achievement. But they stopped short of full citizenship and social equality.

POSTSCRIPT

For two hundred years, slave owners and the yeomanry in slave colonies and slave states lived in fear of an uprising of bondsmen. Many counties in the South by the eighteenth century had a larger population of blacks than whites, and whites understood that if a committed uprising happened, there would be large numbers of whites killed.

One of the many contradictions and ironies of Southern slavery was that while whites raged against abolitionists as naive and bragged about how happy and contented their slaves were, they fully expected to be hacked to death in a slave rising. The black population outnumbered whites in many counties across the South, and whites were certain, for generations, that blacks would rise against them. In fact, blacks shaved the necks of whites, entered their rooms at night while they slept to carry out chamber pots and to stir fires, raised the children of whites, cared for white elderly, yet whites were convinced of their murderous intent.

Southern legislators ritually passed restrictive laws against slaves and free blacks for two hundred years and enacted the same laws over and over as a kind of talisman that might protect them from their bondsmen. While slave owners bragged about how good they were to their slaves and how contented their charges were, at the same moment they preached and warned against a future slave rising that would lay waste to the land. Even as planters boasted about their slaves as "part of the plantation family," their slaves kept running away and looking for freedom. When the Civil War ignited, they hit the roads and the woods in droves in search of Union lines.

Whites tended to think that blacks shared their same worldview, that just as colonists had rebelled against English rule, blacks would eventually rebel against their owners and overseers. The Haitian Revolution of the 1790s brought the fears to a close realization when black slaves rose against their French rulers and Toussaint L'Overture led a slave army against Napoleon's forces and won. Hundreds of mulatto slave owners and their mulatto and black security forces and supporters escaped to America's southern cities and brought tales of horror about the overthrow.

Slave owners were wrong in most of their assumptions. While enslaved Americans truly wanted their freedom, practically none of them thought in terms of wresting it from their owners in an uprising. True, slaves and free blacks listened closely to whites talk about abolition and freedom and the values of the Revolutionary War: the natural rights of man, freedom, liberty, and the pursuit of happiness. In the decades following the Revolutionary War, those slogans and the principles behind them likely resonated as loudly with slaves and free blacks as with whites.

Blacks also took to heart biblical teachings and sermons and Christian teachings. Henry Bibb, the undaunted Kentucky slave, recalled his interest in Christianity when he "had some very serious religious impressions," along with a number of slaves in the neighborhood "who felt very desirous to be taught to read the Bible." But he and his neighbors understood why they were not allowed to hear any gospel but that approved by the owners, which was "Servants be obedient to your masters; and he that knoweth his master's will and doeth it not, shall be beaten with many stripes."

Slaves heard the hypocrisy of plantation religion and felt the anger and injustice of the lash and witnessed the cruelty of selling children away from their mothers, and they had difficulty squaring the circle. There were preachers, especially black ones, who could and did preach the owners' religion in a fashion to entice slaves. But there were many other black preachers who preached the religion of Jericho and the Israelites who were led out of captivity by their god, a not-very-subtle metaphor for emancipation. There were also preachers who held fast to superstition and voodoo as an alternative to the white man's religious teachings.

In most cases, with the few dramatic exceptions such as Nat Turner and Denmark Vesey, slaves looked to freedom as they did to religion: with a very long-term perspective, as something that would come to them as a reward, not as something that they could pursue, certainly not as something they could force from white people at the point of a gun. Ironically, despite white anguish and wringing of hands and prophecies of blood running in the streets and the flood of laws and acts against slaves for a hundred and fifty years, "[n]o white person was killed in a slave rebellion in colonial Virginia. Slaves proved, in fact, less dangerous than free or semi-free laborers."[23]

The constant threat of colonial slave rebellion was mostly a figment of the agitated imagination of whites, inspired by their guilt of enslaving other humans. Many whites observing the bondage of blacks glimpsed an analogy of American colonials versus their British overlords and believed that blacks had the same dreams of overthrowing their own tyranny. It was to the planters' benefit for white yeomanry and laborers and artisans to fear a black uprising; the notion played well into the designs of the ruling elite to pass ever more restrictive laws against blacks, to shore up the underpinnings of slavery, and to elevate the large slave-owning planters as the pillars of white society and security.

Edmund Morgan has drawn a convincing heritage between treatment and attitudes toward the poor in seventeenth-century England and white attitudes toward blacks in colonial Virginia. Institutionalizing the poor began in England with the erection of a "house of correction" in the late sixteenth century, places of confinement for the poor and to put beggars to work. Before the penal concept had lost its initial enthusiasm, it had ensnared the ill, the insane, and the criminal and treated all but the insane as a common curse requiring a common treatment.

These workhouses not only required the confined to contribute to the total wealth with their labor, they also had the advantage of removing the idle and the poor from the view of a disapproving society. The poor were labeled with all the adjectives a proper Englishman could devise to describe the undesirable: miserable, diseased, ignorant, seditious, vicious, lazy, drunk, debauched. By the end of the century, members of this despised class of the disadvantaged were required to wear a prominent red or blue P on their shoulders in the event that the public should not recognize them, its intent to publicly stigmatize them. American whites displayed similar attitudes toward blacks.[24]

By the 1840s there was an awakening of political consciousness among some free blacks who were listening to abolitionist views and weighing the prospects of real freedom against their limbo life of oppression. Slaves too were more receptive to the siren call of the North, and the large number of runaways in the 1840s spoke of their determination to seek freedom regardless of the cost.

Free black had always been a contradiction in terms. Neither free nor necessarily black, non-slave colored people in the South challenged every premise that shored up Southern arguments in support of slavery: slavery was good for blacks, slavery took care of blacks, slaves were happy in their bondage, slaves could not function as free people, nature equipped blacks for slavery.

Visiting Englishman Captain Marryat called the "free Negro" designation "the mere abuse of language."

Independent, self-sustaining nonwhites belied the foundation myths that supported the institution of slavery. Every free colored person undermined the rationale for enslavement and threatened the moral basis for the white system. Prosperous free blacks were especially dangerous to the system; they were proof that free blacks could take care of themselves, that they could find rewarding work and care for their families, that some could raise themselves to a level well above most whites in education and wealth. And very few voiced an appreciation for the slave system from which most had escaped, unless they belonged to the miniscule black slave-owning community.

If free blacks as individuals or a community of free blacks did well, accomplished something with their lives, or competed equally against whites, their successes challenged the whites' basic assumptions about race and slavery and threatened their place in society. The greater the number of free blacks among them, the harder whites fought to deny them a place; and the more strident the criticism of slavery from the Northern press, the more shrill the Southern defense of its peculiar institution.

In their ceaseless attempts to shore up arguments of slavery as a "positive good" and as yet another scheme to rid the state of free blacks, the Virginia General Assembly in 1856 passed a law that would enable free blacks to regress into slavery. According to the law, a free black could choose a master and apply through the courts to become his slave. It was not the first time that planters had fallen victim to their own fantasy notions about slavery and the slave psyche. Three free blacks in Prince Edward County did apply for "assignment to masters," but "it appears that fewer than two dozen free blacks enslaved themselves in the entire state of Virginia between 1856 and 1861."[25] Many free blacks were destitute in the 1850s, but they were not *that* desperate.

By the 1850s the Southern states were more determined than ever to remove free blacks from their borders or return them to slavery. Arkansas, with the smallest free-black population in the Southern states, was the first to pass legislation in 1858 ordering free blacks to leave the state by January 1, 1860, or face enslavement. The state's economy had less to lose than larger economies in states that boasted far larger free-black populations who served as a ready labor supply. Money from the sale of the property of the evicted free blacks in Arkansas was designated to an education fund for white children.

Every democratic society requires a strong consensual history in order to survive. Those conditions could not exist in a democracy with enslaved people. Democracy and slavery cannot coexist without twisting democratic institutions beyond recognition. In the end, the free-black community was too small and too impoverished to effect change in the slave South. Individuals managed to escape some of the constraints of anti-black laws and attitudes, but the ones who truly escaped their caste did so by joining the ranks of the ruling class. The free-black caste was an aberration that emerged through the fissures in the schizophrenic nature of a slave society that aspired to be Christian and democratic. Free blacks were trapped between American ideals, as expressed in American constitutional documents, and American white prejudice, as expressed in the nation's anti-black laws. The history of America cannot be told without the story of its free-black caste, which backlights the chasm between national ideals and national reality.

ACKNOWLEDGEMENT

Who can say why one student looks for answers in dusty records and another in test tubes, why one seeks out the great novelists and another the great philosophers? All are looking for the same answers, the answers to *why*.

My search for answers began at Elon College (now University) in North Carolina. Higher education was nicotine for me; I absorbed it like a drug, at least those subjects I liked. Several of my professors stoked my interests in the humanities, especially in History and English, and kept my grades high enough to see me through. Horace H. Cunningham (*Doctors in Gray*), as Southern in manners as his name and as gracious, taught by example the duty and integrity of the historian. Ferris E. Reynolds, a caricature of the rumpled old philosopher, nodding off afternoons in his cluttered office, nudged me toward critical thinking and taught me to question my own senses. James P. Elder, Jr. was a mentor who prepared me for graduate studies at Virginia Tech and the University of Virginia and remains a close personal friend.

After numerous false starts and flawed detours, I returned to the pursuit of history with the Division of Archives & History (Department of Cultural Resources) in North Carolina. Two Museum of History exhibits, *The Black Presence in North Carolina* and *Thomas Day, Cabinetmaker* introduced me to regional history and taught me the meaning of "All politics (and history) is local." I was fortunate to begin my career with those exhibits when the researcher might be also script writer, exhibit curator, collector of artifacts, and information person.

No regrets. Pulling together the many facets of *The Black Presence in North Carolina*, with the able assistance of Neil Fulghum, later Keeper of the North

Carolina Room at the University of North Carolina, I met an incredible number of African Americans who changed my understanding and my perspective of the history of my home state. Some examples.

Sally Jones and I would sit on her front porch on Main Street in Winton hard by the Chowan River and chuckle about the possibilities of our being family. Sally was a latte-colored lady of post-retirement age who had spent her adult career teaching in New York. She returned to her home where her heritage ran deep to live out her days. There is a river landing on the Chowan near Winton called Tuscarora Beach that in the early 19th century was a ferry landing named Old Barfield's. Hence the joke between us that we might be related.

Sally owned a scrap of paper signed by a magistrate that allowed her grandfather to vote in state elections in the early 20th century despite the state's "grandfather clause" constitutional amendment of 1900 that kept 95% of the state's blacks from the polls. Her grandfather earned that scrap of paper by proving to skeptical election officials of the day that his ancestors had voted in North Carolina prior to the 1835 constitutional convention that disfranchised blacks. Sally was a beautiful person who loved her state despite its refusal to reciprocate for most of her life. I learned from Sally how people with dignity refused to respond in kind to indignities.

I met descendants of the Young family of Raleigh, a grandchild of James Young who served in the Spanish-American War; descendants of Thomas and John Day who carry on the Day tradition of higher education; officers of North Carolina Mutual Life Insurance Company who nurtured a small street-corner insurance venture into one of the major insurance companies in America.

And Beatrice Robbins, daughter-in-law of Parker D. Robbins. Yes, daughter-in-law. Parker D., a "free person of color" tinged with Indian blood, farmer, inventor, landowner, Civil War sergeant major, steamboat captain, builder and one-time legislator, lived until 1917. He had a son late in life whose widow moved into a house built by Parker D. in Magnolia. Every time I met with Mrs. Robbins I felt as if I were holding history in my hand. Her father-in-law was such a resourceful man in the second half of the 19th century that he could not be contained by the post-Civil War efforts to return black citizens to secondary citizenship. When the state ruled that blacks could no longer ride as passengers on steamboats, Parker D. built his own steamboat, the *St. Peter.* Until a few years ago, there were houses in Magnolia built by Parker D. All have been razed. There is yet one standing which will remain unnamed lest it meet a similar fate.

That's where I learned regional history, in the homes and garages and sheds of people who held onto modest family images and artifacts that told large stories about our history and our culture, stories that mostly went ignored until the second half of the 20th century.

I would be remiss not to acknowledge the help of my sister, Nancy Lynn Cregg, who labored in the labyrinth of the Internet on my behalf to make connections that I did not even know I needed. And of my partner, Gail Lockwood, who did tedious manuscript work and listened sympathetically to my outbursts at the loss of a footnote or the misplacement of a book. And to my son, Jean Paul Barfield, who, with my sister and my partner, refused to entertain any doubts that this project would see the light of day. Thank you.

LAWS ON SLAVERY
IN VIRGINIA

1655   Indian slavery prohibited.

1662   The first legal act defining slavery was to determine the status of mulatto children: "All children borne in this country shall be held bond or free only according to the condition of the mother."

1667   A law stating that baptism did not affect the status of a Negro. A baptized slave was still a slave.

1668   An act making free-black females tithable (taxable).

1670   An act further defining who shall be slaves. Forbade free blacks from owning white servants as had been custom.

1680   An act forbidding slaves from carrying guns, clubs, staffs, swords, or any other weapon. Slaves were forbidden to leave his/her plantation without a certificate.

1681   An act to forbid the emancipation of any Negro or mulatto unless the owner paid for transportation outside Virginia within six months. Also outlawed marriage between English (white) to any Negro, mulatto, or Indian.

1696   An act to reiterate the status of children of Negro/mulatto women.

1705   An act to forbid Negro, mulatto, or Indian to own "any Christian servant" except of their own complexion. Also determined that slaves would be held as real estate, not chattel, and could be passed to heirs; reaffirmed travel and weapons ban; decreed that children of a Negro man and white servant woman would be bound out for thirty-one years.

1715　An act to prevent voting by free blacks. Given back in the Constitution of 1767, taken again in 1835 in North Carolina; the act also prohibited interracial marriages.

1723　Negro and Indian slaves could not be freed except for meritorious service as judged by the governor and the council. Abolished voting rights for free blacks and Indians in Virginia.

1741　Manumission limited to meritorious services to be adjudged by the county courts (in superior courts after 1830).

1748　Slave ownership changed from real estate to personal property.

1765　An act that bastards of women servants and Negroes be bound out, males to twenty-one years and females to eighteen.

1782　Restrictions on personal manumissions removed (at this date, there were only 2,800 free blacks in Virginia).

1793　Fugitive Slave Act recognized the rights of slave owners to recover their property from Northern states and free territories.

1798　Passage of the Alien and Sedition Acts.

1806　Act to remove manumitted slaves from Virginia within twelve months.

1820　Missouri Compromise extended slavery to Missouri, with Maine as free state.

1826　North Carolina prohibits free blacks from entering the state.

1831　Act to forbid teaching blacks to read and write.

1832　Act to forbid preaching by blacks.

1856　An act to allow free blacks to enter a state of slavery by applying for an "assignment to masters."

Important Dates

c.1764   John Day Sr. born.

1778   Slave trade in Virginia ended.

1790-1820   A period of "quiescence" on the slavery issue. c. 1795 John Day married Mourning Stewart, daughter of Dr. Thomas Stewart (Dinwiddie).

1797   John Adams elected president, Jefferson, vice president.
John Day Jr. born at Hicksford.

1791   Saint Dominique slave revolt against the French.

1798   Alien and Sedition Acts.

1799   Jefferson at work on Monticello.

1799   George Washington dies at Mt. Vernon.

1800   Unites States capital moved from Philadelphia to Washington City. US electors tie on Jefferson and Burr for president.

1800   Gabriel Prosser, a Richmond blacksmith, planned slave revolt; twenty-five hanged.

1801   Thomas Day born.

1801   US House elects Jefferson president on the thirty-sixth ballot, Burr, vice president.
New York passes Emancipation Act.
US population 5.3 million; one million African Americans.

1802   Ohio outlaws slavery.
James Callender writes first article about Thomas Jefferson and Sally Hemings.

1803	Louisiana purchase: United States pays France $15 million for eight hundred thousand square miles of western land, doubling the landmass of the United States.
	Toussaint L'Overture defeats Napoleon's army in Saint Domingue.
1804	Lewis and Clark Corps of Discovery venture to the Pacific.
	Alexander Hamilton dies in duel with Aaron Burr.
	Thomas Jefferson reelected, George Clinton, vice president.
1806	Act to remove freed slaves from Virginia within twelve months from emancipation.
	Burr conspiracy to seize Spanish territory in the west.
1807	John Day Sr. purchases a farm in Sussex.
1807	Aaron Burr captured at New Orleans, on trial at Richmond—acquitted, makes flight to England.
1808	James Madison elected president—takes Florida from Spain.
1808	Will of Thomas Stewart filed.
1809	Will of Thomas Stewart proved.
1812	US Congress declares war on Britain—15 percent of American troops are black.
1814	British burn US Capitol.
1815	Napoleon defeated in Waterloo.
1815	John Macadam used crushed stone, water, and gravel to pave a road in England.
1815	Major Petersburg fire; five hundred buildings destroyed.
1816	"The year without a summer" caused by Tambora volcanic eruption, which spread sulfuric acid across the planet, causing crop failure and food shortage.
1816	American Society for Colonizing Free Blacks in the United States was formed in New Jersey.
1817	John Day and family moved to Warren County, North Carolina.
1818	Georgia prohibits personal manumissions.
1819	John Day Jr. moved to Warren County.
1819	Alabama admitted as a slave state.
1820	Missouri Compromise: Missouri slave, Maine free. Forbade slavery in Louisiana territory (to be repealed by Kansas-Nebraska Act in 1854).
1821	New York allows free blacks to vote.
1821	John Day Jr. married Polly Wickham in Greensville County.
1822	Denmark Vesey plot in Charleston.
1824	Mexico becomes a republic, outlaws slavery.
1825	Erie Canal completed.
1826	Thomas Jefferson and John Adams die on July 4.

1827	New York outlaws slavery.
1828	Andrew Jackson's inaugural.
1829	David Walker's *Appeal*.
1830	Underground Railroad launched.
1830	Erie Canal completed.
1831	Nat Turner massacre, slave preacher in Southampton County kills fifty-five whites.
1850	Compromise that introduced the Fugitive Slave Law.
1854	Kansas-Nebraska Act.
1859	John Brown attacks Harpers Ferry.

WORKS CITED

Introduction

1. Journal of the House of Commons of North Carolina, 1830-1831, 238. Hereinafter cited as *N.C. House Journal.*
2. *Ibid,* 238.
3. *Marriages of Halifax County, 1801-1831.* Compiled by Marian Dodson Chiarito & James Hadley Pendergast. (Nathalie, Virginia: The Clarkton Press, 1985), 39.
4. John Hope Franklin, *The Free Negro in North Carolina, 1790-1860* (Chapel Hill: The University of North Carolina Press, 1943), 18-19; hereinafter cited as *The Free Negro.*
5. Ira Berlin, *Slaves Without Masters: The Free Negro in the Antebellum South* (New York: Pantheon, 1975), 7-9; hereinafter cited as *Slaves Without Masters.*
6. Captain Frederick Marryat, *A Diary in America* (1837), 117; hereinafter cited as *Diary in America.*
7. David Dodge, "Free Negroes in North Carolina," *The Atlantic Monthly* (January, 1886), 4; hereinafter cited as "Free Negroes in North Carolina."
8. Rodney Barfield, "Thomas and John Day and the Journey to North Carolina," *North Carolina Historical Review* (January, 2001), Volume LXXVIII, Number 1.
9. Franklin, *The Free Negro,* 4.

Chapter One

Slavery in the Making

1. U.B. Phillips, *American Negro Slavery* (New York, 1918), 54; hereinafter cited as *American Negro Slavery.*

2. Allan Kulikoff, *Tobacco and Slaves: The Development of Southern Cultures in the Chesapeake, 1680-1800* (Chapel Hill: The University of North Carolina Press, 1985), 29; hereinafter cited as *Tobacco and Slaves.*

3. Kenneth M. Stampp, *The Peculiar Institution: Slavery in the Ante-bellum South* (New York: Alfred A. Knopf Inc., 1956), 3-23; hereinafter cited as *The Peculiar Institution;* Franklin, *The Free Negro,* 3-13; John H. Russell, *The Free Negro in Virginia, 1619-1865* (Baltimore: 1913), 8; hereinafter cited as *Free Negro in Virginia.*

4. Stampp, *The Peculiar Institution,* pp. 3-23; Phillips, *American Negro Slavery,* 49-61.

5. Kulikoff, *Tobacco and Slaves,* 23.

6. *Ibid,* 11-12.

7. Eugene D. Genovese, *Roll Jordan Roll: The World the Slaves Made* (New York: Pantheon Books, 1974), 299-300; hereinafter cited as *Roll Jordan Roll.*

8. Loren Schweninger, *Black Property Owners in the South, 1790-1915* (Urbana: University of Illinois Press, 1997), 4; hereinafter cited as *Black Property Owners.*

9. *Ibid,* 14.

10. *Ibid,* 13

11. *Ibid,* 14

12. *Ibid,* 14.

13. *Ibid,* 15.

14. *Ibid,* 16.

15. *Ibid,* 15-16.

16. *Ibid,* 15.

17. *Ibid,* 16.

18. *Ibid,* 16.

19. *Ibid,* 11.

20. John J. Zaborney, *Slaves for Hire: Renting Enslaved Laborers in Antebellum Virginia* (Baton Rouge: Louisiana State University Press, 2012), 11-13; hereinafter cited as *Slaves for Hire.*

21. *Ibid,* 12.

22. Lunsford Lane, *The Narrative of Lunsford Lane, Formerly of Raleigh, N.C.* (J.G. Torrey, Printer, 1842); hereinafter cited as *Lunsford Lane.*

23. Jeffrey J. Crow & Robert E. Winters, Jr., eds., *The Black Presence in North Carolina* (Raleigh: North Carolina Museum of History, 1978), 26.

24. Russell, *Free Negro in Virginia*, 10.

25. James Curtis Ballagh, *A History of Slavery in Virginia* (Baltimore: The Johns Hopkins Press, 1902), 1; hereinafter cited as *Slavery in Virginia.*

26. *Ibid*, 31-32.

27. Schweninger, *Black Property Owners*, 17.

28. William Waller Hening, *The Statutes at Large; Being a Collection of all the Laws of Virginia from the First Session of the Legislature, in the Year 1619.* 13 Volumes. (New York: R&W&G Bartow, Printer, 1823), III, 155; hereinafter cited as *Statutes at Large.*

29. Schweninger, *Black Property Owners*, 16-17.

30. *Ibid*, 17.

31. Russell, *Free Negro in Virginia*, 34-35.

32. *Ibid*, 34.

33. Ballagh, *Slavery in Virginia*, 39.

34. *Ibid*, 37.

35. Hening, *Statutes at Large*, II, 170.

36. Ballagh, *Slavery in Virginia*, 39.

37. *Ibid*, 39.

38. Hening, *Statutes at Large*, I, 4.

39. *Ibid*, II, 195.

40. Ballagh, *slavery in Virginia*, 4.

41. *Ibid*, 45.

42. Dodge, "Free Negroes in North Carolina," 4.

43. Ballagh, *Slavery in Virginia*, 47.

44. Hening, *Statutes at Large*, II, 267.

45. Ballagh, *Slavery in Virginia*, 78.

46. Edmund S. Morgan, *American Slavery, American Freedom: The Ordeal of Colonial Virginia* (New York: W. W. Norton, 1975), 313; hereinafter cited as *American Slavery.*

47. Hening, *Statutes at Large*, II, 280-281.

48. *Ibid*, II, 491.

49. *Ibid*, II, 491.

50. Ballagh, *Slavery in Virginia*, 49.

51. Schweninger, *Black Property Owners*, 17.

52. Ballagh, *Slavery in Virginia,* 52.
53. Hening, *Statutes at Large,* III, 298.
54. *Ibid,* III, 298.
55. *Ibid,* III, 453.
56. *Ballagh, Slavery in Virginia,* 59.
57. Ira Berlin, *Slaves without Masters: The Free Negro in the Antebellum South* (New York: The New Press, 1974), 7; hereinafter cited as *Slaves without Masters.*
58. Ballagh, *Slavery in Virginia,* 53.
59. Allan Kulikoff, *Tobacco and Slaves: The Development of Southern Cultures in the Chesapeake, 1680-1800* (Chapel Hill: The University of North Carolina Press, 11985), 387-388; hereinafter cited as *Tobacco and Slaves.*
60. Charles F. Irons, *The Origins of Proslavery Christianity* (Chaple Hill: The University of North Carolina, 2008), 44-45; hereinafter cited as *Proslavery Christianity.*
61. *Ibid,* 44-45.
62. *Ibid,* 44-45.
63. Berlin, *Slaves without Masters,* 29.
64. *Ibid,* 30-31.
65. *Ibid,* 40.
66. Paul Heinegg, *Free African Americans of North Carolina, and Virginia, and South Carolina,* 5th edition, 2 vols. (Baltimore: Clearfield Company, Inc., 2005), Vol. I, 9; hereinafter cited as *Free African Americans.*
67. Heinegg, *Free African Americans,* I, 7.
68. Kenneth M. Stampp. *The Peculiar Institution: Slavery in the Ante-Bellum South* (New York: Alfred A. Knopf, inc. 1956), 425-426.
69. Johnson, *Birth of the Modern,* 306.
70. Morgan, *American Slavery,* 375.

Chapter Two

The Free-Black Caste

1. Schweninger, *Black Property Owners,* p. 18; Franklin, *The Free Negro,* 14-17.
2. Berlin, *Slaves without Masters,* 46-48.
3. *Ibid,* 46-47.

4. Henry Wiencek, *Master of the Mountain: Thomas Jefferson and His Slaves* (New York: Farrar, Straus and Giroux, 2012), 6; hereinafter cited as *Master of the Mountain.*

5. "Thomas Jefferson Correspondence, July 27, 1821," *Thomas Jefferson Papers Series 1, General Correspondence, 1751-1827. The Works of Thomas Jefferson in 12 Volumes.* Collected and edited by Paul Leicester Ford.

6. L. Diane Barnes, *Artisan Workers in the Upper South, Petersburg, Virginia, 1820-1865* (Baton Rouge: Louisiana State University Press) 2008, 127.

7. *Register of Free Negroes and Mulattoes, 1794-1819* (Petersburg, Va.: Library of Virginia Microfilm Reel No. 47), August 16, 1794.

8. Franklin, *The Free Negro*, 27.

9. *Isle of Wight Deed Book 11, 1794-1802*, 171.

10. *Ibid*, 171.

11. *Ibid*, 171.

12. *Will of George Corbin, Accomack County, 1787.*

13. Franklin, *The Free Negro*, 35.

14. *Isle of Wigt Book 2, 1804-1808.*

15. Tommy L. Bogger, *Free Blacks in Norfolk, Virginia, 1790-1860: The Darker Side of Freedom* (Charlottesville: University of Virginia Press, 1997), 30; hereinafter cited as *Free Blacks in Norfolk.*

16. *Petersburg Deed Book 2.*

17. Franklin, *The Free Negro*, 157 & 228-236.

18. *Index of Free Negroes of Greensville County, Virginia.*

19. Harriette Thorne Kent, *Swampers: Free Blacks and the Great Dismal Swamp*, 1991.

20. Charles F. Irons, *The Origins of Proslavery Christianity* (Chapel Hill: The University of North Carolina Press, 2008), 45; hereinafter cited as *Proslavery Christianity.*

21. *Ibid*, 46.

22. *Ibid*, 46-47.

23. Garnett Ryland, *The Baptists of Virginia, 1699-1926* (Richmond: The Virginia Baptist Board of Missions and Education), 1955, 36-38; hereinafter cited as *Baptists of Virginia.*

24. Irons, *Proslavery Christianity*, 46.

25. Berlin, *Slaves without Masters*, 25.

26. Irons, *Proslavery Christianity*, 46-48.

27. *The Black Presence in North Carolina* (Raleigh: Division of Archives and History, 1978), 15; hereinafter cited as *The Black Presence.*

28. Ballagh, *Slavery in Virginia*, 110-111.

29. *Ibid*, 111.
30. *Ibid*, 112.
31. Bishop William Meade, *Old Churches, Ministers and Families of Virginia* (Philadelphia, 1857), 469.
32. "John Day to Rev. J.B. Taylor, October 16, 1847," *John Day Missionary Correspondence*, Southern Baptist Foreign Mission Board, Southern Baptist Historical Library and Archives (Nashville, Tennessee), hereinafter cited as John Day Letters. This particular letter to the Home Mission Board is especially revealing of John Day's life and that of his family and is referred to extensively in this work.
33. *The Black Presence*, 13.
34. *Ibid*, 13.
35. *Ibid*, 13.
36. W.M. Wightman, *Life of William Capers* (Nashville, 1902) 73.
37. Howard McKnight Wilson, *The Lexington Presbytery Heritage* (Lexington, Va.: The Presbytery of Lexington, 1971), 78-79; hereinafter cited as *The Lexington Presbytery*.
38. *Ibid*, 79.
39. *Ibid*, 79.
40. Franklin, *The Free Negro*, 24-25.
41. *Ibid*, 25.
42. James David Essig, "A Very Wintry Season: Virginia Baptists and Slavery, 1785-1797," *The Virginia Magazine of History and Biography*, Vol. 88, No. 1, 1980-1981, 170-180.
43. *Ibid*, 170-180.
44. Marie Tyler-McGraw, *An African Republic: Black and White Virginians in the Making of Virginia* (Chapel Hill: The University of North Carolina Press, 2007), 95; hereinafter cited as *An African Republic*.
45. Tommy L. Bogger, *Free Blacks in Norfolk, Virginia, 1790-1860: The Darker Side of Freedom* (Charlottesville: University Press of Virginia, 1997), 30.
46. Suzanne Lebsock, *The Free Women of Petersburg: Status and Culture in a Southern Town, 1784-1860* (New York: W. W. Norton & Company, 1984), 90; hereinafter cited as *Free women of Petersburg*.
47. Bogger, *Free Blacks in Norfolk*, 28.
48. Carl N. Degler, *Neither Black Nor White: Slavery and Race Relations in Brazil and the United States* (New York: The MacMillan Company, 1971), 83; hereinafter cited as *Neither Black Nor White*.
49. Schweninger, *Black Property Owners*, 23.

50. Eve Sheppard Wolf, *Almost Free: A Story About Family and Race in Antebellum Virginia* (Athens: The University of Georgia Press, 2012), 54-55; hereinafter cited as *Almost Free.*

51. Patrick Melvin Ely, *Israel on the Appomattox,* (New York: Alfred A. Knopf, 2004), 117; hereinafter cited as *Israel on the Appomattox.*

52. Wolf, *Almost Free,* 50-51.

53. Ely, *Israel on the Appomattox,* 48.

54. *Ibid,* p. 420.

55. Berlin, *Slaves without Masters,* 93.

56. *Ibid,* 273-275.

57. Richard Hildreth, *The Slave: Or, Memoirs of Archy Moore* (Boston: Whipple and Damrell, 1840), 2nd edition, 127-128; hereinafter cited as *Memoirs of Archy Moore.*

58. Frederick Law Olmsted, *A Journey in the Seaboard States in the Years 1853-1854* (New York: G. Putnam's Sons, 1904), I, 92; hereinafter cited as *Journey in the Seaboard States.*

59. Paul Johnson, *Birth of the Modern: World Society 1815-1830* (New York: HarperCollins, 1991), 306.

60. Luther Porter Jackson, *Free Negro Labor and Property Holding in Virginia, 1830-1860* (New York: D. Appleton-Century Company, 1942), 3; hereinafter cited as *Free Negro Labor.*

61. Berlin, *Slaves without Masters, xiii.*

62. Martha Hodes, *White Women, Black Men: Illicit Sex in the 19th-Century South* (New Haven: Yale University Press, 1997), 1-5; hereinafter cited as *White Women, Black Men.*

63. *Diary of Augustus G. Fogle,* Moravian Archives, Old Salem, North Carolina, p. 4.

64. Suzanne Simmons, *They Too Were Here: African-Americans in Augusta County and Staunton, Virginia, 1745-1865* (Harrisonburg, Va.: Thesis for Master of Arts degree, Department of History, James Madison University, 1994, 12.

65. *Ibid,* 12.

66. Joshua D. Rothman, *Notorious in the Neighborhood: Sex and Families across the Color Line in Virginia, 1787-1861.* (Chapel Hill: The University of North Carolina Press, 2003), 4-5; hereinafter cited as *Notorious.*

67. 67.Heinegg, *Free African Americans,* II, 3.

68. *Ibid,* 3-4.

69. Walter Clark, ed., *The State Records of North Carolina* (Winston, N.C.: 1905), XIII, 106-107.

70. Olmsted, *Journey in the Seaboard States,* I, 19.

71. *Ibid,* 20.
72. Eugene D. Genovese, *Roll Jordan Roll: The World the Slaves Made* (New York: Vintage Books, 1976), 336; hereinafter cited as *Roll Jordan Roll.*
73. Berlin, *Slaves without Masters,* 251.
74. *Ibid,* 261.
75. *Ibid,* 262.
76. Henry Bibb, *The Narrative Life and Adventures of Henry Bibb, an American Slave, Written by Himself,* 1849, 50; hereinafter cited as *Life of Henry Bibb.*
77. Hodes, *White Women, Black Men,* 3.
78. John W. Blassingame, *The Slave Community: Plantation Life in the Antebellum South.* Revised Edition (New York: Oxford University Press, 1979), pp. 153-155; hereinafter cited as *The Slave Community;* Harriet Jacobs, *Incidents in the Life of a Slave Girl* (Boston, 1862), 32; hereinafter cited as *Life of a Slave Girl.*
79. Hildreth, *Memoirs of Archy Moore,* 14.
80. Jacobs, *Life of a Slave Girl,* 12.
81. *Ibid,* 34.
82. Norman R. Yetman, ed., *Voices from Slavery* (New York: Holt, Rinehart and Winston, 1970), 68.
83. Jacobs, *Life of a Slave Girl,* 8.
84. *Ibid,* 8.
85. *Ibid,* 10.
86. *Ibid,* 11.
87. Tyler-McGraw, *An African Republic,* 96.
88. Jacobs, *Life of a Slave Girl,* 26-27.
89. *Ibid,* 28.
90. *Ibid,* 27.
91. *Ibid,* 13-14.
92. *Ibid,* 15.
93. Mary Boykin Chesnut, *A Diary From Dixie, as Written by Mary Boykin Chesnut.* Edited by Isabella D. Martin and Myrta Lockett Avary (New York: D. Appleton and Company, 1906), 21-22.
94. Joshua D. Rothman, *Notorious in the Neighbor: Sex and Families across the Color Line in Virginia, 1787-1861* (Chapel Hill: The University of North Carolina Press, 2003), 25-26.
95. *Ibid,* 25-26.
96. Wiencek, *Master of the Mountain,* 29.
97. Ely, *Israel on the Appomattox,* 29.
98. *Ibid,* 113.

99. *Ibid*, 134.
100. Rothman, *Notorious*, 57-91.
101. *Ibid*, 57-64.
102. *Ibid*, 65.
103. *Ibid*, 65.
104. *Ibid*, 70.
105. *Ibid*, 131.
106. *Ibid*, 131.
107. Genovese, *Roll Jordan Roll*, 417.
108. *Ibid*, 413.
109. Jackson, *Free Negro Labor*, 87; John H. Russell, *The Free Negro in Virginia, 1619-1865* (General Books, 2009), 159.
110. Russell, *The Free Negro in Virginia*, 104.
111. *Ibid*, 105.
112. Lane, *Lunsford Lane*, 9.
113. *Ibid*, 17-19.
114. *Ibid*, 22-25.
115. *Ibid*, 25-26.
116. *Ibid*, 29-31.
117. Guion Grifis Johnson, *Ante-Bellum North Carolina, A Social History* (Chapel Hill: The University of North Carolina Press, 1937), 587.
118. Robert McColley, *Slavery and Jeffersonian Virginia* (Urbana, Ill.: University of Illinois Press, 1942), 75.
119. Jackson, *Free Negro Labor*, 62-63; Bogger, *Free Blacks in Norfolk*, p. 68.
120. Berlin, *Slaves without Masters*, 76-78.
121. James Sidbury, *Ploughshares into Swords: Race, Rebellion, and Identity in Gabriel's Virginia, 1730-1810* (Cambridge: Cambridge University Press, 1997), 214; hereinafter cited as *Ploughshares into Swords*.
122. *Ibid*, 215; Berlin, *Slaves without Masters*, 76-77.
123. Schweninger, *Black Property Owners*, 88-89.
124. *Ibid*, 89.
125. *Ibid*, 89.
126. Lane, *Lunsford Lane*, 39.
127. *Ibid*, 39.
128. *Ibid*, 39.
129. *Ibid*, 41-42.
130. *Ibid*, 41-42.
131. Mary K. Bratton, ed., "Fields's Observations: The Slave Narrative of a Nineteenth-Century Virginian," *The Virginia Magazine of History and Biography*, vol. 88, no. 1 (1980-1981), 78.

132. Jacobs, *Life of a Slave Girl*, 47-49.
133. *Ibid*, 109-122.
134. Rothman, *Notorious*, 1-5.
135. *Ibid*, 1-5.
136. Schweninger, *Black Property Owners*, 89.
137. Sidbury, *Ploughshares into Swords*, 216.
138. W. M. Wightman, *Life of William Capers* (Nashville, 1902), 75.
139. Berlin, *Slaves without Masters*, xiv.

Chapter Three

The Days in Southside

1. Heinegg, *Free African Americans*, 399-400.
2. Southern Baptist Mission Board, John Day Missionary Correspondence, "John Day to Rev. J. B. Taylor, October 16, 1847," Southern Baptist Library and Archives, Nashville, Tennessee; hereinafter cited as "John Day Letters."
3. Hodes, *White Women, Black Men*, 4-5.
4. Heinegg, *Free African Americans*, I, 399-400.
5. Schweninger, *Black Property Owners*, 87.
6. Jacobs, *Life of a Slave Girl*, 53.
7. Bibb, *Life of Henry Bibb*, 82.
8. Berlin, *Slaves without Masters*, 277.
9. Isaac Harrell, *Gates County to 1860* (Durham, N.C., 1916), 67.
10. Henry Bibb, *The Narrative Life and Adventures of Henry Bibb, an American Slave. Written by Himself.* 1849, 82; hereinafter cited as *Life of Henry Bibb*.
11. Heinegg, *Free African Americans*, I, 22-23; Berlin, *Slaves without Masters*, 50-60.
12. Berlin, *Slaves without Masters*, 56-57.
13. *Ibid*, 56-57.
14. Hildreth, *Memoirs of Archy Moore*, 16-17.
15. *Ibid*, 15.
16. Ibid, 15.
17. *Ibid*, 30
18. Berlin, *Slaves without Masters*, 271.
19. Dodge, "Free Negroes in North Carolina," 26.
20. Lebsock, *Free Women of Petersburg*, 1-3.

21. *Ibid*, pp. 10-12; L. Diane Barnes, *Artisan Workers in the Upper South: Petersburg, Virginia, 1820-1865* (Baton Rouge: Louisiana State University Press, 2008), 33 and 131; hereinafter cited as *Artisan Workers*.

22. Joseph Clarke Robert, *The Tobacco Kingdom: Plantations, Market and Factory in Virginia and North Carolina, 1800-1860* (Gloucester, MA: Peter Smith, 1965), 186; hereinafter cited as *The Tobacco Kingdom*.

23. Lebsock, *Free Women of Petersburg*, 9.

24. *Ibid*, 6-7.

25. Jackson, *Free Negro Labor*, 93.

26. Lebsock, *Free Women of Petersburg*, 6.

27. *Ibid*, 95-96.

28. *Ibid*,1-14.

29. *Ibid*, 1-14.

30. John Ferdinand Smyth, *A Tour in the United States of America: containing an account of the present situation of that country; With a description of the Indian nations*, Vol. 1 (Dublin: G. Perrin, 1784), 41; hereinafter cited as *A Tour in the United States*.

31. Robert, *The Tobacco Kingdom*, 185.

32. Barnes, *Artisan Workers*,161.

33. *Ibid*,131.

34. Jackson, *Free Negro Labor*, 201.

35 Schweninger, *Black Property Owners*, 124.

36. Barnes, *Artisan Workers*, 137.

37. *Ibid*, 137.

38. *Ibid*, 137; Tyler-McGraw, *An African Republic*, pp. 168-169.

39. Tyler-McGraw, *An African Republic*, p. 176; Berlin, *Slaves without Masters*, 170.

40. Lensock, *Free Women of Petersburg*, 105.

41. *Isle of Wight Deed Book* 2.

42. Franklin, *The Free Negro*, 31-32.

43. Smyth, *A Tour in the United States*, 6-7.

44. Robert, *The Tobacco Kingdom*, 202.

45. Smyth, *A Tour in the United States*, 37.

46. *Ibid*, p. 30; Samuel Johnson, *Samuel Johnson's Dictionary: Selections from the 1775 Work that Defined the English Language* (London: Levenger Press, 2004), 367-368.

47. Hening, *Statutes at Large*, II, 268-269.

48. Smyth, *A Tour in the United States*, 39.

49. Ely, *Israel on the Appomattox*, 152.

50. *Ibid*, 154.

51. *Ibid,* 154-155.
52. m,m Maud Carter Clement, *The History of Pittsylvania, Virginia* (Baltimore: Regional Publishing Company, 1987), 239.
53. Ely, *Israel on the Appomattox,* 154-155.
54. *Ibid,* pp. 154-155; Ballagh, *Slavery in Virginia,* 109.
55. *Robert, The Tobacco Kingdom* 57-59.
56. Cecil D. Eby, Jr., ed., *The Old South Illustrated by Porte Crayon* (Chapel Hill: The University of North Carolina Press, 1959), 158-159; hereinafter cited as *The Old South Illustrated.*
57. *Ibid,* 158-159.
58. Jay B. Hubbell, "A Persimmon Beer Dance in Ante-Bellum Virginia," *Southern Literary Magazine,* Vol. 5, no. 5 (November-December 1943), 461-466; Dr. William B. Smith, "A Persimmon Beer Dance, *Farmers' Register,* VI, No. (February, 1838), 59; hereinafter cited as *Farmers' Register.*
59. Smyth, *A Tour in the United States,* 194.
60. Smith, *Farmers' Register,* 59-60.
61. Michael Sobel, *The World They Made Together: Black and White Values in Eighteenth-Century Virginia* (Princeton: Princeton University Press, 1987), 34.
62. Dena J. Epstein, *Sinful Tunes and Spirituals: Black Folk Music to the Civil War* (Urbana, Ill.: University of Illinois Press, 1977), 141; hereinafter cited as *Sinful Tunes and Spirituals.*
63. *Ibid,* 141.
64. Bibb, *Life of Henry Bibb,* 47.
65. *Ibid,* 47.
66. Epstein, *Sinful Tunes and Spirituals,* 142.
67. Heinegg, *Free African Americans,* 399-400; *Dinwiddie County, Virginia. Data,* 43.
68. "The Courts Valuation of Property Impressed for the Use of the Public in Greensville County, Virginia, During the Latter Period of the Revolutionary War, *Virginia Military Records* (Baltimore: Genealogical Publishing Co. Inc.), 161.
69. "Unrecorded Wills of Dinwiddie County, Virginia," contributed by Mrs. Sadie E. H. Short, *The Virginia Genealogist,* Volume 16, Number 4 (October-December, 1972), 94; hereinafter cited as "Unrecorded Wills of Dinwiddie County.
70. John Day Letters to Rev. J.B. Taylor; Augustus Fothergill and John Mark Naugle, comp., *Virginia Tax Payers, 1782-1787* (Baltimore: Genealogical Publishing Company, 1966); Fothergill, *Virginia*

Tax Payers; Dinwiddie County, Virginia. Data. 1762-1865, comp.
Thomas P. Hughes, Jr., 1975, 43; Heinegg, I, 399.

71. John Day Letters to Rev. J.B. Taylor

72. *Surveyors Platt Book, 1755-1796,* Virginia, Dinwiddie County;
1815 Directory of Virginia Landowners (and Gazetteer) (Athens, Ga.:
Iberian Publishing Company, 1997), 5 vols., vol. I; hereinafter cited
as *Directory of Landowners.*

73. John Day Letters, October 16, 1847.

74. John Day Letters, October 17, 1847.

75. Wolf, *Almost Free,* 50-51.

76. Jackson, *Free Negro Labor,* 71-74.

77. Olmsted, *Journey in the Seaboard States.*

78. *Jackson, Free Negro Labor,* 89.

79. *Ibid,* 100.

80. *Ibid,* 84-86.

81. Russell, *Free Negro in Virginia,* 104-106.

82. *Ibid,* p. 104; Jackson, *Free Negro Labor,* 84-86.

83. Russell, *Free Negro in Virginia,* 104.

84. *Ibid,* 104.

85. Berlin, *Slaves without Masters,* 14.

86. Heinegg, *Free African Americans,* I, 9.

87. Fothergill, *Virginia Tax Papers; Seventh Census of the United States
1850. Caswell County, North Carolina. Population Schedule.* National
Archives. Microfilm.

88. Heinegg, *Free African Americans,* I, 7.

89. *U.S. Census, Greensville County, Virginia, 1810; Index of Free Negroes,
Greensville County, 1815.*

90. Smyth, *A Tour in the United States,* 45-46.

91. *Ibid,* p. 46; de Marquis Chastellux, *Travels in North America in the
Years 1780-1781-1782* (New York, 1827), 222 for similar descriptions
of colonial Virginia.

92. Smyth, *A Tour in the United States,* 30.

93. *Ibid,* 29.

94. Rhys Isaac, *The Transformation of Virginia, 1740-1790* (New York:
W.W. Norton & Company, 1988), 25-27.

95. *Ibid,* 26-27.

96. Smyth, *A Tour in the United States,* 58-59.

97. *Ibid,* 58-59.

98. Richard Champion Rawlins, *An American Journal, 1839-1840*
(Madison, N.J.: Associated University Presses, 2002), 142.

99. Smyth, *A Tour in the United States,* 42-43.

Chapter Four

The Days Move to North Carolina

1. Franklin, *The Free Negro*, 15-19.
2. Dodge, "Free Negroes in North Carolina," 11.
3. Michael PArquette, "Thomas Day: Inquiry into Business and Labor in an Antebellum Cabinetshop, master thesis, University of North Carolina at Greensboro, 1996, 4.
4. Franklin, *The Free Negro*, pp. 192-193; William R. Taylor, *Cavalier & Yankee: The Old South and American National Character* (New York: Anchor Books, 1963), 8.
5. Mary J. Bratton, ed., "Field's Observations: The Slave Narrative of a Nineteenth-Century Virginian," *The Virginia Magazine of History and Biography*, Vol. 88, No. 1 (1980-1981), 93.
6. Franklin, *The Free Negro*, 193.
7. Jacobs, *Life of a Slave Girl*, 53.
8. *Ibid*, 53.
9. *Ibid*, 16-17; Heinegg, *Free African Americans*, I, 9.
10. Heinegg, *Free African Americans*, 9; William L. Saunders, ed., *The Colonial Records of North Carolina* (Raleigh, N.C., 1890), 10 vols., vol. VI, 902.
11. *The Colonial Records of North Carolina*, I, 903.
12. Franklin, *The Free Negro*, p. 106; Dodge, "The Free Negro in North Carolina," 7; Roger Wallace Shugg, "Negro Voting in the Ante-Bellum South," *Journal of Negro History*, Vol. XXI, No. 4 (October, 1936), 358.
13. Franklin, *The Free Negro*, 106; Shrugg, "Negro Voting in the Ante-Bellum South," 358.
14. Shugg, "Negro Voting in the Ante-Bellum South," 358.
15. R.H. Taylor, *The Free Negro in North Carolina: Some Colonial History of Craven County* (Chapel Hill: The University of North Carolina Press, 1920), 11.
16. Heinegg, *Free African Americans*, I, 10
17. Franklin, *The Free Negro*, 173.
18. Wilson, *The Lexington Presbytery*, 80.
19. Heinegg, *Free African Americans*, I, 10-11.
20. *Ibid*, I, 9.
21. Dodge, "Free Blacks in North Carolina," 23.
22. Smyth, *A Tour in the United States*, 77.

23. Eric Lincoln, "Black Religion in North Carolina: From Colonial Times to 1900," *The Black Presence in North Carolina*, 19.
24. *Roanoke Advocate*, Halifax, North Carolina (January 5, 1832), Vol. III, No. 44, 14.
25. Lebsock, *Free Woman of Petersburg*, 8.
26. Jonathan Prown, "A Cultural Analysis of Furniture-Making in Petersburg, 1760-1820," *Journal of Early Southern Decorative Arts* 17 (May 1992), 87.
27. John Day Letters, October 16, 1847.
28. *Ibid*, October 16, 1847.
29. *Ibid*, October 16, 1847.
30. *Ibid*, October 16, 1847.
31. *Ibid*, October 16, 1847.
32. Hugh Talmage Lefler and Albert Ray Newsome, *North Carolina: The History of a Southern State* (Chapel Hill: The University of North Carolina Press, 1954, 314.
33. *Ibid*, 316-320.
34. John Day Letters, October 16, 1847.
35. *Ibid*, October 16, 1847.
36. Jeremiah B. Jeter, *A Memoir of Abner W. Clopton, A.M.* (Richmond: Published by Yale & Wyatt, 1837) for a flattering biography of Clopton.
37. *Ibid*, 92.
38. *Ibid*, 97.
39. Taylor, *Lives of Ministers*, 344.
40. North Carolina, *Caswell County Deeds*, Book A, 261.
41. North Carolina, *Caswell county Deeds*, Book W, 74-75.
42. *Hillsborough Recorder* (Hillsborough, N.C.), February 23, 1823.
43. *Caswell County Deeds*, Book W, 43 & 74-75.
44. Robert Baylor Semple, *History of the Baptists in Virginia*, 1810. Revised and extended by G.W. Beale (Lafayette, TN: Church History Research and Archives, 1976), 464-465; hereinafter cited as *History of the Baptists in Virginia*.
45. Irons, *Proslavery Christianity*, 55-56.
46. Semple, *History of the Baptists in Virginia*, 146.
47. John Day Letters, October 16, 1847.
48. Rev. Edward C. Blyden, "Rev. John Day." Extracts from a Eulogy delivered by Rev. Edward C. Blyden, *The Commission* 4 (July 1859), Southern Baptist Convention, Nashville, TN., 2.
49. Leonard P. Curry, *The Free Black in Urban America: The Shadow of the Dream* (Chicago: The University of Chicago Press, 1981), 226-227;

hereinafter cited as *The Shadow of the Dream*; David Walker, *Walker's Appeal, in Four Articles, Together with a Preamble, to the Colored Citizens of the World, But in Particular and very Expressly to those of the United States of America* (Boston, 1829).

50. Berlin, *Slaves without Masters*, 200-206; Curry, *The Shadow of the Dream*, 233-235.
51. Curry, *The Free Black in Urban America*, 208-210.
52. *Ibid*, 208 & 210.
53. Tyler-McGraw, *An African Republic*, 37.
54. Scott L. Malcomson, *One Drop of Blood: The American Misadventure of Race* (New York: Farrar Straus Giroux, 2000), 188; hereinafter cited as *One Drop of Blood*.
55. *Ibid*, 188.
56. Taylor, *Lives of Ministers*, 398.
57. Ibid., 399.
58. Ibid., 404.
59. Ibid., 396.
60. Ibid., 410.
61. Ibid., 412.
62. Ibid., 400.
63. Tyler-McGraw, *An African Republic*, 19.
64. *Ibid*, 67.
65. Curry, *The Shadow of the Dream*, 233.
66. *Ibid*, 233.
67. Tyler-McGraw, *n African Republic*, 6-7.
68. *Ibid*, 7.
69. Malcomson, *One Drop of Blood*, 188.
70. Curry, *The Shadow of the Dream*, 233.
71. Tyler-McGraw, *An African Republic*, 2.
72. Curry, *The Shadow of the Dream*, 233.
73. Malcomson, *One Drop of Blood*, 189.
74. *Ibid*, 190.
75. Tyler-McGraw, *An African Republic*, 39.
76. Curry, *The Shadow of the Dream*, 234.
77. Superintendent Joseph C.G. Kennedy, *Preliminary Report on the Eighth Census, 1860* (Washington, D.C.: Government Printing Office, 1862).
78. John Day Letters, December 15, 1846.
79. *Ibid*, March 30, 1852.
80. Olmsted, *Journey in the Seaboard States*, I, 115.
81. Frances Anne Kemble, *Journal* (London, 1836), 7.

82. John Day Letters, December 15, 1846.
83. *Ibid*, December 15, 1846.

Chapter Five

"To Wear a Free and Easy Expression"

1. *Milton Gazette and Roanoke Advertiser* (Milton, N.C.) March 1, 1827.
2. *North Carolina House Journal, 1830-1831*, 238.
3. *Ibid.*, 238.
4. Schweninger, *Black Property Owners*, 37.
5. "Meeting of April 23, 1841," *Records of the Presbyterian Church of Milton, N.C.*, Historical Foundation of the Presbyterian and Reformed Churches Archives, Montreat, N.C.
6. Lannae Graham letter to Rodney Barfield, August 1, 1875, Thomas Day Vertical File, North Carolina Museum of History; *Presbyterian Session Meetings*, April 22, 1841 and April 6, 1845, Presbyterian Records, Presbyterian Archives, Montreat, N.C.
7. Prown, "A Cultural Analysis of Furniture-Making in Petersburg," 223.
8. "David L. Swain to Thomas Day, November 24, 1847," *Papers of the Philanthropic and Dialectic Societies*, Southern Historical Collection, Chapel Hill, The University of North Carolina Library.
9. *Seventh Census of the United States, 1850. Caswell County, North Carolina, Industry Schedule.* North Carolina State Archives, Microfilm.
10. "Diary of Augustus G. Fogle," *Family Record Book A*, Moravian Archives, Old Salem, North Carolina. Typed copy.
11. *Seventh Census of the United States, Caswell County*. Industry Schedule.
12. Letter from Dr. Thomas Day IV to Mary Satterfield, North Carolina State Archives, Vertical File, Raleigh, N.C.; W.A. Robinson, *et.al.* "Thomas Day and His Family," *The Negro History Bulletin*, Vol. XIII, Number 6 (March 1950), 125-126.
13. Robinson, "Thomas Day and His Family," 125.
14. *Ibid*, 125-126.
15. Letter from Dr. Thomas Day IV to Mary Satterfield."
16. *Raleigh Register*

17. "Thomas Day to David Reid," Bill of Sale, October 14, 1858. Thomas Day File, North Carolina State Archives.

18. *Caswell County Deed Book KK*, 265-266.

19. Meetings of April 22, 1841 and April 6, 1845, *Records of the Presbyterian Church of Milton, N.C.*

20. Author's personal files; also Vertical file on "Milton Presbyterian Church: Historical Background" at the Presbyterian Archives, Montreat, N.C.; See Paul Ader, "Tom Day" in *The State*, February 15, 1941, Volume VIII, Number 38 for the typical paternalistic fiction about Day that circulated in the 20th century press.

21. Patricia Phillips Marshall, "The Legendary Thomas Day: Debunking the Popular Mythology of an African American Craftsman," *The North Carolina Historical Review*, Volume LXXVIII, Number 1 (January, 2001).

22. Gordon Bendall, editor, *The Caswell Messenger* (August 7, 1991), Yanceyville, N.C.; Sharon Overton, *The News & Observer* (August 10, 1991), Raleigh, N.C. The photograph purporting to be Thomas Day originally appeared in the *Afro-American* (January 3, 1953).

23. Morgan, *American Slavery, American Freedom*, 309.

24. *Ibid*, 320-326.

25. Ely, *Israel on the Appomattox*, 374.

SELECTED BIBLIOGRAPHY

Documents

Births, Deaths and Sponsors 1717-1778 from the Albemarle Parish Register of Surry and Sussex Counties, Virginia. Comp. John Bennett Boddie. 1958. Reprint, Baltimore: Clearfield Company, Inc., 1998.

Caswell County Deeds, "North Carolina Mutual Insurance to Thomas Day," November 12, 1849, Book HH, p.44 (microfilm). North Carolina State Archives.

Caswell County Deeds, Book KK, 1871.

Caswell County, North Carolina Deeds, 1817-1840. Abstracts by Katharine Kerr. Franklin, N.C.: Genealogy Publishing Services, 1992.

Caswell County, North Carolina Marriage Bonds, 1778-1868. Comp. by Katherine Kerr Kendall. Baltimore: Clearfield Company, 1990.

Caswell County North Carolina Marriage Records, 1778-1876. Comp. by Francis T. Ingmire. St. Louis, Mo.: Ingmire Publications, 1984.

Daily Express, Petersburg, Virginia, October 23, 1857.

"Diary of Augustus G. Fogle," Family Record Book A, Moravian Archives, Old Salem, North Carolina. Typed copy.

Dinwiddie County, Virginia, Data. 1762-1865. Comp. Thomas P. Hughes, Jr. 1975.

Dinwiddie County, Virginia. Surveyor's Platt Book, 1755-1865. Virginia.

"Free-born Residents of Petersburg, Virginia." *Register of Free Negroes and Mulattos, 1794-1819.*

First Census of the United States, 1790. Virginia. Heads of Families at the First Census of the United States taken in the Year 1790. Baltimore: Genealogical Publishing Co., Inc. 1979.

Greensville County Marriages, 1781-1853. Comp. John Vogt & T. William Kethley, Jr. Athens, Ga.: Iberian Publishing Company, 1989.

Hening, William Waller. *The Statutes at Large; Being a Collection of all the Laws of Virginia from the First Session of the Legislature, in the Year 1619.* 13 Vols. New York: R&W&G Bartow, Printer, 1823.

Hughes, Thomas P. and Jewel B. Standefer, comp. *Petersburg, Virginia Hustings Court. Marriage Bonds—Marriage Register and Ministers' Returns, 1784-1854.* Memphis: Thomas P. Hughes, Publisher, 1971.

Journal of the House of Commons of North Carolina, 1830-1831. Raleigh, N.C.

Land Records. Dinwiddie County, Virginia, 1752-1820. Comp. Thomas P. Hughes, Jr. And Jewel B. Standfer. 1973.

Lewis, James F. and J. Motley Booker, M.D, comp. *Northumberland County Virginia: Wills 1770-1793 and Administrations, 1770-1790.* 1964.

Marriage Bonds and Ministers' Returns. Marriages of Greensville County Virginia, 1781-1825. Comp. Catherine L. Knorr. Pine Bluff, Arkansas: The Perdue Company Duplicating Service, 1955.

Marriage Bonds and Ministers' Returns of Sussex County Virginia, 1754-1810. Cop. Catherine L. Knorr. Pine Bluff, Arkansas: The Perdue Company, Duplicating Service, 1952.

Marriage Bonds and Ministers' Returns of Surry County Virginia, 1768-1825. Comp. Catherine L. Knorr. Pine Bluff, Arkansas: The Perdue Company, Duplicating Service, 1960.

Marriages of Halifax County Virginia, 1801-1831. Comp. by Marian Dodson Chiarito & James Hadley Prendergast. Nathalie, Va.: The Clarkton Press, 1985.

"Milton Presbyterian Church: Historical Background." By Florence Bailey, WOC President. Typed manuscript in vertical file in Presbyterian Archives at Montreat, N.C.

Virginia Military Records. Baltimore: Genealogical Publishing Co., Inc. 1983.

Papers of the Philanthropic and Dialectic Societies, "David L. Swain to Thomas Day, November 24, 1847." Southern Historical Collection, University of North Carolina Library, Chapel Hill, N.C.

—. "Thomas Day to John D. Mallett, January 5, 1848."

Records of the Presbyterian Church of Milton, N.C. Historical Foundation of the Presbyterian and Reformed Churches Archives, Montreat, N.C.

Register of Albemarle Parish Surry and Sussex Counties, 1739-1778. Trans. Gertrude R.B. Richard. Richmond, Va.: National Society Colonial Dames of America in the Commonwealth of Virginia, 1958.

Register of Free Negroes and Mulattoes, 1794-1819, Petersburg, Virginia, Library of Virginia microfilm reel no. 47.

Roanoke Advocate (Halifax, N.C.), January 5, 1832.

Saunders, William L, Ed. *The Colonial Records of North Carolina.* 10 Vols. Raleigh, 1890.

Seventh Census of the United States, 1850. Caswell County, North Carolina, Population Schedule, National Archives (microfilm, North Carolina State Archives).

Southern Baptist Foreign Mission Board, John Day Missionary Correspondence. "John Day to Rev. J.B. Taylor, October 16, 1847." Southern Baptist Historical Library and Archives, Nashville, Tennessee.

"Thomas Day to David Reid," *Bill of Sale,* October14, 1858. Thomas Day File, North Carolina Museum of History. Raleigh, N.C.

Virginia Historic Marriage Register. Greensville County Marriages, 1781-1853. Comp. John Vogt and T. William Kethley, Jr. Athens, Ga.: Iberian Publishing Co., 1989.

Wills and Administrations of Surry County, Virginia, 1671-1750. Elizabeth Timberlake Davis, comp. Baltimore: Clearfield Company, 1995. Reprint.

Articles

Ader, Paul. "Tom Day. *The State.* Volume VIII, Number 38, February 15, 1941.

Barfield, Rodney D. "Thomas and John Day and the Journey to North Carolina," *The North Carolina Historical Review,* January 2001, Volume LXXVIII, Number 1.

Barnes, L. Diane. "Southern Artisans, Organization, and the Rise of the Market Economy in Antebellum Petersburg." *Virginia Magazine of History and Biography,* Vol. 107, No. 2 (Spring 1999). Pp. 159-188.

Berkley, Edmund, Jr. "Prophet without Honor: Christopher McPherson, Free Person of Color." *The Virginia Magazine of History and Biography,* Vol. 77, April, 1969. Pages 180-187.

Blyden, Rev. Edward C. "Rev. John Day." Extracts from a Eulogy delivered by Edward C. Blyden in Providence Baptist Church, Monrovia, Liberia, March 2, 1859. *The Commission* (July 1859), Vol. 4, No.1.

Bratton, Mary J., Ed. "Fields's Observations: The Slave Narrative of a Nineteenth-Century Virginian," *The Virginia Magazine of History and Biography*, Vol. 88, No. 1, 1980-1981. Pages 75-93.

"Dinwiddie County, Virginia, 1800 Tax List," *The Virginia Genealogist*, Volume 18, Number 3. July-September, 1974.

Dodge, David. "Free Negroes in North Carolina," *The Atlantic Monthly* (January, 1886).

Essig, James David. "A Very Wintry Season: Virginia Baptists and Slavery, 1785-1797."

The Virginia Magazine of History and Biography, Vol. 88, No.1, 1980-1981. Pages 170-185.

Hubbell, Jay B. "A Persimmon Beer Dance in Ante-Bellum Virginia," *Southern Literary Magazine*, Vol. 5, no. 5 (November-December 1943), pages 461-466.

Kent, Harriette Thorne. "Swampers: Free Blacks and the Great Dismal Swamp." Harriette Thorne Kent, 1991.

Marshall, Patricia Phillips. "The Legendary Thomas Day: Debunking the Popular Mythology of an African American Craftsman." *The North Carolina Historical Review*, Volume LXXVIII, Number 1, January, 2001.

Nichols, Michael L. "Passing Through This Troublesome World: Free Blacks in the Early Southside." *The Virginia Magazine of History and Biography*, Vol. 92, No. 1 (January 1984). Pages 50-70.

Prown, Jonathan. "A Cultural Analysis of Furniture-Making in Petersburg, 1760-1820," *Journal of Early Southern Decorative Arts* 17 (May 1992).

—. "The Furniture of Thomas Day," *Winterthur Portfolio* 33 (Winter 1998).

"Rev. John Day. Extracts from a Eulogy delivered by Edward C. Blyden, in Providence Baptist Church, Monrovia, Liberia, March 2nd, 1859." *The Commission*, July, 1859, Vol. 4, No. 1.

Robinson, W.A. et.al. "Thomas Day and His Family," *The Negro History Bulletin*, Volume XIII, Number 6 (March 1950), pages 123-140.

Russell, John H. "Colored Freemen as Slave Owners in Virginia," *Journal of Negro History*, I, 233-242.

Shugg, Roger Wallace. "Negro Voting in the Ante-Bellum South." *The Journal of Negro History*. Volume XXI, No. 4 (October, 1936). Pages 357-364.

Smith, Dr. William B. "A Persimmon Beer Dance," *Farmers' Register*, VI, No. 1, February 1838. Pages 58-60.

Schweninger, Loren. "Prosperous Blacks in the South, 1790-1880." *The American Historical Review* 95 (February 1990): 31-56.

—. "The Roots of Enterprise: Black-Owned Businesses in Virginia, 1830-1880.

—. "The Vass Slaves: County Courts, State Laws, and Slavery in Virginia, 1831-1861. *Virginia Magazine of History and Biography*, 114 (Winter 2006) 464-497.

Sneed, Laurel & Christine Westfall. "Uncovering the Hidden History of Thomas Day: Findings and Methodology." Durham: North Carolina Humanities Council, 1995

Short, Sadie E.H. Comp. "Unrecorded Wills of Dinwiddie County, Virginia." *The Virginia Genealogist*, October-December, 1972. Vol. 16, Number 4. Pages 255-257.

The Commission 4 (July 1859)): 1-9. Southern Baptist Convention. Extract from a Eulogy delivered by Rev. Edward C. Blyden.

Monographs

Adams, Nehemiah. *A Southside View of Slavery or, Three Months at the South in 1854*. Port Washington, N.Y.: Kennikat Press, Inc. 3d Ed. 1969.

Ballagh, James Curtis. *A History of Slavery in Virginia*. Baltimore: The Johns Hopkins Press, 1902. Johns Hopkins University Studies in Historical and Political Science. Vol. XXIV.

—. *White Servitude in the colony of Virginia*. Maryland: Heritage Books, 2004.

Barnes, L. Diane. *Artisan Workers in the Upper South: Petersburg, Virginia, 1820-1865*.

Baton Rouge, La.: Louisiana State University Press, 2008.

Berlin, Ira. *Slaves without Masters: The Free Negro in the Antebellum South*. New York: The New Press, 1974.

Blassingame, John W. *The Slave Community: Plantation Life in the Antebellum South*. Revised Edition. Oxford: Oxford University Press, 1979.

Bibb, Henry. *The Narrative Life and Adventures of Henry Bibb, an American Slave, Written by Himself*. 1849.

Bleser, Carol, Ed. *Secret and Sacred: The Diaries of James Henry Hammond, a Southern Slaveholder*. New York: Oxford University Press, 1988.

Bogger, Tommy L. *Free Blacks in Norfolk, Virginia, 1790-1860: The Darker Side of Freedom*. Charlottesville, Va.: University Press of Virginia, 1997.

Boddie, John Bennett. *Colonial Surry*. Baltimore: Clearfield Company, 1989. Reprint.

—Comp. *Southside Virginia Families*. Baltimore: Genealogical Publishing Company, 1966. 2 vols.

Breen, T. H. & Stephen Innes. *"Myne Owne Ground": Race and Freedom on Virginia's Eastern Shore, 1640-1676*. Oxford: Oxford University Press, 2005.

Brown, Douglas Summers, Ed. *Historical and Biographical Sketches of Greensville County Virginia, 1650-1967*. Emporia, Va.: The Riparian Woman's Club, 1968.

Bruce, Philip A. *The Plantation Negro as a Freeman. Observations on His Character, Condition, and Prospects in Virginia*. New York: G.P. Putnam's Sons. 1889.

Chastellux, de Marquis. *Travels in North America in the Years 1780-1781-1782*. N.Y.: Gallaher & White, 1827. Reprint N.Y.: Augustus M. Kelley Publishers, 1970.

Chesnut, Mary Boykin. *A Diary from Dixie, as Written by Mary Boykin Chesnut*. Edited by Isabella D. Martin and Myrta Lockett Avary. New York: D. Appleton and Company, 1906.

Clarke, James Freeman. *Present Condition of the Free Colored People of the United States*. New York: American Anti-Slavery Society, 1859.

Clement, Maud Carter. *The History of Pittsylvania County, Virginia*. Baltimore: Regional Publishing Company, 1987.

Curry, Leonard P. *The Free Black in Urban America, 1800-1850: The Shadow of the Dream*. Chicago: The University of Chicago Press, 1981.

Daudert, Charles. *Andrew Durnford: Portrait of a Black Slave Owner*. Kalamazoo, MI: Hansa-Hewlett Publishing Company, 1999.

Degler, Carl N. *Neither Black Nor White: Slavery and Race Relations in Brazil and the United States*. New York: The Macmillan Company, 1971.

Dinwiddie County: '*The Countrey of the Apamatica*.' Workers of the Writers Program of the Work Projects Administration in the State of Virginia. Dinwiddie County School Board. 1942.

1815 Directory of Virginia Landowners (and Gazetteer). Abstracted by Roger G. Ward. Athens, Ga.: Iberian Publishing Company, 1997. 5 vols.

Doran, Michael F. *Atlas of County Boundary Changes in Virginia 1634-1895*. Athens, Ga.: Iberia Publishing Company,1987.

Duvall, Lindsay O., comp. *Virginia Colonial Abstracts*. Series 2, Vol.1. Northumberland County, Virginia 1678-1713. Easley, S.C.: Southern Historical Press, 1979.

Eby, Cecil D. Jr., Ed. *The Old South Illustrated by Porte Crayon*. Chapel Hill, N.C.: The University of North Carolina Press, 1959.

Elliott, Katherine B. Comp. *Emigration to Other States from Southside Virginia*. South Hill, Va.: Katherine B. Elliott, 1966. Reprint 1990 by Southern Historical Press, Inc. Greenville, S.C. 2 vols.

Ely, Patrick Melvin. *Israel on the Appomattox*. New York: Alfred A. Knopf, 2004.

Epstein, Dena J. *Sinful Tunes and Spirituals: Black Folk Music to the Civil War*. Urbana: University if Illinois Press, 1977.

Fitzpatrick, John C. *The Diaries of George Washington, 1748-1799.* 4 vols. Boston: Houghton Mifflin Company, 1925.

Fothergill, Augustus B. and John Mark Naugle, comp. *Virginia Tax Payers, 1782-1787.* Baltimore: Genealogical Publishing Company, 1966.

Franklin, John Hope. *The Free Negro in North Carolina, 1790-1860.* Chapel Hill: The University of North Carolina Press, 1943.

Franklin, John Hope and Loren Schweninger. *Runaway Slaves: Rebels on the Plantation.* Oxford: Oxford University Press, 1999.

—. *In Search of the Promised Land: A Slave Family in the Old South.* New York: Oxford University Press, 2006.

Garnet, Henry Highlander, Editor. *Walker's Appeal, with a Brief Sketch of His Life by Henry Highland Garnet.* New York: Printed by J.H. Tobitt, 1848.

Genovese, Eugene D. *Roll Jordan Roll: The World the Slaves Made.* New York: Vintage Books, 1976.

Gill, Harold B. Jr. *Apprentices of Virginia, 1623-1800.* Salt Lake City: Ancestry, 1989.

Greene, Robert Ewell. *Black Courage, 1775-1783. Documentation of Black Participation in the American Revolution.* Washington, D.C.: National Society of the Daughters of the American Revoluiton, 1984.

Guild, June Purcell. *Black Laws of Virginia.* Comp. Karen Hughes White & Jean Peters. Afro-American Historical Association of Fauquier County, 1996.

Gutman, Herbert G. *The Black Family in Slavery and Freedom, 1750-1925.* New York: 1976.

Gwathmey, John H. *Historical Register of Virginians in the Revolution, 1775-1783.* Baltimore: Genealogical Publishing Co. Inc., 1979.

Hale, John. *A Historical Atlas of Colonial Virginia.* Staunton, Va.: Old Dominion Publications, 1978.

Hamilton, Thomas. *Men and Manners in America.* Edinburgh: William Blackwood, 1833. Vols. I & II.

Harrell, Isaac. *Gates County to 1860.* Durham, 1916.

Hatcher, William E. *John Jasper, the Unmatched Negro Philosopher and Preacher.* New York: Fleming H. Revell Company, 1908.

Heinegg, Paul. *Free African Americans of North Carolina, and Virginia, and South Carolina.* 5th Ed. 2 vols. Baltimore: Clearfield Company, Inc., 2005.

Henderson, Archibald. *Washington's Southern Tour, 1791.* 2 Vols. Boston, 1925.

Hildreth, Richard. *The Slave: Or, Memoirs of Archy Moore.* 2nd Ed. Boston: Whipple and Damrell, 1840.

Hodes, Martha. *White Women, Black Men: Illicit Sex in the Nineteenth-Century South.* New Haven: Yale University Press, 1997.

Horowitz, Tony. *Midnight Rising: John Brown and the Raid that Sparked the Civil War.* New York: Henry Holt and Company, 2011.

Howe, Daniel Walker. *What Hath God Wrought: The Transformation of America, 1815-1848.* Oxford: Oxford University Press, 2007.

Irons, Charles F. *The Origins of Proslavery Christianity.* Chapel Hill, N.C.: The University of North Carolina Press, 2008.

Isaac, Rhys. *The Transformation of Virginia, 1740-1790.* New York: W.W. Norton & Company, 1988.

Jackson, Luther Porter. *Free Negro Labor and Property Holding in Virginia, 1830-1860.* New York: D. Appleton-Century Company, 1942.

Jacobs, Harriet (pseud. Linda Brent*). Incidents in the Life of a Slave Girl. Written by Herself.* Boston, 1861.

Jeter, Jeremiah B. *A Memoir of Abner W. Clopton, A.M.* Richmond: Published by Yale & Wyatt, 1837.

Johnson, Guion Grifis. *Ante-Bellum North Carolina, A Social History.* Chapel Hill: The University of North Carolina, 1937.

Johnson, Paul. *The Birth of the Modern: World Society 1815-1830.* New York: HarperCollins Publishers, 1991.

Johnson, F. Roy. *The Nat Turner Slave Insurrection.* Murfreesboro, NC: Johnson Publishing Company, 1966.

Samuel Johnson. *Samuel Johnson's Dictionary: Selections form the 1755 Work that Defined the English Language.* Edited by Jack Lynch. London: Levenger Press, 2004.

Johnston, James Hugo. *Race Relations in Virginia and Miscegenation in the South, 1776-1860.* Amherst, Mass.: The University of Massachusetts Press, 1970.

Jones, Richard. *Dinwiddie County, Carrefour of the Commonwealth.* Dinwiddie, Va.: Dinwiddie County Board of Supervisors, 1976.

Kemble, Frances Anne. *Journal.* London, 1836.

Kennedy, Joseph C.G., Superintendent. *Preliminary Report on the Eighth Census, 1860.* Washington, D.C.: Government Printing Office, 1862.

Koger, Larry. *Black Slaveowners: Free Black Slave Owners in South Carolina, 1790-1860.* Columbia: University of South Carolina Press, 1995.

Kulikoff, Allan. *Tobacco and Slaves: The Development of Southern Cultures in the Chesapeake, 1680-1800.* Chapel Hill: UNC Press, 1985.

Landon, C. Bell, Comp. *Sunlight on the Southside: List of Tithes, Lunenburg County, Virginia, 1748-1783.* Philadelphia, 1931.

Lane, Lunsford. *The Narrative of Lunsford Lane, Formerly of Raleigh, N.C.* 1842.

Lassing, Benson J., Ed. *The Diary of George Washington from 1789-1791*. Richmond: 1860.

Lebsock, Suzanne. *The Free Women of Petersburg: Status and Culture in a Southern Town, 1784-1860*. New York: W>W> Norton & Company, 1984.

Lefler, Hugh Talmage and Albert Ray Newsome. *North Carolina: The History of a Southern State*. Chapel Hill: The University of North Carolina Press, 1954.

Little, Lewis Peyton. *Imprisoned Preachers and Religious Liberty in Virginia*. Lynchburg: J.P. Bell Co., Inc., 1938.

Litwack, Leon F. *North of Slavery: The Free Negro in the Free States, 1790-1860*. Chicago: The University of Chicago Press, 1961.

Lynch, Jack, Editor. *Samuel Johnson's Dictionary*. Delray Beach, Fl.: Levenger Press, 2004.

Malcomson, Scott L. *One Drop of Blood: The American Misadventure of Race*. New York: Farrar Straus Giroux, 2000.

Martin, Joseph, Editor. *A New and Comprehensive Gazeteer of Virginia, and the District of Columbia*. Charlottesville, 1835.

Marryat, Captain Frederick. *A Diary in America*. 1839.

Mason, George Carrington. *Colonial Churches of Tidewater Virginia*. Richmond: Whitlet and Shepperson, 1945.

McColley, Robert. *Slavery and Jeffersonian Virginia*. Urbana: University of Illinois press, 1964.

Meade, Bishop William. *Old Churches, Ministers and Families of Virginia*. Philadelphia, 1857.

Mitchell, Joseph. *The Missionary Pioneer or a Brief Memoir of the Life, Labours, and Death of John Steward, [Man of Colour] Founder, under God of the Mission among the Wyandotts at the Upper Sandusky, Ohio*. New York, 1827.

Morgan, Edmund S. *American Slavery, American Freedom: The Ordeal of Colonial Virginia*. New York: W.W. Norton, 1975.

Morton, Louis. *Robert Carter of Nomini Hall*. Williamsburg: Colonial Williamsburg, 1941.

North Carolina Architects & Builders: A Biographical Dictionary. North Carolina State University. Database.

Nugent, Nell Marion. *Cavaliers and Pioneers: Abstracts of Virginia Land patents and Grants, 1623-1782*. 8 vols.

Olmsted, Frederick Law. *A Journey in the Seaboard States in the Years 1853-1854*. 2 vols. N.Y.: G.P. Putnam's Sons, 1904. Reprint

Phillips, Ulrich Bonnell. *American Negro Slavery*. Middlesex: The Echo Library, 2006.

Powell, William S., Editor. *Encyclopedia of North Carolina*. Chapel Hill: The University of North Carolina, 2006.

Rawlins, Richard Champion. *An American Journal, 1839-1840*. Madison, N.J.: Associated University Presses, 2002. Reprint.

Reniers, Perceval. *The Springs of Virginia: Life, Love, and Death at the Waters, 1775-1900*. Chapel Hill: The University of North Carolina Press, 1941.

Richards, Gertrude R.B. *Register of Albemarle Parish, Surry and Sussex Counties, 1739-1778*. The National Society Colonial Dames of America—the Commonwealth of Virginia. 1958.

Robert, Joseph Clarke. *The Tobacco Kingdom: Plantation, Market, and Factory in Virginia and North Carolina, 1800-1860*. Gloucester, Mass.: Peter Smith, 1965.

Roberts, Robert. *The House Servant's Directory: An African American Butler's 1827 Guide*. Mineola, N.Y.: Dover Publications, Inc., 2006.

Rothman, Joshua D. *Notorious in the Neighborhood. Sex and Families across the Color Line in Virginia, 1787-1861*. Chapel Hill: The University of North Carolina Press, 2003.

Russell, John H. *The Free Negro in Virginia, 1619-1865*. Baltimore, 1913,

Ryland, Garnett. *The Baptists of Virginia, 1699-1926*. Richmond: The Virginia Baptist Board of Missions and Education, 1955.

Schreiner-Yantis, Netti and Florence Speakman Love, comp. *The Personal Property Tax Lists for the Year 1787 for Greensville County, Virginia*. Springfield, Va.: Genealogical Books in Print, 1987.

Schweninger, Loren. *Black Property Owners in the South, 1790-1915*. Urbana: University of Illinois Press, 1990.

Semple, Robert Baylor. *History of the Baptists in Virginia*. Revised and Extended by G.W Beale. Lafayette, TN.: Church History Research and Archives, 1976. (orig. 1810)

Shaw, G.W. *John Chavis, 1763-1838, A Remarkable Negro Who Conducted a School for White Boys and Girls*. Binghamton, N.Y.: Vail-Ballou Press, Inc. 1931.

Sidbury, James. *Ploughshares into Swords: Race, Rebellion, and Identity in Gabriel's Virginia, 1739-1810*. Cambridge: Cambridge University Press, 1997.

Simmons, Susanne. "They Too Were Here: African-Americans in Augusta County and Staunton, Virginia, 1745-1865." Harrisonburg, Va.: Thesis for Master of Arts degree, Department of History, James Madison University, 1994.

Simpson, William S., Jr. *Virginia Baptist Ministers, 1760-1790: A Biographical Survey*. Richmond: William S. Simpson, Jr., 1990. 2 vols.1

Smith, Annie Laurie Wright, Comp. *The Quit Rents of Virginia, 1704.* Baltimore: Genealogical Publishing Company, 1977.

Smyth, John Ferdinand D. *A Tour in the United States America: containing an account of the present situation of that country; With a description of the Indian nations.* Vol.1. Dublin: G. Perrin, 1784.

Sobel, Mechal. *The World They Made Together: Black and White Values in Eighteenth-Century Virginia.* Princeton: Princeton University Press, 1987.

Stampp, Kenneth M. *America in 1857: A Nation on the Brink.* Oxford: Oxford University Press, 1990.

—. *The Peculiar Institution: Slavery in the Ante-Bellum South.* New York: Vintage Books, 1989.

Taylor, James. *The Lives of Baptist Ministers.* Richmond: Yale & Wyatt, 1837.

Taylor, R. H. *The Free Negro in North Carolina. Some Colonial History of Craven County.* Chapel Hill: University of North Carolina, 1920.

Taylor, William Robert. *Cavalier and Yankee: The Old South and American National Character.* New York: Oxford University Press, 1993.

The Black Presence in North Carolina. Raleigh, N.C.: Division of Archives and History, 1978. NEH-sponsored book of essays on North Carolina Black History.

Trollop, Frances. *Domestic Manners of the Americans.* London: 1833. Vol.2. Reprint Gloucester, Mass.: Peter Smith, 1974.

Tyler-McGraw, Marie. *An African Republic: Black and White Virginians in the Making of Virginia.* Chapel Hill: The University of North Carolina Press, 2007.

Walker, David. *Walker's Appeal, in Four Articles, Together with a Preamble, to the Colored Citizens of the World, But in Particular and very Expressly to Those of the United States of America.* Boston, 1829.

Wardell, Patrick G., Comp. *War of 1812: Virginia Bounty Land & Pension Applicants.* Bowie, Md.: Heritage Books, Inc. 1987.

Weeks, Nan F. and Blanche Sydnor White. *Liberia for Christ: Presenting the Story of Virginia Baptists in the Colonization, Development, and Christian Conquest of the Republic of Liberia.* Richmond, Va.: Woman's Missionary Union of Virginia, 1959. John Day photograph, p.10.

Wiencek, Henry. *Master of the Mountain: Thomas Jefferson and His Slaves.* New York: Farrar, Straus and Giroux, 2012.

Wightman, W.M. *Life of William Capers.* Nashville, 1902.

Wilson, Howard McKnight. *The Lexington Presbytery Heritage.* Lexington, Va.: The Presbytery of Lexington, 1971.

Wolf, Eva Sheppard. *Almost Free.* Athens, Ga.: The University of Georgia Press, 2012.

Woodson, Carter G. *The Education of the Negro Prior to 1861: A History of the Education of the Colored People of the United States from the Beginning of Slavery to the Civil War*. New York: G. P. Putnam's Sons, 1915.

—. *Free Negro Owners of Slaves in the United States in 1830; Together with Absentee Ownership of Slaves in the United States in 1830*. Washington, D.C.: Association for the Study of Negro Life and History, 1924.

Yetman, Norman R. *When I was a Slave. Memoirs from the Slave Narrative Collection*. Mineola, N.Y.: Dover Publications, Inc. 2002. (From the Federal Writers' Project, 1936-1938).

INDEX